DIPLOMACY AND THE BORDERLANDS

LUIS DE ONÍS

From a portrait in the possession of Professor Federico de Onis

DIPLOMACY AND THE BORDERLANDS

The Adams-Onís Treaty of 1819

BY

PHILIP COOLIDGE BROOKS

1970

OCTAGON BOOKS

New York

Reprinted 1970

by special arrangement with the University of California Press

OCTAGON BOOKS

A DIVISION OF FARRAR, STRAUS & GIROUX, INC.

19 Union Square West

New York, N. Y. 10003

LIBRARY OF CONGRESS CATALOG CARD NUMBER: 73-120235

PREFACE

THIS ACCOUNT of the Transcontinental Treaty of 1819 between Spain and the United States has resulted from an investigation of its background and of the interests and activities of all the countries represented in the negotiation. In it I have essayed to weigh the comparative influences of frontier conditions and of political considerations upon the diplomats. Certain aspects of the agreement involved inevitable recognition of existing occupation of territory, whereas others were largely matters of arbitrary bargaining on paper by the negotiators, who faced some circumstances unknown on the frontiers.

Heretofore the treaty has been subjected to limited interpretations because of its having been studied in the archives and libraries of only one of the nations concerned. Profiting by an examination of materials in Spain, France, and England, as well as in the United States, this portrayal, it is hoped, will give a broad view of all the major complications involved.

The rôle played by Spain has been the phase most neglected by historians, and it forms the core of this narrative. Accordingly, the central theme is the career of Don Luis de Onís as Spanish minister in this country from 1809 to 1819. The intricacies of following the thread of a single negotiation through the kaleidoscopic tangles of the post-Napoleonic period have made the selection of materials a difficult task.

The treaty was intimately concerned with the boundaries of the Louisiana Purchase, but it did not define them as such. The decisions reached were not based upon the rights acquired in that purchase, but were determined by the comparative power of the two nations, the conditions of settlement on the frontiers, and the skill of the negotiators.

Certain of the territorial claims which were advanced are still disputed among historians. These claims did not determine the delineation of 1819, nor were they settled by it; some conclusions regarding them, however, are reached in this study. It appears that the United States had no justifiable title to West Florida as a part of the Louisiana Purchase, but the fact that the United States had occupied the region was a strong bargaining point. Partly through the dexterity of Onís in concealing the nature of his instructions, the United States was led to relinquish a claim to Texas based on the French title. His Catholic Majesty gave up a strong claim to the Oregon territory, and the acquisition of that claim by the United States added appreciably to those the latter country already had by discovery and settlement. Aside from the bartering of these conflicting territorial interests, an agreement was made concerning financial obligations. There was no pecuniary purchase of territory.

The aggressiveness of popular opinion in this country was somewhat offset by the fine sense of legal rights and international amenities displayed by Secretary of State John Quincy Adams. Nevertheless Adams had unbounded confidence in the future growth of the nation and devoted himself to it. In defining and extending the nation's boundaries in this treaty he gained a diplomatic victory which he regarded as the greatest achievement of his career. In its accomplishment he deftly availed himself of Spain's embarrassments and of the desire of the European Powers to maintain peace.

Onís, with the aid of only one constructive statesman among the officials of his own government, and with the fires of revolution consuming the empire more rapidly than his superiors in Spain realized, acquitted himself ably. He prevented the United States from taking Texas, established a definite boundary for the colonies which Spain still dreamed of saving, and freed his country from financial obligations which would have plagued her long afterward and in far greater amount. This he accomplished cleverly, but I do not believe, as Adams charged, that Onís himself intended to defraud the United States in the notorious matter of the Florida land grants, although King Ferdinand was probably culpable.

I have designated the agreement as the "Adams-Onís Treaty" to give credit to the diplomatists who achieved a solution to complex problems of many years' standing. At other times I have employed the phrase "Transcontinental Treaty" (originated by Dr. Samuel Flagg Bemis) to give alliterative emphasis to the broad scope of the subject. The necessity of recognizing the true significance of the western boundary issues has led to the rejection of such a limited term as the "Florida Treaty."

Many persons have assisted me in this study, but space allows the mention individually of only a few who have taken especial interest beyond their regular lines of duty. Thanks can be but small measure of my gratitude to Dr. Herbert E. Bolton, by whose breadth of vision and inspiring guidance I have profited. As one of the concluding chapters in the narrative of the "Spanish Borderlands" and as one of many illustrations of the finely interwoven texture of United States and Hispanic American affairs, this work is, I am pleased to feel, a contribution in the great field he has developed.

Dr. Bemis has aided incalculably through his knowledge of diplomatic history and its sources, and with editorial counsel. It was at his suggestion that this research was begun.

To the Native Sons of the Golden West my thanks are extended for financing a sojourn in Europe. Their generosity was accepted in the belief that this demonstration of the sea-to-sea aspect of the treaty would add to the knowledge of Pacific Coast history. Professor Federico de Onís, of Columbia University, a direct descendant of Luis de Onís, graciously allowed me to use a manuscript biography in his possession, and to reproduce the portrait which appears as frontispiece to this work. The late Professor John C. Parish, sometime managing editor of the *Pacific Historical Review*, kindly consented to the reprinting of quotations used in an article of mine in that journal.

Dr. Charles C. Griffin, of Vassar College, has cordially conferred with me on various matters. It should be noted, however, that my research and that which led to the publication of his *United States and the Disruption of the Spanish Empire, 1810–1822* (New York, 1937) were done independently of each other. His work is a commendable study emphasizing the Spanish political background and the Spanish American Revolution, rather than territorial problems.

I wish to acknowledge the aid and encouragement received from Señor Don Miguel Gómez del Campillo, chief of the Archivo Histórico Nacional in Madrid; Señor Don Juan Tamayo y Francisco, former chief of the Archivo General de Indias in Sevilla; Professor Charles E. Chapman, Professor Herbert I. Priestley, Mrs. Edna M. Parrat, Dr. Victor M. Hunt, and Dr. Lawrence Kinnaird, all of the University of California; the late Dr. J. Franklin Jameson, Colonel Lawrence Martin, Miss Grace Gardner Griffin, and Miss

Clara Egli, of the Library of Congress; Mrs. Natalia Summers, formerly of the Department of State but now of the National Archives, and Mr. Fred W. Shipman, Dr. Vernon D. Tate, and Mr. Jesse S. Douglas, all of the latter institution; the late Dr. James A. Robertson, of the Maryland Hall of Records; the late Mr. W. Harold May, of Columbia University; Dr. and Mrs. Louis C. Nolan and Mr. and Mrs. Frank Louraine, of Washington, D. C.; also Martha Latimer Willard, assistant editor of the University of California Press. My wife, Dorothy Holland Brooks, has given invaluable technical assistance and encouragement.

PHILIP C. BROOKS

THE NATIONAL ARCHIVES
June 12, 1939

CONTENTS

ILLUSTRATIONS

ABBREVIATIONS

A.G.I.: Archivo General de Indias, Sevilla

A.G.S.: Archivo General de Simancas, Simancas

A.H.N.: Archivo Histórico Nacional, Madrid

A.M.A.E.: Archives du Ministère des Affaires Etrangères, Paris

A.M.E.: Archivo del Ministerio de Estado, Madrid

A.S.P., F.R.: *American State Papers* (Washington, 1832–1861), Class I, *Foreign Relations*

B.N.M.: Biblioteca Nacional, Madrid, Sección de Manuscritos

D.S.: Division of State Department Archives, the National Archives, Washington

P.R.O., F.O.: Public Record Office, London, Foreign Office Papers

These abbreviations are employed in the notes. Arabic numerals after "A.G.I.," "A.G.S.," "A.H.N.," and "A.M.E." represent *legajo* (bundle) numbers. Arabic figures are used to indicate volumes after "A.M.A.E." Two sets of Arabic numerals after "P.R.O., F.O." denote series and volumes, respectively. Roman numerals after "D.S." indicate volumes.

CHAPTER I

FOUNDATIONS OF CONTROVERSY, 1803–1816

DIPLOMATIC COMPLEXITIES

OVER A TRANSCONTINENTAL FRONTIER our brilliant if cantankerous secretary of state and an able, suave Spanish minister struggled in 1818 and 1819. John Quincy Adams and Luis de Onís, the diplomatic combatants, faced controversies involving territories from the Floridas to Oregon, as well as complex maritime difficulties. Their treaty of February 22, 1819, concluded a quarter-century of kaleidoscopic diplomatic and frontier rivalries.[1] For the United States this agreement involved the longest border concerned in any negotiation since her founding, and marked the end of the first great wave of territorial expansion with her first treaty title to land on the Pacific. For Spain it was a phase of a desperate conflict to protect her American colonies at once from foreign intrusions and from seething internal uprisings, and to maintain her own prestige.

The negotiations took place during a postwar period of colonial uprisings, maritime competitions, economic rivalries, and anxious efforts to avoid another war. There were difficulties enough to test the abilities not only of such famous statesmen as Adams and Castlereagh, but also of Onís, Pizarro, and Erving, men whose names have until now been obscure but who merit real attention in Spanish and United States history.

Despite these complexities Adams and Onís managed to secure the following major settlements: the cession of the Floridas to the United States, a disposition of numerous claims growing out of the European wars, and (the issue most prominent in the final stages of the negotiations) the delineation of the international boundary from the Gulf of Mexico to the Pacific Northwest.

It will be seen that in the three years of his actual official negotiations with our secretaries of state Onís considered the solution of the territorial problems to be a vital factor in the larger field of Spanish colonial and foreign policy. To give the colonies a well-defined border line on the north would help in defending and controlling them, and would set a limit at which, it was hoped, restless

---

[1] For notes to chap. i, see pp. 26–28.

[1]

adventurers who desired to aid the revolutionary movement could be stopped. Further, and more significant, the settlement of controversies with the United States would ease diplomatic tension, and perhaps ward off the evil day when that Power might become the open protagonist of the insurgent Spanish American provinces. In that tension the most disturbing factor to the people of the United States was the question of boundaries.

The disposition of much of the territory was to be fixed by conditions of settlement which the diplomats were obliged to recognize. In other directions ambitions for occupation were still in the stage of mere projects, so that the negotiators could bargain on paper, sometimes with scant geographical information. Inasmuch as the eastern part of the frontier was better known and settled, its rôle in the narrative is more obvious and offers less demonstration of diplomatic skill than does the farsighted Oregon-California boundary delineation. Even in that, however, the diplomats depended for their interest in and their knowledge of the region on the men who had explored it and who coveted its wealth—men who were proving history to be the concrete experience of human life, and not merely political and diplomatic vicissitudes.

Effective negotiations were long delayed. Onís, when he arrived in 1809, was not recognized as minister by the United States government owing to civil war in Spain, and he could do no bargaining until his acknowledgment in December, 1815. Long before he was recognized, however, the basic points of contention had been voiced, not alone by Onís, but by his predecessors. These issues had their origin in the very nature of European colonial rivalry in the Americas, and their development must be traced before one can intelligently view the work of Onís.

Even in his time, Onís' country still dreamed of maintaining the colonial empire which had arisen with Pope Alexander's division of the colonial world between Spain and Portugal in 1493. From that date Spain claimed virtually all of the Americas. Actually, her holdings had been modified appreciably by the encroachments of competing nations in sections she herself had not occupied. "La Florida," once vaguely delineated as all the known region east of the Mississippi River, had been reduced, roughly, to the area south of the Thirty-first Parallel. As the result of disputes marked by the treaty of 1670, which recognized English claims as far south as Charleston, and by the activities of Oglethorpe in the War for Georgia (1739 to 1743), Spain had had to yield to the English the Atlantic Coast above the 'St. Mary's River (now the northern boundary of the state of Florida). She likewise had had to yield to France on the Gulf, allowing that Power to colonize the region about Biloxi, Mobile, and New Orleans. After a petty war in 1718 and 1719 the boundary was tacitly admitted as being at the Perdido River (the western limit of the state of Florida today).

England held the region for twenty years after the French and Indian War. During this time it was again, at least in name, extended to the Mississippi, and was separated into two parts, a division which gave rise to the terms "East" and "West" Florida.

After Yorktown, more and more had to be conceded to the United States. Spain's military actions saved the Southwest for what was to be the new republic, and in the treaties of 1783 she regained the Floridas, although they were again limited by the Thirty-first Parallel on the north, instead of being enlarged as they had been under English domination. In spite of Spanish protest, the same parallel was agreed upon in the treaty signed by Thomas Pinckney in 1795,[2] and it remained the boundary line until Onís' time. That agreement also provided that the rapidly growing settlements in Kentucky, Tennessee, and western Georgia, in transmitting goods to market via the Mississippi, should have the right to deposit them at New Orleans to await transfer to sea-going vessels.

Out of Pinckney's Treaty grew one aspect of the desultory diplomatic controversies which centered in Madrid from 1802 to 1805. The right of deposit, although originally guaranteed for only three years, was continued until 1802. Then it was suddenly suspended by the Spanish intendant at New Orleans, but without the substitution of another port—a stipulation made in the treaty to care for such a situation. Resentment over this cessation was only one element in the bitter bickerings between the two countries in succeeding years.

Maritime Claims and Louisiana

Representing their respective countries in these dealings were Charles Pinckney, United States minister at Madrid; James Monroe, sent to Spain as special agent of the United States after the purchase of Louisiana; Don Pedro Cevallos, Spanish foreign minister; and the Marquis of Casa Irujo, Spanish minister in this country. Major points of contention were the right of deposit, claims for damages to United States shipping during the European wars, Spain's objections to the Louisiana Purchase, and the continued efforts of the United States to obtain the Floridas.

Pinckney began the debate over claims, which included those for the spoliations by Spanish vessels in the European wars just ended and those for prizes captured by French ships and sold or condemned in Spanish ports.[3] In negotiations with Cevallos, he was able to arrange a convention, signed on August 11, 1802, by which the claims of the United States against Spain were to be adjudicated by a joint commission. That body was to meet in Madrid and was to conclude its business within eighteen months after the ratification of the agreement. Rights of the two parties concerning the French spoliations were to be determined later.[4]

The convention was rejected by the United States Senate in 1803, but was approved when reconsidered a year later. By this time, however, other events had made Spain change her mind about ratifying. Robert R. Livingston, minister to France, had been instructed to ascertain the possibility of acquiring New Orleans and the Floridas, it being erroneously suspected that both had been ceded to France. Out of French embarrassments in Europe and Livingston's designs on the lower Mississippi came the sudden engineering of the Louisiana Purchase. Monroe arrived in Paris as a special commissioner, just in time to help clinch the transaction.

Louisiana, originally a huge French colony, had been lost to France in 1763. England at that time acquired the part east of the Mississippi by conquest and Spain gained the western part through a diplomatic maneuver, without, however, having its limits definitely established.[5] At the same time, the transfer of the Floridas to England had cut off from Louisiana, at least temporarily, the region between the Mississippi and the Perdido rivers. Livingston, during his negotiations over the Floridas, learned that by the secret Treaty of San Ildefonso, October 1, 1800, Spanish Louisiana had been retroceded to France at the demand of Napoleon. Later Livingston realized that a now-famous ambiguity in the treaty left uncertainty whether West Florida was included in the retrocession (as if it had always been a part of Louisiana) or remained Spanish (as having been separated from Louisiana by the Anglo-

Spanish treaties of 1763 and 1783). Livingston, after the purchase, began arguing for the former interpretation.

Great consternation on the part of Spain arose over the Louisiana Purchase. Irujo at Washington protested its illegality, on two counts. First, the French ambassador in Madrid had signed a promise that Louisiana would not be alienated by France. The United States contended that this in no way affected her title, which could not be impaired by such an agreement. A similar rebuttal was offered to Irujo's complaint that the French title was void owing to nonfulfillment of Napoleon's promise, likewise in the Treaty of San Ildefonso, to provide for Charles IV's son-in-law, the Duke of Parma, the kingdom of Tuscany, enlarged to have a population of a million. Failing in these protests, Irujo in 1804 was instructed to withdraw his contentions.[6]

Shortly before the transfer of Louisiana to the United States, Spain had restored the right of deposit at New Orleans. But her consternation over the Louisiana Purchase was expressed when she declined to ratify the Convention of 1802, brought back to Madrid in 1804 after its final approval by the United States Senate. This convention hung in the balance for the next fourteen years.

More trouble ensued over the vagueness concerning West Florida. Spain maintained that, having received the Floridas back from England, she still held them, with the same western limits that the English had enjoyed, but with allowance for the establishment in 1795 of the limit of thirty-one degrees on the north. Quoting the Treaty of San Ildefonso, and the Louisiana Purchase treaty in its definition of Louisiana as having "the Same extent that it now has in the hands of Spain, & that it had when France possessed it; and Such as it Should be after the Treaties subsequently entered into between Spain and other States," the United States countered that this provided for the extension of Louisiana to the Perdido, the Franco-Spanish boundary of 1719. The latter opinion was so definitely held that in 1804 the Mobile Act authorized the organization of the territory as a United States customs district.

Meanwhile Pinckney had threatened war if the Convention of 1802 were not ratified. He went to the foreign office with a chip on his shoulder, only to find that it became a heavy burden when his bluff was called. Monroe arrived in Spain as a special commissioner in January, 1805, to act with Pinckney.

Monroe and Pinckney endeavored to obtain Spanish recognition of the Louisiana Purchase, including West Florida, and to purchase East Florida. Instructions to them stipulated that, in the event of a money payment by the United States, the funds involved should be applied to claims of United States citizens against Spain. Though their mission was a failure, certain of the points in their discussion are of interest because they were revived after the fall of Napoleon.

An alternative proposal in their advances concerned the western limits of Louisiana, which, as the United States had contended since shortly after the purchase, extended to the Río Grande, thus including the present Texas. This opinion was that of Livingston, Secretary of State Madison, and President Jefferson, and has been shown to have been originally that of Napoleon.[7] Pinckney and Monroe were instructed to offer a compromise, accepting the Colorado River of Texas (about 250 miles east of the Río Grande) as the boundary, if Spain would cede East Florida and withdraw claims to West Florida.

Cevallos, answering peremptory notes of Monroe and Pinckney with voluminous evasiveness, reinjected the Claims Convention of 1802, and the right of deposit, into the argument. He demanded that for ratification of the convention the time for filing of claims should be extended; that the clause reserving rights in the French spoliation claims should be canceled on the ground that France and the United States had completely settled their controversies by their conventions of 1803; and that the part of the Mobile Customs Act which affected Spanish territory should be rescinded. He also stated that the right of deposit at New Orleans, which had been extended for four years beyond the stipulation of Pinckney's Treaty, had been abused by contraband trading. Finally, Cevallos did come to the boundary issue. But instead of answering the proposal on western limits, he presented a letter from Talleyrand, who, wanting Spanish aid against England, now said that Spain had not ceded West Florida to France. Cevallos also stipulated that French spoliations on United States commerce be ignored by Spain. Later, he expounded Spain's claims to Texas.

Monroe and Pinckney, following an assurance of the French foreign office to the United States minister, General John Armstrong, that France would back Spain even in a war, resolved on abandoning the project, after one more effort. Accordingly, they stated that the United States was willing to set the western line at the Colorado River, with a thirty-league no-man's land on the eastern bank, and, by accepting Spain's cession of both East and West Florida, to admit that West Florida was not a part of the Louisiana Purchase. Cevallos declined, and Monroe left, followed shortly after by Pinckney, in the summer of 1805.

There now entered the foreign service of the United States, as chargé d'affaires in Spain, George W. Erving, who was to be minister during the final negotiation of the Adams-Onís Treaty. Appointed secretary of legation under his cousin James Bowdoin, whom Jefferson had named minister, Erving became chargé when Bowdoin decided to avoid Madrid and was sent instead to Paris as a special commissioner.

Erving continued the discussions with Cevallos, but to slight avail. He had to protest a renewal of seizure of United States ships by Spanish officials, but, in view of the close backing of Spain by France, the United States could not press matters too firmly. The same difficulty deterred action on the boundaries. Strong opinions were held that Texas should be seized, but fear of antagonizing Napoleon, as well as the Republican party's hesitation to befriend England through such an attack on Spain, combined to prevent its seizure.

In increasing measure the close relationship between the French and Spanish ministries complicated the efforts of United States agents abroad. In Madrid the court of Charles IV was dominated by men of the type of Prime Minister Don Manuel de Godoy, and Cevallos.[8] Though thoroughly schooled in the traditions of eighteenth-century diplomacy, they were not well versed in the geographical details of American problems. Their activities were at this time largely governed by their subordination to Napoleon, who continued to hold the whip hand in Spanish affairs until the entry of the British in 1809. Consequently, the well-known francophile tendencies of the Republican party made any affront to Spain a disavowal of its prevailing diplomatic policy.

In the hope of obtaining concessions from Spain through French intercession, Madison instructed Armstrong to continue at Paris the effort to get the Floridas. Armstrong proposed an arrangement much like that offered at Madrid. The Floridas were to be purchased for five million dollars, and both France and Spain were to be allowed commercial privileges there equal to those of the United States; four million dollars were to be paid by Spain in satisfaction of all claims; and the Colorado River was to be the boundary on the west. A counterproject, inspired by the French prime minister, Talleyrand, was broader in scope. It included the payment of six million dollars to meet claims against Spain by bills on the Spanish colonies, the payment of ten million dollars by the United States for the Floridas, and the extension of the western boundary northward from the source of the Colorado along the headwaters of the Mississippi tributaries. Both schemes included the earlier proposal of a thirty-league desert or neutral zone along the border. The expectation of French assistance was based in part on Armstrong's well-founded belief that any money which might be paid to Spain would promptly find its way to the coffers of Napoleon.[9]

It was necessary to make provisions at home for the execution of such arrangements as those proposed at Paris. Although the net amount to be paid by the United States had been reduced to four million dollars, Jefferson had difficulty in obtaining any appropriation. After a bitter dispute with John Randolph, chairman of the House committee which considered the matter, he managed to get a two-million-dollar grant for the purchase of the Floridas. But the whole negotiation fell through, chiefly because Napoleon's financial needs had been relieved by his successful campaigns in Central Europe.

It is important, for a proper perspective on the later development of United States policy, to note that, in his instructions of 1806 to Armstrong and the newly appointed Bowdoin, Madison held the Floridas to be of much greater importance than the western boundary. He considered West Florida "essential" and East Florida "important," and was willing to yield if necessary to the Sabine River as the western limit in order to obtain the Floridas. That concession meant the relinquishment of all Texas. Thus Monroe's plan foreshadowed the agreement which was ultimately consummated in 1819.

Irujo, meanwhile, was becoming increasingly unpopular with the government at Washington. In 1804 he raised a storm of protest over the Mobile Act; shortly thereafter it was discovered that he had offered inducements to a Philadelphia newspaper man for the publication of articles presenting the Spanish side of the Florida question. And like Merry, the British minister, he developed quite obvious wrath over the informality of Jefferson's and Madison's social customs.

His protests against the Mobile Act were followed by bitter comments on Jefferson's message of 1805 leading to the two-million-dollar Florida appropriation. At that time, with a request for his recall, the Cabinet determined to hold no further correspondence with him. Irujo, unable to communicate directly, voiced his opinions and his complaints against developments, such as the arming in this country of an expedition to revolutionize Venezuela, by means of the press and through the French minister, L. M. Turreau de Garambouville, who took some of his messages to Madison orally. Irujo's efforts were futile, however, and in 1807 he was removed to Milan.

Irujo's departure brought to an end any effective representation of Spain in this country, although there were two men left to dispute between themselves the rights and duties of *encargado de negocios,* or chargé d'affaires. Valentín de Foronda had been consul-general during the ministry of Irujo, and had quarreled with that minister. The arguments were continued between Foronda and José Ignacio Viar, the other *encargado,* who had been in the Spanish service in this country as early as 1792.[10] The two reported on affairs in the United States, and attempted to convey complaints to the government, but did so with difficulty, inasmuch as they were permitted no official diplomatic intercourse. Finally in July, 1809, fearing war between England and the United States, they appealed for the appointment of a minister with sufficient rank and powers to cope with the situation.[11]

Their request was in fact anticipated by the appointment of Onís in the summer of 1809. He left for the United States at once, but was doomed to wait for seven years before he could open official negotiations. In order to understand the causes of that embarrassment, and the difficulties of the rôle Onís undertook, one must turn to the development of the civil war in Spain. It was due to the ostensibly neutral but really pro-French policy of Madison that the government failed to acknowledge Onís' credentials from a Spanish patriot assembly.

NAPOLEON, FERDINAND, AND THE WELLESLEYS

That Spanish diplomacy was ineffective in these years is far from surprising in view of the interference of France. Godoy had won a dubious honor by signing the Treaty of Basel in 1795, by which Spain deserted the first anti-French coalition. In the next year a treaty of alliance with the French government of the Directory had been signed. And now Napoleon, since his accession to power, had become oppressive. Following his defeat at Trafalgar, he sought economic instead of naval aid from Spain; and after imposing heavy tribute on the country, and obtaining her adhesion to the Continental blockade, he forced her into a scheme to bring Portugal into the same system. French troops were to march through Spain, and, following the joint conquest, a tripartite division of Portugal was to be effected.[12]

Napoleon made this arrangement with Godoy, his chief henchman in the Peninsula. He had been dealing also, treacherously, with Crown Prince Ferdinand, Godoy's bitter enemy. The new treaty concerning Portugal brought rebellion from Ferdinand, but in October, 1807, with the discovery of a plot which had been hatched by the Crown Prince and some of the nobility, Ferdinand was again brought under the Emperor's thumb. French troops conquered Portugal, and were turned back on Spain itself to make French domination complete.

Popular uprisings then began the movement which ultimately led to the downfall of Napoleon. King Charles IV, caught between the French and his own subjects, abdicated on March 19, 1808. His son, supported by the populace who lauded his anti-French conspiracy, reigned briefly as Ferdinand VII. But Napoleon's diplomacy and troops soon caused the complete and abject yielding of the Spanish royal family. They were all forced to gather at Bayonne, in southern France, where on May 5 father and son renounced their rights to the crown, and remained virtual captives of Napoleon.[13]

The Emperor called an assembly of Spanish notables in Bayonne to draw up a constitution for the country. And to be constitutional monarch, he chose his brother Joseph, who for the two years previous had been king of Naples. Joseph set out for his new capital in July of 1808.

Terrific resistance was encountered almost immediately. Spectacular public resentment had flared forth in Madrid on the famous second of May, when the youngest prince was forced to leave for Bayonne. Local *juntas,* or governing bodies, sprang up all over Spain; and guerrilla armies fell on the French, distinguishing themselves at the battle of Bailén, on the day before Joseph's entrance into Madrid. That and other successes forced Joseph to retire to northern Spain, and to appeal to his brother for aid. Napoleon himself was forced to campaign in Spain that autumn to reëstablish the *"rey intruso"* (intruder king).

A *Junta Suprema de Gobierno* (supreme governing body), formed in April, 1808, under the French commander Joachim Murat, failed to hold the people, who followed their organization of local *juntas* by drawing up a rival to the Murat group under the presidency of Count Floridablanca. This institution, the *Junta Central Suprema Gubernativa del Reino* (central supreme governing body of the kingdom), carried on in the name of Ferdinand VII, refusing to acknowledge his renunciation in favor of the Bonapartes. It met first at Aranjuez in September, 1809, then moved to Sevilla; and in the fall of 1810, when Napoleon again invaded Spain, it was driven to the Island of León in the harbor of Cádiz, the one spot that could be defended against the French forces.[14]

This organization, or its successors, the *Consejo de Regencia* (regent council) and the *Cortes* (assembly), both first formed in 1810, maintained a government in opposition to the French throughout the Napoleonic Wars which followed, and provided the legal continuation of the monarchy as a truly Spanish institution. But their efforts would have been fruitless without the powerful aid of England.

The English, especially after the battle of Trafalgar and Napoleon's invasion of Portugal, Britain's ally, bent their efforts to attacking the French through the Peninsula. It was the most vulnerable point in the Continental system. Thus Britain was amenable to diplomatic advances made by the Spanish *Junta* and Regency—in fact encouraged and guided them. On January 14, 1809, a treaty of alliance against France was drawn up in London, which laid the foundation for the Peninsular campaign and the eventual expulsion of the Corsican.[15]

British interests in Spain were largely carried forward by members of that notable family the Wellesleys. Richard, Marquis Wellesley, former viceroy of India, was minister to Spain in the latter half of 1809, and foreign secretary during the early part of the Peninsular campaign; his brother Arthur, later Duke of Wellington, led the combined troops; and another brother, Henry, later Baron Cowley, will appear in this study as secretary of legation in 1809, minister in 1810, and ambassador from 1811 to 1822.

A detailed military account of the war is hardly needed here; but for the background of Onís' narrative it should be remembered that until 1813 there were two active governments in Spain, Ferdinand finally being restored in 1814; and that the intervening period was one of bitter fighting in the northern part of the Peninsula between the French under various generals and the Anglo-Spanish under Wellington.

An interested, though no doubt discouraged, spectator of the beginning of these troubles was George W. Erving, the United States chargé, who chose to follow the *Junta Central* to Sevilla and Cádiz. His position, however, was only that of an observer. Since his government declined to acknowledge either Joseph or the *Junta Central* as the ruler of Spain, it could not officially accredit Erving to either. In instructions sent by Robert Smith, secretary of state, November 1, 1809, this policy was explained, and Erving was told to use his own judgment about remaining.[16]

Erving had obtained the release of some United States ships which had fallen afoul of the commercial restrictions of the European wars, had complained against British impressments in the harbor of Cádiz, and had answered Spanish denunciations of Jefferson's embargo.[17] But finally he decided nothing could be accomplished through informal relations with such an unstable administration, and he left in August, 1810.

In the interim after Erving's departure, three men represented the United States: Anthony Morris, special agent; the Reverend Thomas Gough, unofficial representative; and Thomas Brent, later named secretary of the legation. Their lack of rank and the disputes among them prohibited any effective diplomacy, even if any could have been carried on between countries without formal relations. Furthermore, it is difficult to believe that much could have been accomplished in connection with the patriot government, which in the years from 1809 to 1814 had no less than fifteen officials successively in charge of its foreign office.[18]

Not only was the Spanish Empire troubled at home. Shortly after the Napoleonic invasion, the American colonies, which had long fretted under an outdated administrative system, became torn by violent rebellions. These popular movements were led by local *juntas* similar to those in Spain, which likewise acknowledged Ferdinand VII, disavowing his renunciation of the crown. In a few years, however, their loyalty had become mere lip service, and their movements had steadily developed into wars of independence. But in 1809 the patriot government at home took it for granted that they would remain true and could be pacified.

Napoleon's ambitions had extended to the colonies as well, and paralleling the Peninsular War a contest developed between the rival governments of Spain for the fealty of the colonies. French agents roamed over both American continents, actively spreading propaganda.

Several circumstances combined to make the presence of an able Spanish representative at Washington imperative. It was essential for Spain to have information concerning, and influence in, the United States; and the extension of our ambitions toward the south and west, the increasing complexity of British-American affairs, and the desirability of learning the position of the United States on European developments made the need more evident. Thus the *Junta Central* at Aranjuez anticipated the plea of Foronda and Viar by appointing a minister.

DON LUIS DE ONÍS

For this position they chose a man who had served the foreign office for more than thirty years, Luis de Onís y González.[19] He was a native of the town of Cantalapiedra, in the province of Salamanca, where his family still maintains its ancestral home. He received the best education available, beginning the study of Latin and Greek at the age of eight, attending the University of Salamanca, and having two years of legal training. In 1780 he went as secretary with his uncle, Don José de Onís, ambassador to Saxony. After four years the uncle (later ambassador to Russia) returned to Spain, leaving Don Luis as chargé for more than ten years. In that office he won the approval of the secretary of state, Count

Floridablanca. He was chosen to be minister to the United States in 1792, but the fall of Floridablanca's Cabinet prevented his serving in that capacity.

Onís remained in Germany until 1798, when he was made an official of the ministry of state in Madrid. He had charge of matters concerning France for some time, and was active in the negotiation of the Peace of Amiens in 1802. Six years later he went with the court to Bayonne, and at the request of Cevallos wrote his opinion of Ferdinand's renunciation. It was a categorical statement to the effect that the King neither could nor should make such a concession. This stand made it necessary for him to flee to Spain, where he at once joined the patriot *Junta Central* at Aranjuez.

During part of his year's service as senior official in the ministry of state under the *Junta Central* he virtually controlled the office as chief adviser to Don Martín de Garay, who succeeded Cevallos as secretary of state in 1809. It was in the summer of that year that he was chosen, no doubt at the instance of Cevallos and Floridablanca, to represent the *Junta Central* (and according to their view the King, in whose name they governed) at Washington.[20] He was then forty-seven years of age.

Onís left immediately, arriving in New York on October 4, 1809, and had his first interview with Secretary of State Robert Smith in Washington on October 21. He noted that, whereas he could understand Spanish, French, German, or Italian better than English, he knew the last well enough to conduct the conversations with Smith.

Surely he had learned to be suspicious from observing and participating in the intrigues of the court of Madrid. Shortly after his arrival he wrote that he understood that

Mrs. Madison and Mrs. Smith receive presents, and that this is one of the means of which the French minister avails himself to obtain all that he wishes. . . . I wish that you would tell me if you believe it advisable that I should follow an example which can be so advantageous to us in whatever case offers itself.[21]

He sent a spy to Washington to investigate the possibilities of such a plan, but apparently had no success; meanwhile his government had discouraged it on account of the expense.

Onís played an important rôle in the scheme of Spanish service in America, and his position had interesting phases aside from his dealings with the United States government. On him naturally fell the organization and direction of the Spanish service in this country. Disgusted by the disputes of Foronda and Viar (the *encargados* who requested his appointment), he demanded and obtained a complete cleanup of the system. Those two officials were removed, the consul-generalship was suspended, and thereafter all the consuls reported to Onís.[22]

Furthermore, he served as purveyor of information on the Spanish colonies, conducting detailed correspondence with such officials as the governors of the Floridas, the captain-general of Cuba, and the viceroy of Mexico. He frequently advised them concerning necessary steps for the defense of the realm, and reported menacing French or United States movements of which he learned. These duties were especially important in view of the Spanish American revolts which were in progress during the whole period of his residence as minister.

Onís also performed valuable service in directing the purchase and expedition of supplies to Spain during the Peninsular War. His purchase of ships, and flour to send in them, formed an important part of his work.[23]

Onís' largest problems, however, lay in his relations with the United States government. His original instructions were not written with the expectation that a treaty would be negotiated at Washington, although he had full powers.[24] He was to sound the possibilities of progress toward a treaty, and coöperate in furthering it. In any event he was to maintain communication with the government at Washington if possible.

In the first interview with Smith, he was told of the policy of this country toward the rival governments in the Peninsula, a policy which would not allow the recognition of any representative of either.[25] One may well suspect that Madison would have welcomed an opportunity to recognize Joseph Bonaparte as the *de facto* ruler of Spain. But in fact neither Joseph nor the Regency was in assured control of all the country at any time before the restoration. Therefore commitment to either side would have been too large a gamble for an administration whose Jeffersonian watchword was to await the definite turn of events in Europe and reap what gains might fall its way.

Jefferson expressed his view of the situation to Madison at the time, saying:

There seems to be a perfect acquiescence in the opinion of the Government respecting Onis. The public interest certainly made his rejection expedient, and as that is a motive which it is not pleasant always to avow, I think it fortunate that the contending claims of Charles and Ferdinand furnished such plausible embarrassment to the question of right; for, on our principles, I presume, the right of the Junta to send a Minister could not be denied.[26]

From this statement it is clear that the administration was simply postponing the issue in the hope that the favored Napoleonic régime might firmly establish itself in the Peninsula.

Intercourse with the United States was by no means stopped, however. Onís, on his departure from Spain, had been instructed to remain in the United States, whether admitted as minister or not.[27] This order was later made more definite by Eusebio de Bardaxi y Azara, one of the foreign ministers under the Regency.

Bardaxi in instructions written April 21, 1810, reviewed the United States' policy of past years as he saw it. He noted that the effort to maintain neutrality had been threatened by the Napoleonic Wars, and that now, although in commerce the country had nothing to fear from France, she had much to fear from England. Bardaxi showed a tendency to overconfidence and complacence quite characteristic of him and of his contemporaries in Spain when he said that the United States government knew its interests too well to risk a war with anybody, and that "it is ridiculous for her to imagine she is in a condition to make a war."[28] Ridiculous as it may have seemed to him, the war was soon to come, and to affect Spanish interests materially. The same complacence is seen in his remark, in reply to Onís' warning of the presence of French conspirators in America, that "they should not give much concern, because happily we live in times in which adventurers make very little progress wherever they present themselves."

For the time being, commercial needs were of paramount importance in the policy toward the United States. This was shown in these same instructions to Onís when Bardaxi said that amicable relations should be sought, chiefly to encourage the continuation of United States shipments of foodstuffs to the Peninsula. Although under ordinary circumstances the nonrecognition of Onís would have been considered an insult, it was now deemed advisable to temporize with the Madison administration. Onís was told to "seek adroitly to find a means to treat of public affairs with that government," to use the newspapers to influence public opinion, and that, "as our only purpose is to maintain friendly relations between the two powers, . . . you must use much prudence and circumspection, in your writings as well as in the conversations which you have."[29]

Onís distrusted the Republican party of Madison and Monroe, and throughout his residence in this country never showed any liking for the two men. He made all the friends he could among the Federalists, using them as sources of information as well as of influence. He followed instructions regarding writings by publishing, among other things, three pamphlets justifying Spain's interests, which appeared in 1810, 1812, and 1817 under the pseudonym "Verus," used earlier by Irujo.[30]

Despite Onís' nonrecognition, communications went on, in part through the British representatives. On Onís' arrival, he reported that he would live in the same house in Washington with Francis James Jackson, minister from England. His failure to be acknowledged caused him to retire to Philadelphia, but only increased his efforts to win favor with the agents of His Britannic Majesty.

When Onís reached Washington, Secretary of State Smith was involved in an argument with Jackson, who had come a month earlier. That summer, Foreign Minister Canning had rejected the Anglo–United States trade revival agreement negotiated by Jackson's predecessor, David M. Erskine. The new minister thus had come into the midst of a dispute concerning whether or not Erskine had exceeded his instructions. This brought from Jackson a barely disguised accusation of falseness on the part of Smith. Relations between Jackson and Smith were broken off completely in November.

Onís maintained Jackson's confidence through 1810, while the discredited Englishman remained in this country, and the two exchanged information on affairs in Spain and in Spanish America. Jackson was followed by John Philip Morier, chargé, who conveyed some of Onís' complaints on Florida to Smith. He was told in reply that England "did not need to interfere in these subjects."[31] Onís in relating the incident commented that England surely had the right to interfere, as guarantor of the Floridas to Spain under the treaty of 1783.

Meanwhile Onís was trying to deal with Smith through Juan Bautista de Bernabeu, Spanish consul at Baltimore, who conveyed messages on numerous occasions, until his departure for Spain in 1815.[32]

The suggestion had been made, indirectly through a private citizen, that Onís might be admitted if he brought credentials from Mexico. The Spaniard would consider no such idea, and in commenting on it to his own government gave Madison this flourish: "The character of Madison is entirely indecisive and pusillanimous. He is completely given over to France." Although, because of the recent seizure of three hundred United States ships by the French, public opinion favored war with France, he stated that "this government has not the determination to declare war on France, nor on England."[33]

Bernabeu finally obtained an interview with Smith, in September, 1810, in which the latter repeated assurances that Onís would be admitted in the event of a Spanish reconquest of the Peninsula. He added that "a better and a more honest man was never sent out by any nation. . . . Señor Onís is truly respectable by all signs, and we all desire as much as you his recognition, regretting that our neutral position has served as an obstacle to it."[34]

Within a few days Onís found a more convenient channel of communication through Alexander J. Dallas, United States district attorney for the Eastern District of Pennsylvania, with whom numerous conferences were held. Of him Onís said, "Mr. Dallas is like all those of the Democratic party, but is a fine man, of much talent and admitted in the society of the Federalists. I was already on friendly terms with him."[35]

This lasted for only a few months, because in March of 1811 Smith was removed. He was succeeded by James Monroe, who held the office continuously from then until his inauguration to the presidency in 1817. Monroe's appointment brought a change in the communication system. To supplement Bernabeu, Onís called on Pablo Chacón, vice-consul at Alexandria, Virginia. The despatches are full of copies of Bernabeu's and Chacón's detailed accounts of their conferences with Monroe.

A blow was thought to have been dealt to Onís' chances for recognition early in 1811, when one of his letters to another Spanish official was intercepted by revolutionary agents. Upon its receipt

at Washington it was submitted to Congress by President Madison.
Among its choicer passages is the following:

> The administration of this government having put the stamp upon the
> servile meanness and adulation in which they stand in relation to their oracle,
> Bonaparte, the day before yesterday, by their direction, Mr. Eppes, the son
> in law of the former president, Jefferson, made a proposition that a min-
> ister should be sent immediately to Joseph Bonaparte. . . . a vote was taken,
> from which it resulted that, for the present no minister should be sent to
> Joseph.
>
> In the annexed paper you will see all the debates, which for want of time,
> I have not been able to have translated: if your excellency should not be in-
> formed by my former despatches of the mode of thinking of the present ad-
> ministration, this alone will show you the little hope there is of obtaining any
> thing favorable from it, but by energy, by force, and by chastisement.[36]

Although the knowledge of such writings would naturally have
made the administration antagonistic, it is essential to remember
that the policy of nonrecognition was adopted immediately upon
Onís' arrival, before his attitude could have been known. Later
developments, at the time of his official acceptance, also support
the view that the administration's stand was based upon European
political exigencies, and not upon objections to Onís.

After Monroe's appointment, Onís complained to his government that the new secretary of state would not communicate with
him satisfactorily. He was then officially instructed to inform the
administration at Washington, "with firmness and dignity," that
Spain would not long suffer such humiliation.[37] Onís was assured
that the favorable progress of the Peninsular War and the pacification of revolting Mexico gave Spain the hope of being able to defend her American frontiers vigorously. In a code message sent
with this instruction, however, Onís received something of a rebuke
in the statement of Bardaxi that "notwithstanding that which I
tell you in my other letter . . . you must modify somewhat your expressions, presenting your notes in language somewhat less harsh."

WARTIME EFFORTS

As a measure of his accomplishments up to the time of his recognition late in 1815, Onís' diplomatic activities may be conveniently
summarized under the following heads: complaints delivered to the
United States, discussion of Spanish policy in the War of 1812,
abortive dealings with Monroe on a Florida cession, and the small

part he played in the attempts of Spain to have her interests considered at the Ghent peace conference. A dominant note throughout the period is Onís' increasing anxiety caused by the rapidly developing sympathy in the United States for the rebellious Spanish Americans.

The complaints were voiced continually, and their narration forms a large part of Onís' despatches. Their subjects were: (1) his nonrecognition as minister; (2) the fitting out in United States ports of privateers and of vessels which aided the insurgent Spanish American provinces; (3) French and United States unofficial propaganda encouraging revolutions in the Spanish colonies; (4) the occupation and assimilation of revolted West Florida by the United States; (5) the invasion of East Florida; (6) high duties and port charges imposed on Spanish ships by this country; and (7) the steps taken by the United States to gain control over the Creek Indians of Florida. Of these complaints, the second, third, and sixth lie somewhat outside the necessary limitations of this study. The remainder will be considered in the succeeding chapter dealing with frontier conditions, supplementing the notes here on the diplomatic aspects.

Monroe had come into office desirous of maintaining peace, but within fifteen months war was declared on England. The close relationship of this struggle to the whole question of Spanish relations is obvious in the fact that Western ambition for the conquest not only of Canada, but of the Floridas as well, was a contributing cause of the war. Two problems immediately arose—that of a possible advance by the United States southward and that of the probable use of the Floridas as bases of operations by the English.

Onís sent word to Spain of the passage of the war bill by the Senate on June 17, with a comment which shows at once his clear analysis and the fact that he was in a position to give valuable advice to his government:

All my effort will be directed toward maintaining our neutrality, so that we can supply all our possessions with flour, under our own flag; if this is to be achieved, as there is a shortage of Spanish ships and a long time must pass before this announcement is known [in Spain], I feel it my duty to notify you that in view of the need of provisions in the Peninsula, I intend to authorize the Consuls of His Majesty who have funds to buy ships, in order that they may send cargoes of flour on their own account to the Peninsula and other possessions of His Majesty.[38]

Rumors of the United States' projects soon prompted him to intensify his frequent warnings of the need of defending the neighboring Spanish colonies. In October he wrote that apparently the first moves would be to prohibit the sending of aid to the Peninsula and to take the Floridas.[39] He always urged close coöperation with England for maritime defense, and on this occasion, as on others, suggested the possibility of secretly stirring up a slave revolt in the South to distract attention and impede the advance toward the Floridas.

Meanwhile a special meeting of the *Consejo de Estado* (council of state) was held at Cádiz in August to consider Spain's policy toward the war. It resulted in a note from the foreign minister, Ignacio Pezuela, to the British representative, Henry Wellesley, stating that "in all our possessions British forces will receive the reception becoming to the intimate friendship and alliance which exists between the two powers."[40] Wellesley asked for a more specific explanation, and a month later Pezuela, in instructions to Onís, described his statement of Spanish policy as follows:

Spain has for a long time had abundant motives for considering herself in a state of war with the United States, but in the critical situation in which she sees herself, having to sustain destructive wars in both hemispheres [against Napoleon and against her own colonies] which absorb all her resources, she cannot count on the necessary forces to oppose the insults of the American government with probability of success. Considering this, and seeing that by a declaration of war on the United States the Peninsula would be deprived of the supplies of flour and other necessary articles of subsistence which she receives from that country, the Regency has determined to adopt a policy of temporizing with the American government. This is conceived in such terms that our relations with the Americans should not prejudice the interests of England, which we must favor by all considerations of gratefulness and due friendship, although being careful not to give pretext to the American government to carry the excess of its complacency toward France to the point of making a war which could suit neither Spain nor England. . . . These views . . . I transmit to you advising you at the same time that the Regency has made opportune exertions to obtain [an agreement] from the English government that its ships should protect the boats, possessions, and properties of Spain, and especially the Floridas from the usurpations of the Americans.[41]

Spain was of course bound to support England, generally speaking, by her treaty of January, 1809; furthermore, she showed here the anxiety which she so frequently demonstrated in leaning for naval, military, and diplomatic support on the island kingdom.

The flour and wheat from the United States, most of which are said to have been consumed by the British armies in the Peninsula, were shipped in greatest quantities in the years 1812 and 1813. Though Onís and his consuls were buying some ships, most of the supplies went in United States bottoms, and their owners profited well until the breakdown of the Continental system released supplies from the Baltic.[42] An act of Congress, in 1813, prohibiting United States vessels to sail under foreign licenses, such as those issued by the British for this trade even during the war, helped to stop this commerce.

During the struggle, although the volume of Onís' correspondence evidences a difficulty of communication and a somewhat necessary lapse in activity, there did develop an interesting effort on the part of Monroe to revive the Florida dealings. In 1811, although he received Congressional authority for occupation under certain conditions, Monroe failed in what was evidently an attempt to obtain East Florida by subornation of a revolt which would have allowed the province to fall into the hands of the United States. When war was declared, only a slim Northern and Federalist majority kept Congress from authorizing the seizure of all of Florida east of the Perdido, in order to keep England from using it as a base. A like attempt of the administration met failure in 1813.

After the first such failure, Monroe approached Onís through Vice-Consul Chacón. In a conference on July 15, 1812, Monroe is reported by Chacón to have said that,

According to the geographical situation of that region, the nature of its habitants, and in order to conserve the peace between the two nations, the Floridas should belong to the United States, and for years the Congress has taken this into consideration, and expects that Spain, in order to avoid a possible war, before exposing herself to that will concede amicably that which ... this government claims so justly over a territory which Spain does not need, not being able to derive any advantage from it, and the maintenance of which costs more labor and expense than one could expect it to be worth.[43]

Two weeks later Monroe presented a set of propositions and questions for Onís' consideration. He stated that the United States would exchange for East Florida, and for Spain's claims to West Florida, its right to be indemnified for damages suffered in the Napoleonic Wars. He asked whether Onís was authorized to make such a treaty, whether the Florida officials would obey his order to evacuate, what effect the Constitution of 1812 would have,[44] and, if Onís had full powers, when it would be convenient for him to come to Washington to negotiate.[45]

Onís, in the despatch which related these propositions, stated that he thought they were "ridiculous" and insincere. He listed a greater number of Spanish grievances toward the United States than Monroe had considered, including the old protest of the illegality of the Louisiana Purchase, the damage caused by Miranda's expedition to Venezuela, that caused by Captain Pike in his journey through northern Mexico, claims for injuries by French privateers who brought Spanish vessels into United States ports, the damage caused by the embargo (which he said should not have applied to Spanish ships), and that done by a presidential proclamation which, Onís stated, urged the provinces of Spanish America to declare their independence.[46]

He then stated his intention, in view of the progress of Spanish arms in the Peninsula and in Mexico, and of the weakness of the United States' military forces, to delay until Spain could send effective reinforcements to protect the Floridas. Accordingly he answered Monroe on only one point, saying he did not have full powers to treat.

The Regency in Spain made short shrift of Monroe's propositions, writing Onís that they had

no great confidence that that government will fulfill what it promises, as it already appears to be its constant maxim to aggravate by deed and make reparations by word.

As to powers it has already been repeated to you, at different times, that only those of an ordinary minister to a friendly government will be sent and not those of a negotiator of cessions, and that neither does the constitution permit nor the decorum of this most punctilious and valiant nation consent that you should even talk of cessions.[47]

Spain, growing more and more confident during the war in view of its successes against Napoleon and the miserable performance of the United States against England, received with avidity all news of the war in America, and planned to be on hand when the spoils were divided. To this end she strove to have her interests considered in any peace negotiations—but she strove vainly. Onís' only participation was to recommend such an effort, to discuss it with the Russian minister in Washington, André de Daschkoff, and to attempt to persuade the United States to instruct its commissioners to consider Spanish affairs. At the same time, no doubt, the Regency in refusing Onís the authority to negotiate was partly moved by its belief that the United States was about to suffer a disastrous defeat.

Daschkoff brought to Monroe in March, 1813, the offer of Czar Alexander to mediate, an offer accepted so promptly that in May commissioners were en route to Europe. Immediately Spain's ambassador in London, Count Fernán Núñez, was instructed to ask England to demand at the conference that the United States evacuate the occupied sections of the Floridas, and that they recognize the Regency and admit Onís.

Fernán Núñez made his approaches to the new British foreign minister, Robert Stewart, Viscount Castlereagh. He failed completely, on account of two stubborn facts: first, Castlereagh had declined the offer of Russian mediation, and, second, as Fernán Núñez reported in his despatch of September 25, 1813, he found the Russians apparently pledged to support British interests, so that Spain could expect no aid from that quarter.[48]

In Washington, Onís had no better fortune. Far from instructing our commissioners to consider a settlement which would suit Spain, Monroe told them that they might "find it advantageous to bring to the view of her Ministers, the relation which the United States bear to the Floridas." That relation, he explained, was expressed in the claim to West Florida as part of Louisiana, the claim to East Florida as indemnity for spoliations, and the effort made by Congress to keep out a foreign threat by passing a bill authorizing occupation of West Florida.[49]

This renewal of Monroe's efforts to obtain some recognition of the United States' claim to the Floridas was thwarted by Albert Gallatin, a member of the commission and an opponent of the administration's Florida policy. He insisted on the withdrawal of United States troops from Florida in order to aid the commissioners in their diplomacy with England and Russia.[50] Thus the efforts of both Spain and this country to further settlement of their issues in this negotiation failed.

When, after Castlereagh's later offer to treat directly for peace, the commissioners finally undertook their work at Ghent in the fall of 1814, Spain again endeavored to intrude upon the negotiations. Fernán Núñez once more received instructions to try to influence the British ministry in that direction. Spain now demanded the return of all of Louisiana (disregarding her approval of the purchase, given in 1806), and asserted that Great Britain had promised the return to Spain of all her territory occupied by the United States.[51] But this gesture was also fruitless, and, as the United States' commissioners again went uninstructed toward any settlement suitable to Spain, the Floridas were omitted from the treaty, as was Louisiana.

Spanish confidence was further shattered by the postwar victory of Jackson at New Orleans; and it was with evident disappointment that Onís wrote, on hearing of the conclusion reached at Ghent, as follows:

If in this treaty nothing has been stipulated relative to the conclusion of the discussions pending between His Majesty and this government, I foresee great difficulties in settling them in an advantageous manner, and I fear that we have lost the most favorable occasion which could present itself for accomplishing that end. Of course Louisiana and New Orleans have been fortified for the attack of the English, there has gathered in them a respectable army, and although it is regular that with the conclusion of peace the militias should disband and return to their homes, to rest on their laurels, I cannot say that General Jackson, moved by his vainglory over the defense of New Orleans, and the taking of Pensacola, will not try energetically to aid the insurgents of the Provincias Internas.[52]

This was not Jackson's first threat to the Spanish outposts, nor was the dangerous situation on the frontier suddenly created at this time. To understand later diplomacy one must turn to a survey of conditions and the development of controversies along that extensive and undetermined line. And one must continually ask how far the territorial claims of the two countries coincided with movements of population, or with exploits of isolated explorers, traders, or settlers; and how far such factors may have guided diplomatic arrangements.

NOTES TO CHAPTER I

¹ "Treaty of Amity, Settlement, and Limits, Signed at Washington, February 22, 1819," in Division of State Department Archives, the National Archives, Washington, Treaties. The most reliable publication of this treaty is in the current series: D. Hunter Miller, *Treaties and Other International Acts of the United States of America* (Washington, 1931—), III:3–20.

² Samuel Flagg Bemis, *Pinckney's Treaty* (Baltimore, 1926), *passim*.

³ Claims against Spain represented some 125 vessels and cargoes, at a valuation of from five to eight million dollars; those against France nearly the same. See Charles E. Hill, "James Madison," in *American Secretaries of State* (New York, 1927–1929), III:48. The complex problems of maritime spoliations run through the whole period. But they affected the Adams-Onís negotiations only slightly, and the claims were renounced in the treaty with little argument.

⁴ Miller, *op. cit.*, II:492–497.

⁵ Circumstantial evidence of a boundary agreement to include Texas in Louisiana made just preceding that treaty is presented in Richard Stenberg, "The Boundaries of the Louisiana Purchase," *Hispanic American Historical Review*, XIV (1934):32–64. But no satisfactory proof that it existed is advanced. Certainly there was no consideration of such a document in the Adams-Onís negotiations.

⁶ Hill, *op. cit.*, p. 46.

⁷ Henry Adams, *History of the United States* (New York, 1889–1891), II:255, 298.

⁸ Of Cevallos in this period a French writer has said: "The new secretary of state had [in 1800] for eight years been the nightmare of foreign ambassadors. . . . Obliging attention and passions of anger, ruses and threats were equally futile against his stammering and confused discourse, his involved notes, pedantic and vacuous, [and] his indolence and inertia. . . . But Cevallos had in the eyes of Godoy, whose cousin he had married, one quality of first rank: absolute submission to the favourite."—André Fugier, *Napoléon et l'Espagne* (Paris, 1930), I:119.

⁹ Hill, *op. cit.*, p. 58.

¹⁰ Onís to Pizarro (Spanish foreign minister), November 14, 1817, in Archivo Histórico Nacional (Madrid), Sección de Estado, Legajo 5642.

¹¹ Foronda and Viar to Garay (Spanish foreign minister), July 21, 1809, in A.H.N., Est., 5635, Apartado 3.

¹² Treaty of Fontainebleau, October 29, 1807, discussed in Fugier, *op. cit.*, II:254–262.

¹³ Pedro Aguado Bleye, *Manual de historia de España* (5th ed., Bilbao, 1927–1931), II:413–417; Fugier, *op. cit.*, II:440–448, and *passim*.

¹⁴ Aguado Bleye, *op. cit.*, II:501–518. Certain papers of the patriot *Junta* in the Archivo Histórico Nacional in Madrid are listed in the *Indice de los Papeles de la Junta Central Suprema Gubernativa del Reino y del Consejo de Regencia* (Madrid, 1904).

¹⁵ Wenceslao R. de Villa-Urrutia, *Relaciones entre España é Inglaterra durante la guerra de independencia, 1808 á 1814* (Madrid, 1911–1914), I:304–310; *British and Foreign State Papers* (London, 1841—), I:667–673.

¹⁶ Smith to Erving, November 1, 1809, in D.S., United States Ministers, Instructions, VII.

[17] Jabez Lamar M. Curry, "Diplomatic Services of George W. Erving," Massachusetts Historical Society, *Proceedings*, Ser. 2, V (1889) :17–33.

[18] Calculation from instructions to Onís, 1809–1814, in Archivo del Ministerio de Estado (Madrid), Estados Unidos, Legajos 216–221.

[19] MS biography of Onís (Madrid, 1827) ; José García de León y Pizarro, *Memorias* (Madrid, 1894–1897), I:201, 206. The assertion that Onís was appointed minister in 1792 is made in the MS biography. We know that the appointment of a minister at that time was projected, without definite reference to the individual, from a memorandum by William Carmichael, United States commissioner plenipotentiary, of a conversation he had with Floridablanca, dated at San Lorenzo, November 7, 1791. See A.H.N., Est., 3890; also Bemis, *op. cit.*, pp. 183–184.

[20] Villa-Urrutia, *op. cit.*, I:219; Jerónimo Bécker, *Historia de las relaciones exteriores de España durante el siglo XIX* (Madrid, 1924–1927), I:136–137; Garay to Foronda, June 29, 1809, in A.M.E., 216.

[21] Onís to Garay, November 16, 1809, in A.H.N., Est., 5635, Apartado 4.

[22] Onís to Pizarro, November 14, 1817, *ibid.*, 5642.

[23] Garay to Onís, July 29, 1809, in A.M.E., 216; Bardaxi to Onís, January 14 and May 5, 1810, *ibid.*, 217.

[24] Narciso de Heredia, *"Exposición ... al rey"* (June 4, 1817), in Pizarro, *op. cit.*, III:271. A copy of the original powers, not the instructions, dated July 26, 1809, appears in D.S., Notes from Spanish Legation, III.

[25] Onís to Garay, October 21, 1809, in A.H.N., Est., 5635, Apartado 4.

[26] Jefferson's reference to Charles IV and Ferdinand resulted apparently from a confusion of the dispute between those two in 1808 with that between the *Junta* and Joseph which raged in 1809. See Jefferson to Madison, November 26, 1809, in Jefferson, *Writings* (Memorial Ed., Washington, 1903–1904), XII:328; also Madison papers, MS, Library of Congress.

[27] Onís to Garay, October 21, 1809, in A.H.N., Est., 5635, Apartado 4.

[28] Bardaxi to Onís, April 21, 1810, in A.M.E., 217. Bardaxi held office from March, 1810, to February, 1812.

[29] *Ibid.*

[30] These "Verus" pamphlets are reprinted in Luis de Onís, *Memoria sobre las negociaciones* (Madrid, 1820), I, Appendix:14–70. That at least one of them was written by someone other than Onís is indicated in chap. iii, p. 63.

[31] Onís to Bardaxi, January 12, 1811, in A.H.N., Est., 5637.

[32] Cevallos to Onís, December 10, 1815, in A.M.E., 237.

[33] Onís to Marqués de las Hormazas (Spanish foreign minister), June 17, 1810, in A.H.N., Est., 5636. Bardaxi had been appointed foreign minister in March, but Onís did not learn of it until July 10, and so continued addressing despatches to Hormazas. Such discrepancies were frequent, and presented a major obstacle to efficient negotiation. It took anywhere from six weeks to four months for mail to reach Madrid from Washington, the latter period sometimes being required when mail was routed through England for safety.

[34] Onís to Bardaxi, September 20, 1810, in A.H.N., Est., 5636.

[35] Onís to Bardaxi, October 31, 1810, *ibid.*

[36] Onís to the captain-general of Caracas, February 2, 1810; translated in MS volume on Spanish affairs, 1810–1816, in the secret file of the secretary of state, now in the Division of Manuscripts, Library of Congress. Inaccurately published in *American State Papers* (Washington, 1832–1861), Class I, *Foreign Relations*, III:404.

[37] Bardaxi to Onís, June 24, 1811, in A.M.E., 218.

[38] Onís to Pizarro (then foreign minister for a few months), June 17, 1812, in A.H.N., Est., 5638.

[39] Onís to Pezuela (Spanish foreign minister), October 26, 1812, *ibid.*

[40] Pezuela to Wellesley, August 10, 1812, *ibid.*, 5556, Expediente 1. Similar instructions went to the viceroy of New Spain regarding the treatment of British ships on the Pacific. See Vernon D. Tate (ed.), "Spanish Documents Relating to the Voyage of the 'Racoon' to Astoria and San Francisco," *Hispanic American Historical Review*, XVIII (1938):183–191.

[41] Pezuela to Onís, September 10, 1812, in A.M.E., 219.

[42] W. Freeman Galpin, "American Grain Trade to the Spanish Peninsula, 1810–1814," *American Historical Review*, XXVIII (1922):24–44.

[43] Quoted in Onís to Pezuela, July 19, 1812, in A.H.N., Est., 5638.

[44] The patriot Cortes at Cádiz had approved a constitution on March 11, 1812. Although it was discarded with the absolutist restoration of Ferdinand VII, it became the battle cry of the rebelling American colonists and later of the Spanish Liberals.

[45] Onís to Pezuela, August 31, 1812, in A.H.N., Est., 5638.

[46] President Madison's annual message of November 5, 1811, contains the only reference in his currently published statements to which Onís could have given this interpretation. The Spaniard's accusation in all probability refers to this paragraph: "... it is impossible to overlook those [scenes] developing themselves among the great communities which occupy the southern portion of our own hemisphere and extend into our neighborhood. An enlarged philanthropy and an enlightened forecast concur in imposing on the national councils an obligation to take a deep interest in their destinies, to cherish reciprocal sentiments of good will, to regard the progress of events, and not to be unprepared for whatever order of things may ultimately be established."—James D. Richardson (ed.), *Messages and Papers of the Presidents, 1789–1899* (Washington, 1896–1899), I:494.

[47] Labrador (Spanish foreign minister) to Onís, December 28, 1812, in A.M.E., 219.

[48] Fernán Núñez to the *secretario de estado*, September 25, 1813, in A.H.N., Est., 5557, Expediente 1.

[49] Monroe to commissioners, April 27, 1813, in D.S., United States Ministers, Instructions, VII.

[50] Julius W. Pratt, "James Monroe," in *American Secretaries of State*, III: 268–270.

[51] Cevallos to Fernán Núñez, December 8, 1814, in Archivo General de Simancas (Simancas), Est., 2675 moderno.

[52] Onís to San Carlos (Spanish foreign minister), February 13, 1815, in A.H.N., Est., 5640.

CHAPTER II

THE BORDERLANDS, 1810–1816

TERRITORIAL COMPLEXITIES

ALONG THE FAR-FLUNG DIPLOMATIC BATTLE LINE lay four great regions of international rivalry for occupation: the Floridas, Louisiana and Texas, New Mexico, and Oregon. Although the interest of the nations was at first largely focused at the eastern end, it gradually became more evenly balanced to include the whole frontier. Thus in the final weeks of the treaty negotiations in 1819, with the cession of the Floridas having been conceded within the councils of the respective protagonists for at least a quarter-century, the Oregon-California boundary was the subject of dispute on which Adams risked the whole agreement.

The fact that these regions were areas of rivalry in exploitation, and were not mere names on the map, is of fundamental significance. The purpose of this chapter is to consider the magnitude of that exploitation, and in doing so to give meaning to the various geographical terms employed. It is also essential to observe wherein lay the territorial claims of the two countries to the regions which were covered by the treaty negotiations.

The United States in 1816, when direct negotiations were resumed with Spain, was a republic of eighteen states and a vast partially undefined public domain. She had gone through a war with little military glory, but had at least maintained her ground, territorially speaking. The northern limit east of the Lake of the Woods had been long established, except for a disputed interpretation of the Maine boundary. The northern boundary of the Louisiana Purchase was in litigation between the United States and England, but it was not a matter vitalized by any wave of settlement.

Along the southern and western frontier, however, lay the possessions of Spain, a monarchy now so weakened by civil war at home and by rebellion flaming through her huge American domain that she appeared to offer little effective hindrance to this country's aspirations, which were rapidly developing into the spirit of "Manifest Destiny." The manner in which Spain notably delayed that expansion, and forced concessions in making a treaty, did her credit for determination and skill, both in administration and in diplomacy.

Spain's governing officials, in 1816, still looked on the colonial uprising as a problem of "pacification," evidently taking for granted what outsiders and colonials considered an impossible reconquest.[1] And, still dreaming of the days when all of North America was Spain's unchallenged possession, they were reluctant to admit the necessity of yielding any more of it than had already been lost. In fact, they were soon to maintain that the King had no right to cede away lands.

The center of Spanish North America was the city of Mexico, long the capital of the viceroyalty of New Spain. But the United States adjoined two subdivisions of that administrative unit. It had long been customary, when a large and important area lay far from a viceregal capital, to make it a semiautonomous unit of the system, with direct reference to Spain in many matters. Such was the captain-generalcy of Havana, governing the West Indies, the Floridas, and Louisiana. This region, vastly important in trade and international political rivalries, had in its capital an important administrative, military, and financial center.

After Havana became a captain-generalcy, a reorganization took place on the northern frontier of New Spain itself. Thus was formed the Provincias Internas (Interior Provinces), also a captain-generalcy, with its capital at Chihuahua. This unit, later separated into two districts, embraced what are now the northern states of the republic of Mexico, and Texas, New Mexico, Arizona, and California. Both at Chihuahua and Havana the governments were essentially military, but there were also present civil and commercial authorities. And all officials indulged in the characteristic Spanish practice of writing the innumerable lengthy and detailed reports which now crowd the archives.

EAST FLORIDA

The Florida peninsula was the first area, geographically speaking, on the line along which the two Powers met. With the region bordering the Gulf Coast as far west as the Apalachicola River (an area somewhat less extensive than the present state of Florida), it constituted the Spanish province of East Florida. The capital and

[1] For notes to chap. ii, see pp. 54–56.

principal center was St. Augustine, Spain's northern outpost on the Atlantic, which harbored most of the white residents of the province. Besides that town there were Fernandina, on notorious Amelia Island at the mouth of the St. Mary's; St. Mark's, on the Gulf shore; and Apalache, at the mouth of the Apalachicola, hardly more than an Indian trading post.

The province was vital in the control of the Bahama channel on the route of the fleets from Mexico to Spain. Had there been effective Spanish marine forces it might well have been the base of operations for the suppression of illicit trade between North and South America, and of privateering. In its own commerce, since a large proportion of its approximately five thousand inhabitants consisted of settlers from the United States, it had more intercourse with Savannah, Charleston, and Baltimore than with Havana. In 1804 immigration from the northern neighbor country was declared illegal, but a close commercial relationship continued.[2] The immigration restriction was hardly a major factor, since the province had never sustained a large permanent agricultural population. Certainly to the land-hungry "Anglo-Americans" it offered less attraction than did the West.

As part of the region desired by the United States at Paris in 1803 and at Madrid in 1805, the province drew its share of attention. At all times it was viewed with alarm and covetousness because of the activities and the trade possibilities of its native inhabitants, an offshoot of the Lower Creek Indians called the Seminoles.[3] The Indian trade of both provinces had been in large part controlled by British agents from the Bahamas since the British occupation of the Floridas, ending in 1783.

In recent years, disputes between the Indians and the frontier settlers of Georgia had increased enough to offer an occasion for interference by the United States. This was based on the accusation that Spain had not lived up to her obligation, incurred in Pinckney's Treaty, to keep the red men pacified. Intervention was made even more desirable on the part of the United States when the threat of war with England arose.

Further cause for contention appeared in the problem of fugitive slaves, who escaped from the southern states into East Florida in sufficient numbers to comprise a troublesome, lawless group. As early as 1733 they had received official attention in an order that they need not be returned nor their owners reimbursed by the Spanish officials. In the second Spanish occupation (1783–1821) the first governor, Vicente Manuel Zéspedes, frequently asked official opinion on the matter. One of his successors, Enrique White, finally reached an agreement with officials of the United States in 1797, on instructions from Spain, by which the fugitives were to be returned.[4] But the agreement was irregularly observed and the number of fugitives increased. More than half of the population of East Florida in 1804 was listed as slaves,[5] but how many of these were fugitives from the north, or how many of the escaped Negroes eluded any census, it would be difficult to say.

It has been shown in the first chapter that Monroe was one of the most active promoters of the United States' designs on the Floridas. Therefore it was natural that during his secretaryship of state another attempt should be made on them. He appears to have been involved in a clandestine plot to revolutionize East Florida by abetting the expedition led there by General George Mathews, former governor of Georgia. Congress in a secret act of January, 1811, had authorized occupation of the Floridas east of the Perdido River in the event the local authorities agreed, or in the event another Power threatened them.[6] The latter condition was made in view of the possibility of the use of the Gulf Coast by England in the war which was then threatening. In accordance with the first condition, Mathews had been sent to take over the section of West Florida included in the act, inasmuch as it had been offered to the United States by a harassed Spanish governor. But, in the meantime, that official, Vicente Folch, had changed his mind and he refused to deliver. Mathews then turned his interest to the eastern province. At the same time a detachment of riflemen and some ships of the navy gathered at the St. Mary's River, to be on hand if an opportunity came to carry out the Congressional authorization.

Mathews hatched a scheme whereby he could conduct a mock revolution with the aid of the "Anglo-Americans" who were already resident in the Spanish territory. Its leaders were to request occupation by the United States. He had already discussed these plans in Washington, in January, 1811, and had received instructions in a letter written by Monroe on June 29 to take charge on the border with the troops already gathered there. Soon after that,

Monroe received from Mathews a complete explanation of the latter's plans. This explanation went unanswered.

Mathews, evidently interpreting silence as consent, proceeded to have his "revolutionary volunteers" (largely Georgia militia, and adventurers who conveniently assumed that rôle) take possession of Fernandina on Amelia Island. They at once invited occupation, which Mathews effected on March 18, 1812. From Fernandina they set out for St. Augustine, eventually camping before its gates. As the volunteers advanced, the troops followed immediately, occupying the territory at the request of the filibusterers who took it in hand just ahead of them.

The government shortly became embarrassed by Mathews' overenthusiasm. On April 4, 1812, Monroe wrote Mathews, dismissing him. But it was not the time to withdraw troops from such a strategic place as East Florida, and Monroe appointed Governor D. B. Mitchell of Georgia to succeed Mathews. He was to hold the troops before St. Augustine, ready to meet contingencies that might arise in the impending war. Although Mitchell quarreled with the Spanish officials, he remained for many months.

The maintenance of United States forces in Spanish territory was justified on the grounds of protecting the "patriots" against the wrath of Spain. Onís reported this condition to his government in his despatch of August 3, 1812. He also sent copies of the correspondence of Mitchell and the new East Florida governor, Sebastián Kindelan.[7] Onís was shortly instructed to tell Monroe that all residents of East Florida "seduced" by General Mathews would be pardoned, if they conducted themselves thenceforth as loyal Spanish subjects.[8] This made the pretext for Mitchell's stay groundless.

From the first this venture had been vehemently protested. Since Onís could not communicate directly with Monroe, Augustus John Foster, the new British minister, presented a protest, in his own name. The source of the complaint is shown in Onís' despatch to his government of September 8, 1811, which included copies of his report from Juan José Estrada, then governor of East Florida, and of his letter to Foster asking that the protest be made.[9] English representatives continued the complaints at Ghent, partly for bargaining purposes in the negotiation of the peace treaty. Following the two efforts of Monroe, already related, to obtain East Florida through Onís, in 1812 and 1813, and after the war was well under way, United States troops were finally withdrawn from before St. Augustine in May, 1813.

Later, Indian troubles on the Apalachicola River directed attention to the apparent English incitement of the red men in another part of East Florida. Major Edward Nicholls, of the British marines, built a fort on that river, gathering Seminole and Creek allies. When he left at the end of the war Negroes, evidently allies of the Indians, seized the place, which thus acquired the name Negro Fort. After various threats from General Jackson in an effort to end its troublemaking, General Gaines, under Jackson's orders, built Fort Scott on the Flint River near-by. In 1816, when a supply convoy moving up the river was attacked, with some casualties, troops from Fort Scott advanced. A redhot cannonball was thrown into Negro Fort, killing many of its defenders. As a result of this reprisal the Negroes and Indians were for a time cowed, if not pacified.

WEST FLORIDA

It is difficult at times to keep the stories of East and West Florida separate, and it is not in all respects desirable. For in their strategic position, their Indian troubles, and their dangerous possibilities in the war, they were much alike. They were separated in some degree by the fact that there were few permanent settlements between St. Augustine and St. Mark's or Apalache, and few between the latter two towns and Pensacola, the capital of West Florida. An important element in the population of the western province was the body of several hundred Indians, mostly of the Creek federation,[10] who were nearly as troublesome as the Seminoles in East Florida.

The chief political dispute over West Florida involved the region west of the Perdido, which was claimed by the United States as part of the Louisiana Purchase. There, owing to this claim and to more rapid occupation, Spain's régime was disturbed sooner than in the peninsula.

After the passage of the Mobile Act in 1804, numerous settlers entered West Florida, as well as Louisiana proper, from the western states. Many of them received land grants from Intendant Ventura Morales; and all were subject, though in a more or less rebellious manner, to the administration of Governor Folch.

British influence was strong in West Florida, as in East. It was exercised generally through the great trading firm of Panton, Leslie and Company, known after the death of Panton in 1802 as John Forbes and Company. With posts at Pensacola, Mobile, and St. Mark's, this institution was of great importance both in Indian affairs and in commerce.

Concessions to this firm, as well as foreign immigration for the purpose of forming a substantial community for self-defense, and trade with France and her colonies, all had been allowed by Spain in her effort to make the province strong enough to stand by itself. The attempt succeeded much too well for Spain, owing largely to the influx of "Anglo-American" frontiersmen. The scattered population was largely foreign, and, despite the adaptation of her colonial system to local conditions, Spain's hold grew increasingly shaky.

Commercially, the United States found that its designs were furthered by the dependence of West Florida on Louisiana for supplies and markets. Spanish restrictions, which imposed duties and allowed trade only in Spanish ships, had become largely impossible to enforce by 1808.[11] The breakdown of the system was completed by Folch. Seeing the needs of his people, and not having the legal righteousness of his archenemy Morales, he let down the restrictive bars in a series of executive acts. His orders brought legal worries to Spanish officialdom, and probably only the war in Spain prevented his punishment. But as an aid to inevitable economic penetration by the United States, his actions were so effective that the process was nearly complete by 1812. This penetration included navigation of the important Mobile and Apalachicola rivers from the western United States, as well as navigation of the Gulf itself.

Folch, despairing of holding the province under existing conditions, in 1810 offered to deliver it to the United States. But by the time former Governor Mathews and Colonel John McKee, an Indian agent sent with him by the secretary of state, arrived to receive the gift, Folch had recanted. The offer of Folch caused his recall later to Spain to answer for it, but not before most of the province had been permanently lost to effective Spanish control by economic penetration.[12]

Folch's offer was caused by lack of support from a home government harassed by civil war, and was occasioned by the uprising of the West Florida residents about Baton Rouge, nine-tenths of whom were immigrants from the United States.[13] These people, in July, 1810, met in convention, declared themselves an independent state, and requested admission as one of the states of the Union. The United States government paid little heed to this request, but did authorize occupation of the region under the title alleged to have been acquired in the Louisiana Purchase. All of West Florida was taken except Mobile. In April, 1812, that section west of the Pearl River was made a part of the new state of Louisiana, and the region between the Pearl and the Perdido was included in Mississippi Territory.

The declaration of war at once brought to the United States the fear of invasion from the territory still under Spanish control. In February, 1813, in response to the call for volunteers and through plans laid by the War Department, three bodies of troops were ready to advance into the Floridas if occasion arose. Brigadier General James Wilkinson, in command in the southwest, was at New Orleans. Andrew Jackson, with two thousand Tennessee volunteers, was at Natchez. On the St. Mary's and St. John's (the latter in East Florida in Spanish territory) were federal troops under Major General Thomas Pinckney (continuing the occupation begun by Mathews and Mitchell) and some Georgia and Tennessee volunteers.

The combined attack was frustrated, however, by the decision of the Senate, on February 12, to authorize the seizure of only that region west of the Perdido—meaning simply Mobile, since it alone remained in Spanish hands there.[14] This necessitated the order for withdrawal, and disbandment or diversion of the troops. Pinckney finally withdrew in May, 1813, but not before the Tennessee volunteers had burned several deserted Seminole villages, taking corn and skins, and driving off cattle. Jackson, refusing to disband his men, kept them under guard on his own responsibility at Nashville.

Meanwhile the peace commissioners who had been sent abroad were afraid that the actions in the Floridas would jeopardize their settlement, and Gallatin urged against even the authorized seizure of Mobile. That occupation was carried out, nevertheless, in April. Wilkinson effected it and had begun the erection of a fort there when he was recalled to the northern frontier.

Now the broader aspects of the war were to be seen in the British encirclement plan and scheme of attacking the United States on all its Indian frontiers. The same Tecumseh who had stirred the Northwest incited the Creeks to battle. And prodded further by the attack of the Tennessee volunteers on their allies, the Seminoles of East Florida, the Indians of the confederation went on the warpath in August, 1813—only to bring upon themselves swift and sure retribution.

Fort Mims, near the junction of the Alabama and Tombigbee rivers, and inside the certain limits of the United States, was the focus of the Indian attack. Several hundred persons were killed by the braves, enough to incite the already militant and land-avaricious Westerners. Jackson's Tennessee volunteers readily accepted the gage of battle, and were led by him through a victorious winter campaign. By the treaty signed at Fort Jackson (an establishment at the junction of the Coosa and Tallapoosa rivers) in August, 1814, the Creeks were forced to surrender two-thirds of their lands.

Jackson, fortifying himself with the widely circulated charges of Spanish support of the Indians, continued into the territory of "the Dons," as he called them. By this time a British fleet under Captain W. H. Percy had brought Major Nicholls with a force of marines, who established themselves at Pensacola for the Gulf campaign. While Jackson awaited more Tennessee troops at Mobile, a United States force successfully defended Fort Bowyer, at the mouth of Mobile Bay.[15] Jackson, on his own responsibility, without instructions from Washington, then marched eastward to Pensacola, which he took by storm on November 7. Thence he returned to Mobile, and soon set out on the campaign which ended in his brilliant defense of New Orleans against the veterans of Wellington's army, January 8, 1815.

After the signing of the Treaty of Ghent, the British finally captured Fort Bowyer. However, under the treaty, no British seizures were to be maintained and, despite Spanish efforts, no change was made in the southern boundaries. During the war, nevertheless, West Florida's occupation by the United States was made complete and permanent. Although theoretically there was no settlement of the West Florida controversy, actually there was no of rare occurrence.

LOUISIANA-TEXAS

The Louisiana Purchase was divided in 1812 into two parts: the southern part became the state of Louisiana, the eighteenth to be admitted to the Union, and the remainder became known as Missouri Territory. The new state was drawn into the vortex of international affairs at once. In the War of 1812 its capital was the scene of mobilization activities, and of one great enemy thrust. Commercially, the state assumed a vital rôle, both as producer and market, and as an avenue for the transport of goods. In the subversive acts of plotters by land and pirates by sea which were continually disturbing the Spanish colonies, Louisiana played a notorious part. And with respect to the boundary question it was an outpost thrust into a disputed frontier.

New Orleans, long an important center as the port of deposit for goods from the southwest, became even more influential commercially when the advent of the steamboat made inland water transport for a time the major factor in western trade. Governor W. C. C. Claiborne in 1809 reported a population of about fifty-five thousand in the Territory of Orleans, which had the same area as the later state. Of these, half were Negroes, most of them slaves. A quarter of the total are described as "natives of Louisiana, for the most part descendants of the French."[16] The remainder included some thirty-five hundred natives of the United States, and French, Spanish, English, German, and Irish nationals.

From Spanish vice-consuls stationed at New Orleans, Natchez, Natchitoches, and St. Louis, Onís received and relayed numerous complaints of threats to the Spanish Texas-Louisiana frontier. These officials, especially those at the upriver points where little Spanish trade could penetrate (the vice-consul at Natchez was later removed on that account), reported as well to other civil and military leaders, in Havana and in San Antonio, or Bexar, the distant capital of Texas.

The new state had as boundaries exactly those it has today, employing on the west the Sabine River. That delimitation lacked treaty basis, but found authority in the usage of the vicinity, especially since the Wilkinson-Herrera neutral-ground agreement of 1806, the development of which should be noted.

After the purchase of Louisiana, Governor Claiborne of Lou-

isiana, the Marquis of Casa Calvo, Spanish commissioner, and
Ventura Morales, former Spanish intendant, had indulged in con-
tumacious bickering. Both the Spaniards remained long after Claiborne thought they were entitled to and argued long over land
titles and the boundary. In the winter of 1805–1806 Casa Calvo
explored the boundary area himself. He concluded that on the basis
of long acceptance the line should be at the Arroyo Hondo, near
Natchitoches and east of the Sabine.[17]

Antonio Cordero, then governor of Texas, took steps to establish that limit, and rumors of his activities, though probably exaggerated, worried the Louisiana officials. In 1805 the Spanish post
of Los Adaes, seven leagues west of Natchitoches, was reoccupied,
and settlements were made at Bayou Pierre and Nana, both east
of the Sabine. The few men at Los Adaes were easily dislodged by
a United States force from Natchitoches in January, 1806. But
soon seven hundred more men were sent to guard the Spanish front.
Various encounters in the disputed area increased the fear of war
between the two countries, until in the spring of 1806 orders came
from Washington for a general dressing up and reinforcement of
the border posts.

Wilkinson was ordered to take charge at New Orleans. He soon
drew up a temporary palliative agreement with the Spanish commander, Herrera, whereby the Spanish troops were to remain west
of the Sabine and the United States forces were to stay east of the
Arroyo Hondo, the intervening few miles being considered neutral
ground. This agreement was a part of Wilkinson's scheme to re-
establish himself as the protector of the West, by staving off the
Spanish threat and by exposing at the same time the Aaron Burr
conspiracy.[18] A later governor of Texas, Manuel Salcedo, in 1809
sought to discredit this so-called "Neutral ground treaty" by saying that the real Spanish line was the Arroyo Hondo and that the
United States' demand for the neutral area was unwarranted. At
the same time he sent to Spain advice on methods of protecting his
province.[19]

Neither government, however, was possessed with a legal conclusion to the argument, and at both Madrid and Washington the
diplomats continued their efforts to establish rival claims. Jefferson's conceptions of the proper boundaries of Louisiana became
more and more comprehensive. He eventually asserted that, in-

stead of being merely the area between the Sabine and the Iberville rivers and including just the watershed of the Mississippi, the province rightfully embraced West Florida, Texas to the Río Grande, and an undefined area beyond the Rockies to the Pacific.

Jefferson thus definitely formulated the United States' claims to Texas. His arguments in defense of his position were substantially the same as those used repeatedly in succeeding discussions, including the negotiations resulting in the Adams-Onís Treaty. The alleged title was of course based on that of France, but on the whole little help was obtained from that Power in defining the rights it had held previous to 1803. Thus Jefferson, Madison, Monroe, and Adams had to study with more or less thoroughness the whole Franco-Spanish colonial story.

Briefly, the French claim was based upon the following activities of adventurer-traders which were alleged to have resulted in permanent title to land west of the Sabine: the futile journey of La Salle to the Bay of St. Bernard (Bahía de San Bernardo, or Matagorda Bay), between the mouths of the Guadalupe and Colorado rivers, in 1686; the grant by Louis XIV in 1712 to Antoine Crozat, for his trading company, of a monopoly over all the territory from New Mexico to the Carolinas, and from the Gulf to the Illinois country; the journeys of Louis Juchereau de St. Denis to Natchitoches in 1713, and to the Río Grande, where he was captured by the Spanish, in 1717; and the expeditions of La Harpe up the Red River and across to the mouth of the Canadian in 1719, and to the Bahía del Espíritu Santo (Bay of the Holy Spirit—Galveston Bay) in 1721.

Jefferson in his memoir on the subject asserted that at the time of La Salle the Spanish frontier was far around on the Gulf Coast, at the Pánuco River, and that the Río Grande was taken as the boundary because it was halfway between the outposts of the two nations. No evidence of any such agreement appears, and certainly the Spanish had established themselves far north of Pánuco.[20] Better grounds might have been found in the almost complete French control of the Indian tribes in northern Texas, and in the lack of effective Spanish occupation either to the north or along the Gulf Coast. Dr. Herbert E. Bolton has pointed out that Los Adaes was but the tip of a wedge thrust by the Spaniards into territory in which the French had control both of the Indians and of trade.[21]

More immediate French support of Jefferson's view was found in the instructions given by Napoleon to General Victor, who had expected to occupy Texas before the Louisiana sale. In 1802 these orders were prepared with the statement that, although the boundaries of Louisiana were not all clearly defined, at least the limit followed the Gulf Coast west to the Río Grande, and north along it to the Thirtieth Parallel. Professor Marshall has shown that this paper is of questionable value, since Napoleon did not study the situation closely. As a matter of fact, certain French maps had traced the line much farther north than the Thirtieth Parallel. Even the United States' faith in the instructions to Victor was equivocal. For, whereas the definition of Louisiana as extending to the Río Grande was prized, the statement that Louisiana did not include West Florida was ignored.[22]

Against these claims the Spanish could confidently hold up the record of their colonization of Texas, a record marked by counters to every French thrust, with most of them leading to permanent establishments. These counterdrives were notably the Alonso de León expedition of 1689 (answering the La Salle threat), which saw the temporary founding of missions on the Neches River and the organization of Texas as a province; the Domingo Ramón venture of 1716 (meeting St. Denis' first intrusion), leading to settlements at Dolores on the Neches, at San Antonio, and at Los Adaes; and that of the Marquis of Aguayo, who in 1720 (answering attacks of the "war" of 1718–1719) made Los Adaes the capital of Texas and the site of a presidio, occupied the Bahía del Espíritu Santo, and reinforced San Antonio. By this time it was clear that the effective outposts of the two nations were at Los Adaes and Natchitoches. Thus in 1736, when a minor dispute called for settlement, it was natural for local officials to agree that the Arroyo Hondo, between those outposts, was the boundary, even though this delimitation obstructed active trade between the two.[23]

Missionary and commercial activity was not notably successful in eastern Texas, and the acquisition of Louisiana by Spain in 1763 removed the necessity for military bulwarks against the French. A reorganization resulted in the withdrawal of the Los Adaes settlers in 1774 and concentration at San Antonio.

While Governor Cordero was reëstablishing Los Adaes, in 1805, Jefferson learned from Louisiana officials of one Spanish map maker (Lángara) and one United States map maker (Sibley) who put the limits at the Sabine and the Arroyo Hondo, respectively, totally disregarding French claims to rights in Texas.[24]

Spain was also studying the problem, and, pursuant to a Royal Order of May 20, 1805, Father Melchor de Talamantes was instructed to prepare a treatise on the Louisiana-Texas boundary. After Talamantes' arrest for complicity in a revolutionary plot, the work was entrusted to Father José Antonio Pichardo.[25] This industrious friar cleric completed in 1812 an argumentative tract of 5,127 sheets (*fojas*). It supported the Spanish claims. A copy reached Spain four years later and appears to have been used in the ministry of state during the negotiation of the Adams-Onís Treaty.[26]

Along the disputed frontier line during the first two decades of the century flourished various illegal or revolutionary activities to which such a heterogeneous population was prone. Throughout the period of maritime uncertainties attendant upon the War of 1812 and the Spanish American revolutions, pirates on Barataria Lake, just west of the mouth of the Mississippi, had been preying upon commerce of all kinds. They ran their contraband into New Orleans, where they sold it, more or less openly, at prices which were lower than could be asked by importers who bought their goods and paid customs duty on them.[27] The chief pirates were two Frenchmen who had begun life in America as immigrant blacksmiths in New Orleans, Jean and Pierre Lafitte. Louisiana authorities made halfhearted efforts to quell them. But, sailing under letters of marque issued by France or by the republic of Venezuela, they continued to seize ships of all nations, especially those of Spain. After serving in the army which defended New Orleans under Jackson, they went back to privateering, making their headquarters on Galveston Island.

Early among the land threats to the border were the horse-trading ventures of Philip Nolan. He made journeys into Texas during the years from 1797 to 1801, when he was finally captured and killed by Spaniards. As a protégé of Wilkinson, it appears that he probably had other motives than those of a horse trader.

Following the years when the frontier was being fortified on both sides, and after the disruption of the Burr plot, came the beginning of Mexico's revolt from Spain, which brought havoc to the Texas settlements.[28] Among the first acts of the revolutionary government set up by the priest Hidalgo in the Mexican uprising of 1810 was the sending to Washington of an agent, one Bernardo Gutiérrez. This man, who was received by high officials there but who failed to win their support, organized an expedition on the border that carried on after the original uprising in Mexico had been quelled.

Gutiérrez enlisted the aid of a former United States army officer, Augustus McGee, who acted as the real leader in an invasion of Texas in 1812. With a large following of "Anglo-American" adventurers and some Indians, the group advanced until in the spring of the following year they captured San Antonio. McGee had died en route, and Gutiérrez was deposed following the brutal execution of Governor Manuel Salcedo. The command then fell to José Alvarez de Toledo, once a deputy in the Cortes at Cádiz, who had only a few months before offered to betray the expedition by selling information of it to Onís.[29] In August, 1813, the enterprise was broken up by the Royalists, who took cruel vengeance on their captives. The eastern part of the province suffered seriously from these encounters.

Toledo continued his propaganda, attempting to organize further revolutionary movements for the invasion of Mexico through Texas. But he quarreled with the two other leaders in the same sort of activity—Humbert, a Frenchman, and Dr. John Robinson. The latter, the surgeon of the Pike expedition, had gone to Mexico as an agent of the United States government in 1812. On his return he used his observations as the basis for appealing to Westerners to join him in an effort to free the Spanish colony. Robinson got as far as holding a meeting at Natchez in 1814, and Toledo gathered some forces on the Sabine in the following year. But neither made an actual invasion. That was to be left for a French venture from the Gulf Coast in 1817, and one more "Anglo-American" episode two years later.

NEW MEXICO

In 1776 the northern frontier of Mexico was reorganized as the Provincias Internas. Through a series of changes the region came to be divided into the Eastern Interior Provinces, including Texas, Coahuila, Nuevo Santander, and Nuevo León; and the Western, including New Mexico, Nueva Vizcaya, Sinaloa, Sonora, and the

Californias, with the capital at Chihuahua. New Mexico embraced more than it does today, though the center, then as now, was on the Río Grande, and the capital at Santa Fé. Long an outpost of New Spain, New Mexico showed greater activity and was more profitable than Texas, but its fringes were even less well known or exploited.

The Spanish governors early in the nineteenth century were concerned chiefly with the regulation of trade with old Mexico, Indian affairs, and the increasing threat of "Anglo-American" intrusions. Along the Río Bravo (also known as the Río Grande del Norte) traders went frequently between El Paso and the leading settlements of the upper country: Santa Fé, Albuquerque, La Cañada, and the rather new Indian trading center of Taos. The province in 1818 has been variously estimated to have had a population of from twenty thousand to forty thousand.[30]

Trade relations and efforts to ward off attacks kept the Spanish continually alert to the Navajos on the west, the Utes on the north, and the Comanches and Apaches on the east. The last-named tribes were also met by the French explorers, who traveled over much of the Southwest during the eighteenth century, and by the eager advance guard from the United States after the purchase of Louisiana in 1803.

The Mississippi-to-Río Grande route was hardly developed sufficiently to be called the Santa Fé Trail until after Mexican independence, but the territory through which it passed was known long before that time to traders of the three countries. In their intercourse the traders had found the Indians generally helpful; and before the first non-Spanish Europeans reached New Mexico across the plains, the French and Spanish were trading with each other through the medium of the natives.

Trade and exploration took the French through nearly all the territory between the Mississippi and the Rockies. Many of them either stayed voluntarily or were detained in New Mexico, thus building up a non-Spanish white group there. The cession of Louisiana to Spain in 1763 cut off their base of action, with the result that the entire West remained under control of the Spaniards.

From Santa Fé, explorations, forays against the Indians, and investigations of foreign intrusions were made, giving the Spaniards some knowledge of the watershed of the Mississippi. Uriburri, Villazur, and Bustamante were prominent explorers. In 1779 Gov-

ernor Juan Bautista de Anza of New Mexico went from Santa Fé
up the Río Grande to the headwaters of the Arkansas, over the
mountains to the plains, where he routed some Comanches, and
thence back to a safer home. These were the frontiersmen of New
Mexico; their reports help make the literature of the southwestern
borderlands.

Upper Louisiana was little explored by its new masters. Desire
for a commercial lane had led to the establishment of the Santa
Fé-to-San Antonio route by Pedro Vial between 1786 and 1789,
and three years later he made a successful trip to St. Louis. But
it remained for ambitious "Anglo-Americans" to further the development of the Mississippi-to-Río Grande passage.

They came in little-known groups of scouts or traders at first,
some staying in the Southwest. Such was the venture of Baptiste
Lalande, who was sent from St. Louis by a merchant in 1804. He
failed to return, and was later found in the New Mexico capital
by Captain Zebulon Montgomery Pike. There also was James Pur-
cell, a Yankee trader who had been commissioned by Indian friends
in the Rockies as their agent to Santa Fé.

Pike's famous expedition in 1806 and 1807 is now believed to
have been motivated by a genuine desire to explore the country,
rather than by the sinister purposes of General Wilkinson.[31] The
story of his trek through the Missouri and Arkansas river countries, his capture by the Spaniards on the upper Río Grande, his
visit to Santa Fé and later to Chihuahua as a prisoner, is a classic
of the West. Because of its semiofficial nature, and because he
published an account of it, Pike's expedition was particularly
significant at the time. Spain later claimed indemnity for losses
caused by his intrusion. Meanwhile rumors of the invasion had
given rise to one more important Spanish undertaking: Captain
Facundo Melgares' advance with six hundred men into what is
now Kansas, partly in an effort to head off the "Anglo-Americans."
The attempt proved futile.

Two later groups from east of the Mississippi entered New Mexico, only to run afoul of the Spanish authorities and to become
later the cause of diplomatic discussions. In 1809 Spanish troops
captured Reuben Smith and his party near the head of the Red
River, and imprisoned them at Santa Fé. Before their release in
1812 their absence had caused sufficient concern to prompt the

sending of an official protest to Onís. In the latter year another group under Robert McKnight was captured, and they were not released until 1821.

Similar difficulties developed during the Adams-Onís negotiations. A boundary argument arose over the activities of Joseph Philibert, Jules de Mun, and Auguste Pierre Chouteau, who set out for the Southwest in 1815. After a cordial reception in Santa Fé and a winter's trapping on the east slope of the Rockies, they were haled before Governor Pedro Allende, who maintained that they had been working in Spanish territory. Philibert countered with the assertion that Louisiana included all the area to the Rockies. The Spanish governor, invoking the Spanish theory that the Louisiana Purchase was illegal, declared that Spain still owned to the Mississippi. The men were ultimately released, but only after their goods had been confiscated. This affair also caused a diplomatic controversy, resulting in a claim by the State Department against the Spanish government, which was not settled until years later.[32]

It was apparent that the frontier, though undefined, followed the general course of the Rockies, from the head of either the Red or the Arkansas River to some point north of the region occupied by the Spaniards. This left a huge area, little known or exploited, between New Mexico, California, and the Oregon country—a high region of mountain and desert, to which the United States, in its westward expansion, had not yet sent its scouts, and which lay vaguely within the realms of King Ferdinand.

Across from New Mexico to California, through Arizona, a way had been opened by Father Francisco Garcés, in 1775–1776. Farther north the only notable enterprise had been the pathfinding tour of Fathers Francisco Domínguez and Silvestre de Escalante, through what is now southern Colorado into Utah, and down into Arizona, instead of across the Sierra as planned.

From the few expeditions and from conjecture, some rather vague ideas of the geography of the region had developed. One interesting example was the idea of a river running from the Salt Lake to the Bay of San Francisco.[33] However, little conception of a boundary existed, and above the Arkansas the vastness of the unexplored mountain and plains area made international conflict of interests of rare occurrence.

THE PACIFIC NORTHWEST

The westward course of the frontier turns our study, as it eventually did the eyes of the pioneers, toward the Northwest. There the narrative is largely of fur, and of a cauldron of international rivalry which was already boiling late in the previous century. Though that region had usually been approached from the sea, to Adams and Onís it was a part of the overland frontier. Exploration across the continent had indeed been infrequent. After the French and Indian War, although the Scotch and English fur companies penetrated western Canada, the exploration of the upper Missouri country lagged until the time of the Louisiana Purchase. Even before Jefferson knew of that great acquisition, he had been instrumental in starting William Clark and Meriwether Lewis on their famous venture. His purpose appears to have been the promotion of the fur trade, rather than eventual territorial aggrandizement. The arrival of that party at the mouth of the Columbia River in 1805 proved to be the soundest basis for the subsequent claim of the United States to the Oregon country. But, although Jefferson had expressed interest in linking upper Louisiana with the Pacific, it was evidently some time after the purchase that he decided it could be done under a legal claim to the Northwest area.[34]

In succeeding years other trappers and traders journeyed up the Missouri, gradually increasing the knowledge, influence, and interest of the United States in the more remote regions. The base for these enterprises was St. Louis, the great trading center of the upper Mississippi. This town, which numbered more than fourteen hundred population in 1810 and was growing steadily,[35] had administrative importance as the capital of Missouri Territory. But it had more significance as the economic metropolis of the great valley.

Among its residents who were early active in pushing westward the sphere of Indian trade was Manuel Lisa. He traded profitably on the Big Horn River in the winter of 1807 and 1808, and a year later helped form the St. Louis Missouri Fur Company, which conducted an unsuccessful trading experiment at the headwaters of the Missouri. Individuals carried the exploration still farther, some of their exploits being definitely recorded and some indicated only by fragmentary evidence. One, Alexander Henry, who had journeyed west with the Lisa group, crossed the mountains into the Snake River valley, where he traded for a winter.

In 1811 the expeditions of John Jacob Astor's Pacific Fur Company got under way. Astor, already the leading fur merchant in the country, was now looking with shrewd business designs toward the Northwest. He sent two groups, one by sea and one by land. The first, aboard the "Tonquin," reached the mouth of the Columbia in April, 1811, and founded a post which was named Astoria. The second, under Wilson Price Hunt, reached there early in 1812. Although Astoria was the first permanent United States settlement on the Pacific, it had been preceded by the explorations and by the establishment of trading posts of other countries.

A review of the earlier history of the North Coast is essential to an understanding of the diplomatic controversies. For many years international dispute had centered about that region. A long narrative of exploration and rivalry may be summarized by saying that the Spaniards, long claiming the entire "South Sea" as their sphere, had found the Russians encroaching from the north, and now between them had come the advance guards of the English, both by sea and by land.

Theoretically, all North America was Spain's until by specific agreements she signed parts of it away. Effectively, this was not true, and in increasing measure Their Catholic Majesties had had to depend upon their explorers, traders, soldiers, and scholars to maintain as much as possible of the domain they claimed.

Spanish sailors, by the late eighteenth century, had run the coast line to latitude 61° north. Meanwhile, by land, Spain had definitely occupied Alta California to the Bay of San Francisco, where her outpost presidio and mission were established in 1776. This site was not only the farthest north of the California settlements; it was also a part of the great frontier defense scheme which, under Charles III, involved a chain of presidios from ocean to ocean, from San Francisco to St. Augustine.

The establishment of San Francisco was a phase of Spanish defensive colonization, inspired by the fear of Russian aggression. Masters of Siberia after their great eastward movement, the Russians under Peter the Great sought further fields for their commercial ventures. Their endeavors were carried forward most ably by the great explorer Vitus Bering. Two voyages, ending in 1741, brought him to Alaska. In that same year his subordinate, Chiri-koff, ran the coast north from latitude 55° 21'.³⁶ That accomplishment appears to have been used subsequently for the definition of the monopoly given to the Russian American Fur Company, organized to manage the lucrative trade between the North Pacific with its skins and China with its silks and other luxuries.³⁷

Estevan José Martínez and Gonzalo López de Haro, able Spanish explorers, were sent to forestall further Russian advance by occupying Nootka Sound, on the west side of what was later called Vancouver Island. On arriving there, the explorers found, not Russians, but English and "Anglo-Americans."

The English early entered the Pacific, with Drake's round-the-world voyage of the late sixteenth century, but they did not come to trade in any great numbers until after the journey of Captain James Cook. In 1778 Cook ran the coast from near Cape Blanco (Lat. 42° 50' N.) to Nootka. He then went up into the Bering Sea, and down to the Sandwich Islands, where he was killed.

Numerous English ships soon entered the rich North Pacific-to-China trade. Three of them happened to be at Nootka in 1789, and Martínez seized them on the ground that they were encroaching on Spanish domain. A diplomatic controversy ensued, resulting in the Convention of October 28, 1790, by which both nations were to be admitted freely to navigation, fishing, Indian trade, and settlement in the unoccupied districts.³⁸ No claims or delimitations were set forth, but the convention was important in that it constituted a departure of Spain from her traditional position of exclusive sovereignty.

Captain George Vancouver, for England, and Juan Francisco de la Bodega y Cuadra, an experienced Spanish navigator, then explored the North Coast as commissioners under the convention. Some questions arose, which led to the signing of another convention, in 1794. This bound each country not to claim sovereignty to the exclusion of the other. Nootka was abandoned.³⁹

The Nootka Sound Convention of 1790 has been considered the first diplomatic controversy over the North Pacific, and the first breach of Spain's exclusive claim. It was not the former, certainly, because conversations, at least, had been carried on previously between Spain and Russia. Whether or not it was the latter is a matter of conjecture, as it is uncertain whether there had been an understanding of delimitation between those two Powers. Certain writers present evidence suggesting the existence of such an agreement, employing Prince William Sound, in latitude 61° north, as the division point.[40] But none has yet proved it.

The uncertainty of the Spanish attitude is shown in the various suggestions of Viceroy Juan Vicente Revilla Gigedo (the second viceroy of the name). He at one time proposed an Anglo-Spanish boundary running straight north from the westernmost point of the Strait of Juan de Fuca;[41] a year later he instructed Bodega to seek a settlement along the Forty-eighth Parallel;[42] and still later, "narrowing his pretensions, [he] urged that Spain cease straining for the Pole and be content with a boundary at the Columbia River or Bodega Bay, either of which, assuming Anian [the much sought mythical strait through the continent] to exist, might be its outlet."[43] None of these proposals developed into a treaty of limits, however. The Russians proceeded with the organization of the Russian American Fur Company, which was active below Prince William Sound, the point suggested as a boundary.[44] Russia eventually issued a provocative assertion to an extensive title in 1821, when a ukase of the Czar declared land and sea above the Fifty-first Parallel a closed sphere. But after four years' negotiations this claim was modified by treaties with the United States and England.[45]

Thus it was that, while England and Spain agreed to leave their titles undefined, at the same time the Russian affronts to Spanish sovereignty were resented. They were not, however, answered by any definite published agreements between those two countries.

Into such a kaleidoscope of territorial interests there entered a fourth Power in the 1780's. The New England traders whom Martínez found at Nootka in 1789 were the vanguard in a series of expeditions which were to lead to the provisions of treaties with England in 1818 and with Spain in 1819 giving the United States an ocean-to-ocean frontier.

The picturesque and active enterprises of the Massachusetts seamen early came to include stops on the North Coast on the route to China. Furs picked up there could be exchanged for luxuries in the Orient more cheaply than merchandise brought from the Atlantic Coast. One of the captains, Robert Gray, wintered at Nootka while on the first "round-the-world" voyage to be made by a ship under the registry of the United States. He returned to the North Pacific, and in the summer of 1793 met Vancouver. Gray believed that he had just discovered the mouth of the Columbia, not knowing that the Spaniard Heçeta had done this seventeen years before. The Columbia was explored a few months later by one of Vancouver's ships, which sailed a hundred miles up the river.

Salem and Boston traders continued in the Orient and North Pacific trade, but no settlement was made on the Coast until John Jacob Astor developed his plan for the Missouri-Columbia fur trade. The arrival of the "Tonquin" and of the Hunt group further strengthened the claim of the United States to the region—based first upon two expeditions of discovery (that of Gray and that of Lewis and Clark) and now upon these two of settlement.

Reinforcements came to the new post with the arrival of the ship "Beaver" and of the land party under Hunt, both early the following year. They were just in time to forestall a British expedition led by David Thompson, who floated down the river with a canoe party. This expedition was but the southern offshoot of extensive explorations which had brought Alexander MacKenzie and Simon Fraser to the Pacific in the region that was then called "New Caledonia," now British Columbia. They gave England the most tangible claims she had to the widely disputed regions. But without bothering to delimit spheres legally, traders of various countries continued their quest for furs.

During the Adams-Onís negotiations, the status of the Northwest was further complicated by circumstances growing out of the War of 1812. When word of the hostilities reached Astoria, early in 1813, the Astorians, knowing that they were outnumbered, arranged a sale of the post to the Northwest Company, which was effected the following November. This provided a peaceful means for the inevitable transfer of the post. But, unfortunately for England, the commander of her frigate "Racoon," which arrived two weeks later, thought it necessary to take possession as an act of war. Astoria became Fort George. British occupation likewise extended during the war throughout the entire upper Mississippi-Missouri system. Above St. Louis the English and their Indian allies found no opposition from a United States hard pressed to defend its hither frontiers.

But these gains were erased by the peace commissioners at Ghent, as was an extravagant denial by our secretary of state of any British claim on the North Coast. Monroe had written instructions that

the post at the mouth of the River Columbia which commanded the River ... ought to be comprised in the stipulation, should the possession have been wrested from us during the war. On no pretext can the British Government set up a claim to territory, south of the Northern Boundary of the United States. It is not believed that they have any claim whatever to Territory on the Pacific Ocean. You will however be careful, should a definition of the boundary be attempted, not to countenance in any manner or in any quarter a pretension in the British Government to Territory south of that line.[46]

Disregarding this vehement declaration, the treaty commissioners simply provided for a mutual restoration of property seized during the war, and left the boundary problem unsettled. Astoria, having been taken as an act of war after its sale in 1813, now had to be returned to the United States. Monroe informed Anthony St. John Baker, the British chargé, in 1815, that the mouth of the Columbia would be reoccupied at once.[47] But that step was not actually taken until 1818.

Out of this territorial rivalry, left unsettled at Ghent, grew the first actual treaty delimitation by any claimants to the region west of the Mississippi; but even it did not extend as such to the Pacific. Four special commissioners who were appointed for the task agreed, in the Convention of October 20, 1818, that the boundary should run along the Forty-ninth Parallel to the Rocky Mountains. But west of that range they left the sovereignty indeterminate, in the famous joint-occupation agreement which allowed use of the region by citizens of both Powers.[48]

It is essential to note that, important as this truce was, it did not provide a delimitation of the area west of the Rockies on either the north or the south. The first step in such a definition came with the Adams-Onís Treaty signed a few weeks after news of the British convention reached Washington.

A review of the rivalries of Spain, Russia, England, and the United States on the Pacific shows, then, that, although each Power had established claims by exploration and settlement, no specific delineation of spheres had taken place before 1819. The international conflicts over Louisiana had narrowed down to two principals—the United States and Spain—but the southern and western limits of that territory still remained uncertain. In dealing with these two sets of problems the diplomats at Washington were to have appreciable leeway. In contrast, the actual circumstances of occupation indicated very nearly the line to be agreed upon between Louisiana and Texas. Over the treatment of the Floridas the negotiators had, between 1815 and 1819, to reach an accord dictated by the long-accepted fact that Spain must yield title to the provinces at the best obtainable bargain.

Another notable contrast between the eastern and western parts of the frontier is that of geographical knowledge. Centuries of experience had led to a thorough comprehension of the Florida terrain, but the farther one looked toward the Pacific the less sure could one be of the location of rivers, mountains, and landmarks. To the credit of the various explorers of intervening years be it said that, although in 1803 the western boundary could not have been drawn effectively, in 1819 enough was known to make possible a practicable delineation.

NOTES TO CHAPTER II

[1] So well accepted was this view of reconquest that the manuscripts relating to the colonial revolutions in the Archivo General de Indias at Sevilla were filed under the general heading of "Pacification."

[2] Arthur P. Whitaker, *Documents Relating to the Commercial Policy of Spain in the Floridas* (Deland, Florida, 1931), p. lii.

[3] These Indians had remained Spanish allies when most of the great confederacy accepted English suzerainty early in the eighteenth century. They merged with the Oconees, a Georgia offshoot, receiving the Creek appellation for "runaway" ("seminole"), which became their common designation. See John R. Swanton, *Early History of the Creek Indians and Their Neighbors* (Washington, 1922), pp. 398–400. They had long occupied the region of the Savannah and Apalachicola rivers. Schooled in the crafty ways of competing Spanish, English, and United States Indian agents, they were naturally a people with little responsibility as a nation, and slight respect for international conventions.

[4] Mabel M. Manning, "The East Florida Papers in the Library of Congress," *Hispanic American Historical Review*, X (1930):393–394.

[5] Whitaker, *op. cit.*, p. liii.

[6] D. Hunter Miller, *Secret Statutes of the United States* (Washington, 1918), *passim*. This episode is well described in Julius W. Pratt, *Expansionists of 1812* (New York, 1925), pp. 60–119.

[7] Onís to Pezuela, August 3, 1812, in A.H.N., Est., 5638.

[8] Labrador to Onís, October 21, 1812, in A.M.E., 219.

[9] Onís to Bardaxí, September 8, 1811, in A.H.N., Est., 5637.

[10] John R. Swanton, *Indian Tribes of the Lower Mississippi Valley and Adjacent Coasts of the Gulf of Mexico* (Washington, 1911), pp. 39, 43–45.

[11] Whitaker, *op. cit.*, p. liv.

[12] Bardaxí to Onís, November 21, 1811, in A.M.E., 218.

[13] Isaac J. Cox, *The West Florida Controversy* (Baltimore, 1918), pp. 312–529.

[14] Pratt, *op. cit.*, pp. 226–229.

[15] Peter J. Hamilton, *Colonial Mobile* (rev. ed., New York, 1910), p. 431.

[16] Charles E. Gayarré, *History of Louisiana* (New York, 1854–1866), IV: 212.

[17] Thomas M. Marshall, *History of the Western Boundary of the Louisiana Purchase* (Berkeley, 1914), p. 23.

[18] Walter F. McCaleb, *The Aaron Burr Conspiracy* (New York, 1903), pp. 136–171; Royal O. Shreve, *The Finished Scoundrel* (Indianapolis, 1933), pp. 171–173, 178, 243.

[19] Salcedo to Miguel de Lardizábal, November 15, 1809, in Biblioteca Nacional (Madrid), Sección de Manuscritos, MS no. 18636:28.

[20] Thomas Jefferson, "The Limits and Bounds of Louisiana," in American Philosophical Society, *Documents Relating to the Purchase and Exploration of Louisiana* (New York, 1904), pp. 5–45; Marshall, *op. cit.*, p. 11. The statement that the Río Grande was the boundary did not even have the backing of Spanish administrative precedent, since the western limit of the Spanish province of Texas was at the Nueces, farther east.

[21] Herbert E. Bolton, *Texas in the Middle Eighteenth Century* (Berkeley, 1915), pp. 33–34.

[22] Marshall, *op. cit.*, pp. 4–5; Henry Adams, *History of the United States* (New York, 1889–1891), II:5–7; E. Wilson Lyon, *Louisiana in French Diplomacy, 1759–1804* (Norman, 1934), pp. 131–140, 225.

[23] Bolton, *op. cit.*, p. 34.

[24] Marshall, *op. cit.*, p. 12; Juan de Lángara y Huarte, *Carta esférica que comprehende las costas del Seno Mexicano* (Madrid, 1799). Dr. John Sibley of Natchitoches, a student of the West, was credited by Jefferson for much of his knowledge of Louisiana.

[25] The history of this report, without mention of the use which was finally made of it, is told in the introduction to Professor Hackett's translation of the treatise. See José A. Pichardo, *Pichardo's Treatise on the Limits of Louisiana and Texas*, Charles W. Hackett, ed. (Austin, Texas, 1931—), I:ix–xx.

[26] Philip C. Brooks, "Pichardo's Treatise and the Adams-Onís Treaty," *Hispanic American Historical Review*, XV (1935):94–99.

[27] Gayarré, *op. cit.*, pp. 289–290, 301–307.

[28] A brief review of border troubles appears in Lillian E. Fisher, "American Influence upon the Movement for Mexican Independence," *Mississippi Valley Historical Review*, XVIII (1932):463–478.

[29] Labrador to Onís, December 8, 1812, and Onís' notation on the same, March 4, 1813, in A.M.E., 219.

[30] Alfred B. Thomas (ed.), "Anonymous Description of New Mexico, 1818," *Southwestern Historical Quarterly*, XXXIII (1929):58.

[31] Zebulon M. Pike, *Zebulon Pike's Arkansas Journal*, Stephen H. Hart and Archer B. Hulbert, eds. (Colorado Springs and Denver, 1932), pp. lxiii–xcvi.

[32] Grant Foreman, *Pioneer Days in the Early Southwest* (Cleveland, 1926), pp. 77–79; and Eleanor L. Richie, "The Disputed International Boundary in Colorado, 1803–1819," *Colorado Magazine*, XIII (1936):171–180.

[33] One of the maps which shows such confusions is that of John Melish, published in 1818. It was used as the basis for the Adams-Onís Treaty.

[34] Ralph B. Guinness, "The Purpose of the Lewis and Clark Expedition," *Mississippi Valley Historical Review*, XX (1933):90–100; Marshall, *op. cit.*, pp. 13–14.

[35] William J. Ghent, *The Early Far West* (New York, 1931), p. 123.

[36] Frank A. Golder, *Russian Expansion on the Pacific, 1641–1850* (Cleveland, 1914), p. 185.

[37] Hubert H. Bancroft, *The Northwest Coast* (San Francisco, 1884), II:349.

[38] Convention signed at the Escorial, October 28, 1790, in *British and Foreign State Papers* (London, 1841—), I:663–667.

[39] William R. Manning, "The Nootka Sound Controversy," American Historical Association, *Annual Report*, 1904:467.

[40] *Ibid.*, p. 309. The possibility of a limitation of Spanish sovereignty by an agreement with Russia is considered in a letter from Count Floridablanca, Spanish foreign minister, to Alleyne Fitzherbert, British ambassador at Madrid, June 13, 1790, reproduced in Robert Greenhow, *History of Oregon and California* (Boston, 1844), pp. 421–425; it is also taken up in Bancroft, *op. cit.*, I:227–228; and in a dissertation by Charles L. Stewart, "Martínez and López de Haro on the Northwest Coast, 1788–1789," to be found in the University of California Library.

[41] Henry R. Wagner, *Spanish Explorations in the Strait of Juan de Fuca* (Santa Ana, California, 1933), p. 61.

[42] Irving B. Richman, *California under Spain and Mexico, 1535–1847* (Boston, 1911), p. 164, footnote 13.

[43] *Ibid.*, p. 167.

[44] The base of supplies on the Russian River in California established later by this company had no bearing on territorial claims, since it was admittedly in Spanish domain.

[45] Convention signed at St. Petersburg, April 17, 1824, in D. Hunter Miller, *Treaties and Other International Acts of the United States of America* (Washington, D.C., 1931—), III:151–162; convention between Great Britain and Russia signed at St. Petersburg, February 28, 1825, in *British and Foreign State Papers*, XII:38–43.

[46] Monroe to commissioners, March 22, 1814, in D.S., United States Ministers, Instructions, VII. "That line" was presumably an extension of the Forty-ninth Parallel.

[47] Monroe to Baker, July 19, 1815, in D.S., Notes to Foreign Legations, II.

[48] Convention signed at London, October 20, 1818, in Miller, *Treaties*, II: 658–662.

CHAPTER III

CEVALLOS AND MONROE REOPEN THE DISPUTE, 1815–1816

AFTER THE WAR

O VER SUCH A COMPLEX PROBLEM of territorial sovereignty and such vicissitudes of frontier rivalry as have been outlined many hours of study and conference were to be spent. Innumerable exchanges of notes resulted. Officials of Spain, the United States, England, and France went through a procedure which one writer has rather impatiently described as "tiresome reiteration," and as "higgling and splitting of hairs, partaking too much of the child's method of quarrelling."[1]

Even with the prodigious system of reports in vogue in the Spanish colonial system, the differences along the North American frontier were a bit remote from the grandiose court of Madrid. The wonder may well be, not that so little accurate knowledge was possessed there, but that the negotiations were handled by the Spanish ministers with as much intelligent understanding of the situation as they were. The misfortune is that the men competent in American affairs were frequently not in control.

Certainly the two Spaniards who were most prominent in the direction of the affair at Madrid in 1815–1816 had no keen understanding of the American scene—King Ferdinand VII and his foreign minister, the same Cevallos who had dealt with Monroe and Pinckney years before.

Ferdinand, restored to his throne following the expulsion of the French troops from Spain, was doomed to a troubled and inglorious reign both because of the controversy over his reëstablishment, and because of his habit of intrigue behind the backs of his responsible ministers. Shortly before Napoleon's defeat early in 1814, the Emperor and Ferdinand, the latter still captive, negotiated a treaty at Valençay which would have provided for the restoration of Ferdinand on condition of the removal from Spain of both the French and the English troops. The Cortes, which had been governing in Ferdinand's absence with the support of English forces, refused to sanction this agreement. But Ferdinand's old-

---

[1] For notes to chap. iii, see pp. 69–70.

time tutor, the Duke of San Carlos, directed a royalist movement in which the leaders of the Cortes were arrested. All of its enactments were declared null and void by a decree of May 4, 1814.[2]

Meanwhile the allied troops had entered Paris, paving the way for a wave of absolutism throughout Europe. Naturally imbued with that spirit, Ferdinand set out to govern not only by innumerable secret maneuverings, but also by a vengeful severity toward the Liberals. He refused to accept the Constitution of 1812, and in this he evidently had the support of the masses, who welcomed him with acclaim.

In his effort to restore the grandeur of the courts of Philip II and Charles III, the King indulged in luxuries which were hardly in keeping with the needs of the country. In the midst of reconstruction, after a grueling civil and foreign war, the major problems of his reign seem to have been, not the rebuilding of Spain, but his marriage alliances and the aggrandizement of his family and favorites.[3]

The position of the country as a diplomatic power is well portrayed in a description of the Spanish ambassadors of the time as

in tow of the others, obscured as inferiors in diplomacy, in spite of the magnificent effort which the nation had just made [in the Peninsular War] which enabled the other European powers to begin their work of crushing the tyrant. The Spanish court, crowned by the repellent figure of Ferdinand VII, appeared here with its constant characteristics of lack of foresight, lack of continuity, disagreement among its ministers, blindness and absence of judgement, defects which were reflected in the work of our ministers abroad, disturbed by insecurity and lack of means and full of continual vexations.[4]

The first foreign minister under the restoration was San Carlos, archabsolutist of the régime. He was followed in November, 1814, by Cevallos, now restored to favor. A poignant estimate of Cevallos comes from Erving, the United States minister, who had had some years' experience in observing European diplomats. It must be remembered that he always showed a bitter attitude toward the Spanish court, which is clearly revealed in the following:

The first minister Cevallos is a cunning, selfish, pusillanimous, weak man. He was once thought to be honest. That opinion has gone by. He lives in penury, and profits of his situation to amass and to hoard money which he sends out of the country, preparing for an evil day which he has just discernment enough to see is not far distant (some say that in this precaution he but follows the example of his King). In the mean time he holds his place by the base servile

crawling of a Courtier; experience has taught him how most meanly to conde-
scend; he never presumes to have an opinion in opposition to his master
though in matters of his own routine of thirty years.—withal he has great
difficulty in keeping his post. His blunders strike even the King from time to
time, and he has constantly to encounter cabals formed for his ruin; this indeed must be the case with any man in his situation under the present system.
Who else has to do with the government I have not yet learnt and who they will
get to replace Cevallos better than him, bad as he is, I am wholly at a loss to
conceive.[5]

Cevallos had a sample of his King's vacillation in January, 1816,
when he was suddenly removed—then reinstated the next day.
Nevertheless he managed to hold office for nearly two years. And
if United States affairs received little of his attention, there was
some excuse for that fact in the number of problems facing him.
The relations of Spain with other European Powers in the complex
postwar settlements were evidently hopelessly engrossing for those
who were trying to promote the interests of Ferdinand.

At the Congress of Vienna, the Spanish ambassador, Pedro
Gómez Labrador, was almost completely helpless. Cevallos had
instructed him to limit his activities to demands for observance of
the Treaty of San Ildefonso of 1800. In other words, Labrador was
to ask for the fulfillment of Ferdinand's great desire that the kingdom of Etruria be returned to his sister, the queen of that realm;
or that Louisiana, which in 1800 Spain had traded for the Etruscan
crown, be returned; or that the fifteen million dollars which France
received for Louisiana in 1803, and the ships and money furnished
by Charles IV to Napoleon, be returned to Ferdinand.[6]

Ignorant of the accord between Spain's natural allies, England,
France, and Austria, Spain turned for assistance to Russia, whose
minister in Madrid, Dmitri Pavlovitch Tatistcheff, was gradually
gaining influence over Ferdinand. "But when the Congress began
to treat of Italian affairs," says the historian of Labrador's mission, "the bad faith of Tatistcheff, the credulity of the King, and
the stupidity of Labrador made themselves evident. The isolation
of Spain and of her representative was complete. . . ."[7] Labrador
signed none of the treaties drawn up, because Spain's desires in
Italy were not met, and, incidentally, because the Powers failed to
support his demand for the return of Louisiana. Spain in 1817
finally adhered to the Vienna treaties of 1814 and to the Paris
agreements of the following year, gaining some measure of satis-

faction in her Italian interests. It is evident, though, that Spain, during the negotiations with the United States, was embarrassed by her weak position in Europe and by inept diplomacy.

During the process of the restoration of the monarchy, the United States was represented in Spain by Anthony Morris, of Pennsylvania. He had remained as a special agent almost from the time of Erving's departure from Spain in 1810. Thomas Brent was also an agent for the United States in Madrid, and the Reverend Thomas Gough, an unofficial representative. The latter was appointed secretary of the legation in 1815. Morris frequently quarreled with both, particularly over their allegation that he was conspiring to have himself appointed minister.

In the summer of 1815 Brent sent to Monroe a copy of a letter purported to have been written by one Francisco Sarmiento, a secret agent who had been in the United States and had assisted Onís. It was addressed to the latter and asked that he influence the United States government to appoint Morris. Morris wrote to Monroe, frankly explaining the affair, and gave the plausible opinion that the letter was merely an attempt of Sarmiento to gain Morris' confidence.[8] No action was taken in the matter.

Though, of course, no negotiations were carried on, Morris had informal conversations with Cevallos. Most interesting of these was the one in which Cevallos categorically denied the rumor that Spain had ceded the Floridas to England.[9] Cevallos was right, but the report of the cession had caused a stir in the United States, and it was not discredited for some time, in spite of contrary assurances given not only at Madrid but at Washington.

On receiving word of Ferdinand's restoration, Madison and Monroe determined to reappoint Erving to Madrid, this time as minister. His instructions were accordingly sent in October, 1814, to Paris, where he had just returned from a special and successful mission to Denmark. He was to take over affairs from Morris and to reëstablish friendly relations, though he did not receive "any distinct and definite powers" for the purpose. He was to rely on the instructions to Pinckney and Monroe which had been issued in 1803–1805.[10]

Erving at once applied, through Morris, for a passport from the Spanish government, only to be refused on the grounds that he could not be recognized as minister until Onís likewise received admittance. Morris called the reply "extraordinary," and declared that he thought he could detect "the cloven foot of the British Government" in it. Erving himself thought the answer was given on grounds of his own "intimacy and negotiations with the king of Naples [Joseph Bonaparte] when he was Lieutenant of Napoleon at Madrid."[11]

Erving was the son of a British Loyalist who had left America during the Revolution. The son had later been in the United States, but much of his life had been spent abroad. He was not in good health, and had a doctor attending him during much of his residence in Spain. He was qualified for the position by his broad experience, but he had a thoroughgoing distrust of Spain. This was illustrated by such comments as "it is difficult to say when that. country was well governed, but surely the exhibition of ineptitude, bigotry & tyranny which it now presents has no parallel."[12]

The new minister had to wait two years, however, before his acceptance by the court at Madrid. Onís had already waited three times that long for recognition by the United States, and Spain held out in insisting that their envoy be recognized first.

ONÍS IS ADMITTED

Onís, following his rejection, had taken up residence in Philadelphia, where he lived until 1817. He had with him his family, which consisted of his wife (who became ill and died in 1818), his mother, his two daughters,[13] and his son. His summers were usually spent at Bristol, some thirty-six miles up the Delaware from Philadelphia.

During the War of 1812, as has been seen, he continued his various complaints to Monroe. He was also interested in schemes to offset probable expansionist threats from the United States. One interesting despatch presented a proposal which he had received from Luis de Clouet, former Spanish consul at New Orleans, to regain Louisiana by a threefold attack. This well-studied plan was to employ from three to ten thousand men: two thousand cavalry were to cross the Sabine, and the other two groups, of infantry, were to be landed at the mouth of the Mississippi and at Lake Pontchartrain.[14] Clouet later went to Spain to discuss the plan, but nothing came of it.

Just at the time of the discussion of this plan at Madrid, while Spain was in the midst of her effort to gain support at the Congress of Vienna and while the negotiations at Ghent were in progress, came Erving's application for a passport. It is natural to presume that part of the Spanish disinclination to receive him was based on a desire to await the outcome of these enterprises.

Onís was still not recognized, and there was no longer reason to base this nonrecognition on the civil war in Spain. Monroe wrote Erving in 1814 that Onís had made himself unacceptable to the Washington government (by such anti-United States expressions as were contained in his letter of 1810, which had been intercepted and presented to Congress), but that, if it were particularly desired that he remain, the objections might be waived "as an act of courtesy to his government."[15] In July, 1815, the same offer was repeated, with the stipulation that Ferdinand "express a desire that the Chevalier de Onís should be received," when "it will be complied with in a spirit of accommodation with the wishes of His Majesty."[16] The Spanish held out for a time, refusing to ask as a special favor what they expected as a right, but finally yielded. Accordingly, Monroe received Onís' credentials on December 19, 1815.

Onís then began an active three and a half years of official service, in which his zeal was certainly evident. The notes he wrote to the United States government were multitudinous. And although all Spanish officials were required to keep their copyists busy, Onís must have been one of the more avid, for at times he complained that even two copyists could not meet his demands. The volume of his despatches for his ten years' residence in this country is approximately ten thousand pages. Almost a third is of his own composition; another third consists of various enclosures; and the remaining bundles of papers are filled with drafts of replies, decipherations, and notations.[17] These comprise his correspondence to the Spanish secretary of state alone, exclusive of regular communication with consuls, other ministers and ambassadors, and officials in Havana, Mexico, and even Peru.

Among the various men who aided him as copyists, secretaries, messengers, or secret agents, the most interesting are José Alvarez de Toledo, the Mexican revolutionary leader who eventually became a confidant and adviser of the minister, and a publicist named Miguel Cabral de Noroña. The latter had incurred absolutist wrath by his publication of a liberal paper in Cádiz, but after many appeals by Onís the government allowed the minister to employ him, without official status, to write propaganda. Noroña had originally intended to publish a Spanish newspaper, in coöperation with the then-insurgent Toledo, but Onís dissuaded him from that design.[18] After his procurement for the royal cause, through financial inducements, Noroña served as translator of French, English, and Portuguese. He also wrote some important *memorias,* including the "Verus" pamphlet of 1812 (generally credited to Onís) and a lengthy discussion of the colonial problem. He was sent in 1819 to England, where until his death a year later he published a Spanish propaganda journal, *El Observador.*

After his recognition, Onís naturally proceeded to formulate all Spain's complaints against the United States, and to set forth his country's territorial claims. Thinking that this was the best time to settle the difficulties, while the United States was still recovering from the war, he tried to find a basis for agreement with Monroe, but to no avail.

Onís demanded, first of all, that West Florida be returned to Spain pending the settlement of its title. Secondly, he asked that the recruiting and arming of expeditions in the United States to revolutionize Spanish provinces be stopped, particularly the enterprise then being organized by Toledo and one Manuel de Herrera at New Orleans. He demanded, further, that ships of the insurgent colonies be excluded from United States ports, and that they be prevented from obtaining supplies.[19]

It should be emphasized here that well into the 1820's Spanish officials assumed that the reconquest of the colonies was possible. Thus the prevention of foreign aid to the insurgents, as well as the protection of the northern frontier of the colonies, vitally affected Spain's diplomacy with the United States.

With respect to his last two demands, Onís eventually received some satisfaction in the Neutrality Act of March 3, 1817, which prohibited the fitting out of expeditions in the United States to fight Powers with which this country was at peace. This prohibition was given added force in an act of April 20, 1818.

With respect to territories, the West Florida demand reopened the arguments of 1803–1805, but the contending ministers reached no accord. Monroe said that, since Spain held Texas, which he considered part of the Louisiana Purchase, the United States was equally justified in continuing to retain West Florida until its title should be established. Onís replied by presenting a lengthy account of Spain's colonization of Texas and the historical bases for her resulting title.[20]

Monroe, furthermore, had presented a list of counterclaims against Spain, including the nonratification of the Claims Convention of 1802, the indemnity claimed because of Spanish maritime spoliations in the Napoleonic Wars and the suspension of the right of deposit at New Orleans, the alleged violation of neutrality by Spain in allowing the British to use the Floridas as a base in the War of 1812, and the rejection of the various peaceful attempts of the United States to buy the Floridas. He also declared that the United States, recognizing the superior right of neither metropolis nor colony, would treat each, and its representatives and ships, alike, as far as the opening of ports was concerned. This became the prevailing policy of the administration in the Spanish American revolutions.

Onís then suggested, orally, that Spain would be willing to cede its claim to all territory east of the Mississippi in exchange for all territory on the western side, but he said that he wished the negotiation could take place in Madrid. Monroe in reporting this to Erving expressed doubt that such a proposal would lead to a prompt agreement.[21]

Shortly thereafter the scene did shift to Madrid. The Spanish government yielded on the recognition of Erving as soon as it learned that Onís had been admitted at Washington, with the result that the United States minister's credentials were received in August, 1816. He proceeded at once to present his government's views to the Spanish authorities.

THE ISSUES STATED

It will be recalled that Erving in 1814 did not receive detailed instructions or powers for negotiation. While awaiting recognition he visited Washington, where he met Onís. Full instructions were sent him only after he had returned, and after Onís' preliminary conferences had failed. The directions given him by Monroe, although they led to no successful negotiations, reveal the secretary of state's policy, somewhat more firmly expressed here than in the notes to Onís.

Monroe wrote on May 30, 1816, empowering Erving to make a settlement with Spain, and stating that he should propose an arrangement on the same bases as those offered in 1805, with an important possible concession on the Louisiana-Texas frontier.[22] He was to ask that Spain cede territory east of the Mississippi, and accept the claims-settlement procedure as given in the Convention of 1802. Finally, he was to suggest that the United States should relinquish its rights to indemnification for the spoliations by French cruisers, and for damages caused by the suppression of the right of deposit at New Orleans.

With respect to territorial delineation, Monroe outlined again the plan for a line up the Colorado River to its source, running thence to the northern limits of Louisiana and embracing all the tributaries of the Mississippi. But he said, in addition:

The President ... is willing, should it be indispensably necessary, to establish the Sabine, from its mouth to its source, as the boundary, in that extent, between the United-States and the Spanish-Provinces; leaving the residue of their boundaries, to be settled by Commissaries to be hereafter appointed by both governments.[23]

Monroe went on to explain the plan of the administration whereby the United States was to depend on the sale of lands in the Floridas for the financing of the payments to be made to its own citizens for claims. He carefully instructed Erving to make certain that no Spanish grants there should be valid after an agreed date, thus assuring the government possession of sufficient property for sale purposes. That this caution was sound became all too evident three years later.

Further advice showed that Monroe was not unmindful of the western land claims, but that he considered them less vital than they later became:

Beyond the conditions above stated you will not go. They are to be your ultimata. I need not remark, that it will be your duty, to obtain as much better as you may be able, rather seeking however an indemnity for spoliations and other wrongs, in money from Spain, to be paid directly by her, than in an extension of the Western Boundary beyond the Sabine, though that is to be obtained, if practicable.

In leaving the Boundary from the source of the Sabine, West and North, to be settled by Commissaries, any adjustment there will be avoided, which might affect our claims on [the] Columbia River, and on the Pacific.

Erving never presented the extreme concessions authorized by Monroe. When Monroe's instructions were presented to Congress and published, the portions quoted above were omitted. But they appear important when appraising the final settlement achieved in the Adams-Onís Treaty and the censure Adams received for relinquishing Texas. It is fairer to evaluate the arrangement finally obtained by John Quincy Adams with a knowledge of the concessions Monroe would have made.

At the same time, Monroe presented his somewhat vague views on the extent of Louisiana in instructions to William Pinkney, who had been sent to Russia shortly after Erving's departure. It is also a commentary on his conciliatory policy that he would have made concessions on the North Pacific sufficient to enrage any "54° 40′ or fight" enthusiast of Polk's time. Whereas thirty years later many would have fought to hold what is now British Columbia, Monroe then would have yielded it peaceably.

Writing to Pinkney on May 10, 1816, he said:

The Northern boundary between the United-States and the British possessions, is formed by a line, which runs from the North-westernmost point of the Lake of the Woods, due West, on the parallel of the 49° of North Latitude. It was limited by the Treaty of 1783, between the United-States and Great-Britain, West, by the Mississippi, which was then supposed, to have its source, North, of that parallel. The territories of the United-States, were afterwards extended, by the acquisition of Louisiana, whose boundaries have not been defined by Treaties, but which according to the principles and usages applicable to such a case, may fairly be considered of vast extent equally to the West and North as well as to the South. In adjusting these claims with the Russian government it will be satisfactory to the United-States to do it, by adopting the parallel of 49° as the boundary between them on the Pacific ocean.[24]

That offer was withdrawn a few months later when Richard Rush, *ad interim* secretary of state, told Pinkney that "the President has some reasons for believing that the Government of Russia will be satisfied with the 55th degree of North latitude as the boundary."[25]

No boundary negotiation was carried on between Erving and Cevallos at the time, because before the Spanish minister answered the note of August 26, in which Erving recounted the complaints of the United States against Spain, instructions had been sent to Onís transferring the negotiations to Washington. The United States minister had tried to obtain an answer from Cevallos, but failed, and the delay gave rise to the following comment, which

suggests that Erving's attitude was not such as to promote successful conversations :

In the midst of all this [financial and political turmoil in Spain] the government seems to be possessed by the most perfect apathy, scarcely any business
is done, of course it accumulates; Mr. Cevallos gives me as a reason why he
has not yet read my note that he has had too much to do, and yet I know that
he wastes much time in audiences with priests and friars. The only two affairs
on which they seem to have any sensibility is the projected marriages with the
Portuguese Princesses: and secondly and least important that of the colonies,
they talk of efforts and I really believe are making them such as they are, in
the mean time a few contemptible boats keep their whole coast in alarm;—by
blistering them in that quarter we may make them wince that's all.[26]

Cevallos and Erving had engaged in an acrimonious conversation on September 14 over the complaints presented by the latter.
When the former maintained that Spain had vehemently protested
the British use of the Floridas in the War of 1812 (a statement to
all appearances contrary to the fact of Anglo-Spanish cordiality
discussed in chapter i), Erving replied that "it would be proper to
shew also that active opposition had been made to the landing &
operations of the english." When Erving referred to the Convention of 1802, Cevallos replied "that the paper I alluded to was no
convention, not having been ratified."[27] But no mention was made
of bases for a settlement.

Meanwhile Monroe had written Onís, on June 10, 1816, expressing his regret that that minister was not empowered to treat. After
hearing of this, Cevallos wrote Erving saying that full powers had
been sent to the minister at Washington. Erving did not know
whether Monroe had really requested that Onís be empowered or
not. Therefore he was not sure how news of the change in place of
negotiation would be received at Washington. He suspected the
Spaniards of taking the step simply to relieve themselves of the
pressure of the negotiation in Madrid, and to delay a settlement.

Erving was obviously offended by the maneuver, and intimated
as much in a conversation with Cevallos on September 17, followed
two days later by a letter giving written form to his views. He
pointed out that he was fully empowered to negotiate without further reference to his government, and that, if Cevallos was too busy
(having three ministries in his charge at the time), a special agent
or commission might deal with him. Cevallos replied that even such
an agent would have to refer to him for instructions step by step,

thus saving no time. Erving protested almost too loudly his own fairness in his letter, saying of the conversation of the 17th:

I concluded by excusing the warmth with which I pressed the subject, assuring you that I was very far from seeking any personal gratification in this matter of high public interest, but that I looked only to the desired result.[28]

As a matter of fact, the instructions to Onís probably had not been *sent* at that time, but they were dated September 10, 1816, and apparently were transmitted by the messenger whom Erving sent to Washington with his despatch of September 22. They gave Onís full powers to treat, but allowed him no further latitude than the offers already made by Spain.[29] This restriction brought a protest from Onís to his government, and made any successful dealing with Monroe in the following winter impossible. So far as boundary demands were concerned, the ministers were still as far apart as the respective demands: from Spain, that the western limit be the Mississippi, and from the United States, that it be the Colorado, or possibly the Sabine.

Long before his letter of instruction reached Onís, however, Cevallos, who had never dealt in a straightforward or conciliatory manner with the United States, and who apparently had not had a new idea on relations with that country in fourteen years, fell victim to a Cabinet intrigue, and on October 30, 1816, he was removed, for the last time.

The stalemate caused by Onís' lack of wider powers held until after the election of James Monroe to the presidency. By the time instructions from Cevallos' successor could be put into effect, the United States also had a new chieftain in its foreign office. Fortunately the change in each country brought a more active, aggressive, and farsighted procedure on the affairs in dispute.

NOTES TO CHAPTER III

[1] Hubert B. Fuller, *Purchase of Florida* (Cleveland, 1906), pp. 217, 225.

[2] Pedro Aguado Bleye, *Manual de historia de España* (5th ed., Bilbao, 1927–1931), II:552–556.

[3] *Ibid.*, pp. 559–560.

[4] Benito Sánchez Alonzo, book review in *Revista de Filología Española*, XVIII (1931):75–76.

[5] Erving to Monroe, August 31, 1816, in D.S., Despatches, Spain, XIII.

[6] Aguado Bleye, *op. cit.*, II:560.

[7] W. R. de Villa-Urrutia, *Fernán Núñez, el embajador* (Madrid, 1931), pp. 215–216.

[8] Morris to Monroe, May 30, 1815, in D.S., Despatches, Spain, XII.

[9] Morris to Monroe, November 7, 1815, *ibid.*

[10] Monroe to Erving, October 6, 1814, in D.S., United States Ministers, Instructions, VII.

[11] Morris to Monroe, November 27, 1814, in D.S., Despatches, Spain, XII; Erving to Madison, March 16, 1815, in Massachusetts Historical Society, Manuscript Letters of George W. Erving.

[12] Erving to Madison, October 6, 1814, in Massachusetts Historical Society, Manuscript Letters of George W. Erving.

[13] Mrs. Samuel Harrison Smith (Margaret Bayard) speaks of the Misses Onís as receiving considerable attention at an "intollerable squeeze" (a reception) in her *First Forty Years of Washington Society*, Gaillard Hunt, ed. (New York, 1906), p. 139. But the Onís family appear to have been generally inactive in society. The illness of Onís' wife was no doubt one reason. Another was perhaps the usual delay in the receipt of his salary, of which the minister continually complained; although Erving, in speaking of the corruption of the Spanish court, alleged (without giving any substantiation) that Onís had "helped himself," and was said to be a partner of Cevallos in draining the public treasury. See Erving to Monroe, August 31, 1816, in D.S., Despatches, Spain, XIII.

[14] Onís to Luyando (Spanish foreign minister), June 8, 1814, in A.G.I., Indiferente general, 1603. Onís' interest in such an objective was in part based on his conviction of the illegality of the Louisiana Purchase. That view was supported by Henry Adams, but has been upheld by few since his time. See Henry Adams, *History of the United States* (New York, 1889–1891), II:56.

[15] Monroe to Erving, October 6, 1814, in D.S., United States Ministers, Instructions, VII. I doubt that Onís was effectively *persona non grata* for other than political causes.

[16] Monroe to Cevallos, July 7, 1815, in D.S., Notes to Foreign Legations, II.

[17] My own rough estimate, difficult to make because of the present distribution of his correspondence among many different bundles, and in various archives.

[18] Noroña, who was Portuguese, originally spelled his name "Noronha." A sizable file of correspondence relating to his connection with Toledo and his later services, with several issues of *El Observador*, is in A.H.N., Est., 5555, Expediente 60.

[19] Onís to Monroe, December 30, 1815, in *A.S.P., F.R.,* IV:422. A fairly complete file of the notes which were exchanged by the two governments was submitted to Congress, and appeared in the *State Papers*, with the Adams-Onís

Treaty (*A.S.P., F.R.*, IV:422–626). Onís complained only once, after 1815, of the suppression of material in the publication—when certain documents which he had sent with a note were withheld. The greatest weakness of the series is to be found in the exclusion of instructions to the United States ministers abroad and their despatches, and in the inclusion of only extracts from many important letters.

[20] Monroe to Onís, January 9, 1816, and Onís to Monroe, February 22, 1816, in *A.S.P., F.R.*, IV:424–426.

[21] Monroe to Erving, March 11, 1816, in D.S., United States Ministers, Instructions, VIII.

[22] Monroe to Erving, May 30, 1816, *ibid.*

[23] *Ibid.*

[24] Monroe to Pinkney, May 10, 1816, *ibid.*

[25] Rush to Pinkney, April 21, 1817, *ibid.*

[26] Erving to Monroe, August 31, 1816, in D.S., Despatches, Spain, XIII.

[27] Erving to Monroe, September 22, 1816, *ibid.*

[28] Erving to Cevallos, September 19, 1816, in *A.S.P., F.R.*, IV:436.

[29] Cevallos to Onís, September 10, 1816, in A.M.E., 222; Jerónimo Bécker, *Historia de las relaciones exteriores de España durante el siglo XIX* (Madrid, 1924–1927), I:448.

CHAPTER IV

PIZARRO AND ADAMS TAKE UP THE BATTLE, 1816–1818

FRESH LEADERSHIP

CHANGES IN THE DIRECTION of foreign affairs in each capital brought to the fore the men who were to achieve the ultimate solution of the difficulties between Spain and the United States in the treaty of 1819. Outstanding among these was John Quincy Adams, a diplomatist highly respected by his contemporaries. In the most far-reaching territorial question the nation had faced since its founding he was to prove himself the best-qualified negotiator the United States could have had. It is largely because of the tenacity and skill which he demonstrated in the negotiation of this treaty that he is widely considered the most able of our secretaries of state.

With Adams, Onís was able to make the first real progress in the negotiation, for now issues were more clearly stated, decisions more firmly made. It must be said that Onís, too, in his ten exciting years in this country, showed admirable determination and diplomatic ability. He was frequently discouraged by the inconstancy of his own government as compared with the firmness of the government to which he was accredited. While Ferdinand's ministers awaited favorable occasions or delayed in the hope of receiving foreign assistance, the United States, in Onís' estimation, was rapidly developing into a most sinister threat to the continuation of Spanish dominion in America.

Onís' foreboding was heightened when United States troops under fiery Andrew Jackson invaded the Floridas without benefit either of instructions or of a war, thereby grossly insulting the Spanish crown. But Jackson's enterprise, undertaken in the spring of 1818, was only the culmination of a series of events which had given Onís reason to view the young republic with uncertainty—events and conditions which included the War of 1812 and previous invasions of the Floridas; an active sympathy of many persons in the United States toward the insurgent Spanish colonies, resulting in shipments of arms, in illegal outfitting of privateers, and in filibustering; the beginnings of an economic expansion marked by such spectacular ventures as the founding of Astoria on the Pacific Coast; and such firm foundations for growth as the inauguration of a great system of internal transportation routes to the west.

In dealing with these problems, Onís fortunately had, from 1816 to 1818, the counsel of one of the few capable ministers of the Spanish restoration. On Cevallos' removal in October, 1816, Ferdinand appointed as secretary of state for foreign affairs José García de León y Pizarro. Pizarro (as he was commonly known) was a man with long experience in the foreign office. His appointment was generally considered to be a distinct step toward able and upright dealings. From the beginning he took an active interest in relations with the United States, conducting a highly complex series of negotiations in that field—so complex, indeed, that it is easy for the student to become lost in the mass of detailed writings. Throughout, he and Onís were evidently agreed on major policies, and confidentially bemoaned to each other the many obstructions they met.

Pizarro, "a man of sound intelligence and political experience, who was expected to give a more humane and liberal turn to the government,"[1] had spent twenty-six of his forty-six years in government service, having held minor positions in legations throughout Europe, then serving as a subsecretary in the foreign office and secretary of the Council of State from 1802 to 1808.[2] He fled to Andalucía in the latter year, and continued his diplomatic career under the patriot Cortes and the Regency, being foreign minister for three months in 1812. Before his second appointment to that office in 1816, he had been named minister to Prussia, but apparently had spent most of the preceding year or two in France.

Pizarro had risen through the service under Floridablanca, Godoy, and Cevallos, and must have known intimately the intricacies of court intrigue at Madrid. In spite of that unwholesome atmosphere, he had developed a reputation for integrity and ability that won the respect of his contemporaries in other countries. He had known Onís for at least sixteen years;[3] and because he had spent ten years as a boy in South America, where his father was serving as a colonial official, he no doubt had a broader appreciation of the problems of empire which Onís had to face than did, for example, Cevallos.

[1] For notes to chap. iv, see pp. 101–104.

Pizarro's memoirs, written many years after his retirement, are characterized by his extreme pique at having been deprived of the honors due him for his important rôle in the negotiation of the Adams-Onís Treaty. He was removed from office just before its conclusion, and he naturally felt that others profited from his good work. The autobiography shows a notable self-esteem, a fact which must influence one's estimate of its reliability. Yet his story appears to be substantiated by the mass of contemporary documents. To authenticate his statements, he included in his *Memorias* a whole volume of correspondence and reports, of which more than 170 pages concern the treaty of 1819.[4]

It has been noted that Erving lacked sympathy for Spanish ways (although at times he displayed interest in phases of Spanish culture) and that he was disgusted with Cevallos. In view of this attitude, it is interesting to read his comments on the ministerial change, which also describe some of Pizarro's problems at home:

Mr. Pizarro ... has much more ability, industry, knowledge of affairs, & habit of business than Mr Cevallos;—he has also a portion of good faith, which the other was entirely deficient in; & his mind is free from those strong prejudices, & those absurd & obstinate errors, which were rooted in that of his predecessor. In the several interviews which I have had with him, I have observed a moderation, good sense, & conciliatory temper, from which I should augur most favorably, if the political affairs of this government were really, as they are ostensibly, under his control;—but this is not the case:—by what degree of infatuation or apathy it is possessed, or under what secret influence it is directed, I will not undertake to say,—but it is obvious that nothing of importance is done to advance the interests of the country in its foreign relations, nor effectually to relieve it from the weight of domestick evils under which it groans.... In that all important department of "Hacienda" (finance) every thing is in ruins, & no measure meriting the name of effort is attempted to repair it, & whatever is attempted, finds a fatal opposition in the interest of the individuals who are employed to effect it....

In my first & second interviews with Mr Pizarro ... he professed the best dispositions to conciliation, took care not to join me in censure of his predecessor, said that he proposed to inform himself fully as to the existing state of our relations, and,—since then,—he has not said a word on the subject.[5]

Erving went on to discuss the dangers which Pizarro faced from the treachery of the King, and from the undermining influence of numerous enemies, especially Cevallos. The latter had been appointed minister to Naples at a high salary, but had remained in Madrid, working against Pizarro. The one bright spot in the pic-

ture was the appointment in December, 1816, of Martín de Garay
as finance minister. Like Pizarro, he was a man who commanded
respect for integrity and ability. He began work immediately upon
a great financial reform plan, with which he made some headway.
It was eventually pushed aside by court intrigue, however, and
Garay went the way of all discredited ministers, into exile from
the court.

SPANISH PROCEDURE AND POLICIES

Pizarro's program did not take effect for some time after his appointment. Long and arduous debate with Erving resulted in only
one or two significant agreements. In Washington, after months of
waiting, Onís at last received instructions from the new *secretario
de estado,* only to find that negotiations there would have to be
postponed until the reorganization attendant upon the inauguration of the new administration could be effected. Adams had been
chosen by Monroe as the new secretary of state, but he was minister to England at the time and did not return from London until
late in 1817. Consequently, conversations with Onís were not
opened until December of that year.

In the interim it was becoming apparent that the change from
Cevallos to Pizarro was a most significant and fortunate event for
Spain. In view of the inactivity which had characterized the régime
of Cevallos, the organization, industry, and policies of the foreign office under Pizarro's administration were striking and merit
analysis.

First it must be noted that, although Pizarro did inform himself
thoroughly on the questions at issue with the United States, he was
greatly assisted by a clerk in the foreign office, Narciso de Heredia
(to whom he gives credit in his·*Memorias*), who handled all the
routine of this negotiation, wrote the instructions to Onís, and
apparently acted as expert adviser. Consequently, it was on Heredia that the real burden of the transaction fell.[6] It appears,
however, from the general tone of Pizarro's work, and particularly
from the accounts of dealings with him written by Erving and
Henry Wellesley, that Pizarro was himself well acquainted with
the situation in America, and that he followed it closely.

Certainly much study and labor were given to the problem. The
notes to foreign ministers and instructions to Spanish ministers in
foreign courts, as well as the reports submitted to the Council of

State, contain a mass of information on the subject which could have been obtained only in the perusal of countless pages of earlier correspondence and reports. And their very number is impressive, particularly the high-water mark of fifty-five letters of instruction sent to Onís in the month of July, 1817, all concerning details aside from the lengthy statements of general policy governing the negotiation.[7]

Special reports, and innumerable accounts from colonial officials of frontier claims and disputes, were sent in to the foreign office. One of especial interest, which it is reasonably certain was used by Heredia, is the famous report on the limits of Louisiana and Texas prepared by Father José Antonio Pichardo. In the archives at Sevilla is a letter from the viceroy of Mexico, dated March 15, 1813, in which he said that the copy of Pichardo's historical memoir could not yet be sent to Spain, as only 1,969 of its 5,127 pages had been copied.[8] Another, dated September 30, 1816, announced that the copy of the report, which had just been completed, was being sent in two boxes containing thirty-one volumes. But it was explained that the plans which were to accompany it had not been completed, because of the illness of the man who was preparing them, the same Gonzalo López de Haro who in 1789 had piloted a vessel to Nootka Sound. On the margin of this letter is a notation made by the *secretario de estado,* requesting that the report be placed at the disposition of three department officials, among them Heredia.[9]

Little was done to further the negotiation for some time after Pizarro's appointment. It will be remembered that Erving, in his despatch quoted above, complained that Pizarro had not mentioned the affair at any time between September 30 and December 15.

Meanwhile, the policy to be followed was outlined in a *Bosquejo* (sketch) of relations with the United States, submitted to the King on November 6, 1816.[10] This paper, unsigned but clearly originating in the foreign office, was prefaced by a castigation of the United States as being ungrateful in view of Spain's aid in her revolution against England, and as being "always anxious to promote rebellion and perfidy." There followed a lament over the sale of Louisiana, allowed by the "perfidy" of France, and the "weakness and stupidity" of Spain. The North American republic was accused of making war, in effect, on Spain, under the guise of scrupulous neutrality, by supporting the insurgent colonies of Spanish America.

Erving, according to the *Bosquejo*, came with full powers, but with a menacing tone, and with unjust demands. Onís, at the same time, had reported that the United States desired a boundary running up the Río Grande to the Thirty-first Parallel, and thence westward to the sea (though such a boundary determination could not have been based on official communications from the government at Washington).

The best policy—so it had been decided when this sketch was written—would be to prolong the negotiation and to seek the aid of some respectable Power. Russia was favored. That nation was chosen because of her "direct interest" in seeing that the Spanish colonies were not freed, since, if they should be, the La Plata country about Buenos Aires would undoubtedly take away Russia's trade in hides and tallow. It was also suggested that a territorial cession in the Floridas might be made to Russia, to recompense her for her aid and to provide a buffer against the United States. Russia, as will be seen later, declined to aid Spain.

Finally, the assertion was made in the *Bosquejo* that it was "urgent to keep the negotiation away from a diplomat as astute and turbulent as Erving," with the recommendation that Onís should negotiate the treaty.

Onís was still fretting in Washington under the limited authority given him by Cevallos to make concessions to the United States. He was desperately afraid that if a settlement were not reached shortly this country would seize the Floridas and Texas, and would openly aid the revolting colonies. That the Spanish government also feared the latter eventuality is evident in the sketch quoted above outlining relations with the United States, on the success of which "depends in great part the fortune of our ultramarine colonies."

Monroe's Last Effort and New Spanish Proposals

Although Pizarro promised to send Onís further instructions at various times, none regarding the major issues at stake appears to have been sent until August, 1817, and no comprehensive set of instructions was forthcoming until November of that year. In the interim the minister to the United States was able to accomplish almost nothing.

During the winter of 1816 and 1817 Monroe's final effort in the affair as secretary of state was made when he tried to persuade Onís to accept the Colorado River of Texas as the boundary line, the United States thereby offering to yield the region between that and the Río Grande in exchange, so it was stated, for all Spanish lands east of the Mississippi. Following the failure of this plan in conference, Monroe wrote Onís, January 14, 1817, declaring the futility of further negotiation on limits, and asking that the Spanish minister take up the question of a convention to provide compensation for spoliations and for the suppression of the right of deposit at New Orleans.[11]

In his reply, Onís attempted to justify his inability to bargain on the boundary issue by explaining that the full powers, of which he had received only the duplicates (the originals having been delayed, lost, or stolen), did not give him sufficient latitude to agree to Monroe's proposals, and that the further instructions which he needed presumably had been delayed in the mail. Onís said he had understood previously that the negotiation concerned only the cession of disputed West Florida; and that he doubted if his King would accede to the loss of East Florida, with the important harbor of Pensacola, "the key to the Gulf."[12] With respect to Texas, he said that Monroe's plan would be no "exchange," repeating the claim that all of Texas belonged to Spain anyway. This statement of Onís is interesting in contrast to his description of the treaty after its signature in 1819, in which he praised it as embodying a fair exchange, the Floridas for Texas.[13]

Early in February Onís wrote Pizarro saying that he feared serious trouble if a prompt settlement were not reached, and again asking for more liberal instructions.[14] Until they came, he said that he would delay, hoping to gain a more favorable opportunity, and not wishing to take any steps which might lead the President to authorize a declaration of war or bring about a recognition of the insurgent Spanish colonies during the current session of Congress.

Although the Neutrality Act of March 3, 1817, gave Spain some satisfaction with respect to her complaints over the equipment of ships and enlistment of forces for Spanish America in this country, Onís still found grounds for protest. All through the spring of 1817 he was greatly discouraged—disgusted with the United States and offended at the treatment given him by his own country. His dislike for Washington no doubt made him more zealous in his efforts to arrive at a settlement, or, as an alternative, to have the negotiations transferred to Madrid. In April he wrote Pizarro a nonofficial communication, beginning with the affectionate diminutives *"Querido Pizarrito,"* in which he complained of his lack of instructions and told of the imminent death of his wife. Señora de Onís had been ill much of the time since coming to America, and her husband frequently blamed her ill health on the climate of the Atlantic seaboard, saying that she could have been saved if he had been allowed to return to Spain. In this letter he says to Pizarro:

My wife . . . despaired of by the doctors, will be dead long before you receive this. . . . My Clementina [one of his daughters] runs the same risk, and if you do not send me the authorization to leave here next spring, you will be her murderer. I can do no more; this is no country for healthy people, and especially in the circumstances in which I have been; send me where you will provided that you take me away from here, even though it be to plant cabbages. . . .

. . . Señor Don Pedro Cevallos made the greatest blunder he could in transferring the negotiations here: for with these people it is impossible to do anything, and one negotiates with them at a disadvantage, [as they] publish the notes they wish, and hide those which do not suit them; in addition to which you must understand that nothing but force can make them give up West Florida which they have occupied, that it will be very difficult to obtain an agreement to put the boundary at the Mississippi, *and that, even in this case, one must wonder if the island of Cuba will not be endangered by the cession of East Florida, unless we always have there a garrison of ten thousand troops and eight warships.* You cannot realize the ambition and pride of this government, nor can you believe that it might be so foolish that, without provocation, it would declare a war which might be very unfortunate for it; but you must believe that the people all want war with Spain, and that only the tact and prudence with which I have conducted myself have been able to prevent it on three distinct occasions. The Government does not want it now, but the people will force the Government to declare it if the differences are not settled before next December.[15]

Señora de Onís died in the following month, but the daughter survived. Onís, in his prediction of war in the following winter, proved to be unduly pessimistic, for, although little progress had been made on the affairs at issue by December, no war came.

The intervening period saw the inauguration of Monroe as president, the appointment of Adams as secretary of state, and the continuation of Onís' protests in maritime matters to Richard Rush, acting secretary. Adams did not even meet the Spanish minister in

Washington until the opening of the Congressional session which the latter so much feared. Concerning Adams' appointment, Onís had little comment, simply voicing the general opinion of Adams' high ability, but saying that he knew nothing of him personally.

In Spain, conversations of interest continued between Erving and Pizarro. Aside from these, an important crystallization of policy took place—finally making possible the sending of the instructions Onís had so long and impatiently awaited.

Pizarro wrote Erving on July 16, noting that Onís' messenger was in Madrid awaiting the preparation of instructions, and asking if in the interim the United States minister was still authorized and willing to save time by undertaking negotiations there.[16] This was a direct reversal of Cevallos' decision that the work should be done in Washington, and Erving complained that the transfer in the preceding fall had put him in the embarrassing position of having powers and not being able to use them. He said that, since frankly there was suspicion already that Spain was simply trying to delay the matter, he could not encourage further procrastination by entering into a discussion of arguments worn out by frequent restatement since 1805.[17] He offered, however, to receive a proposal for a settlement, which could be either accepted or rejected without long consideration. Pizarro hesitated, but finally sent the *projet* of a treaty with his note of August 17.

In Pizarro's view the arguments were not soured by long standing, because of new developments since 1805. These were, specifically, the addition of claims of Spain (hitherto unvoiced) against the United States for spoliations, the collection of more proofs of the Spanish title to Texas, and the seizure of West Florida by the United States. "So great is the mass of documents and authentic and indisputable proofs . . ." he said, "particularly relative to the western boundary of Louisiana, that I doubt whether there be a point which is susceptible of more exact and rigorous demonstration."[18]

In this note Pizarro restated the claim of Spain to West Florida, but said that the King would now yield on the point of asking its restoration before any negotiations could be entertained, a condition imposed on Onís' earlier dealings.

The *projet* included the establishment of a claims commission much like that of the Convention of 1802, but did not involve a revival of that unratified agreement. The declaration was to be made that Spain would assist the United States in appealing to France for payment of the claims for spoliation by French corsairs, but not that Spain herself was liable.

With respect to limits, Pizarro's plan included the cession of the Floridas to the United States, with the western boundary of this nation being put at the Mississippi River from its source to its mouth. Further, the scheme was to be contingent upon the approval of the Powers signatory to the Treaty of Utrecht of 1713, which, Pizarro maintained, had guaranteed the integrity of Spain's dominions as they stood before the death of King Charles II of Spain (1700).[19]

Pizarro, realizing that the United States would probably not accept the Mississippi as a western limit, proposed an alternative to his *projet*, namely, to submit the whole affair to the mediation of one or more Powers friendly to both nations.

Erving replied that he could not consider such an agreement, and offered some explanations, but said nothing of the mediation plan.[20] He professed ignorance of the new proofs of the Spanish title to Texas as well as of the new claims of Spain for spoliations since 1805 and declared the eighth article of the Treaty of Utrecht no longer effective. Furthermore, he referred to the United States' Neutrality Act of March 3, 1817, as fulfilling certain demands of Pizarro on that point.

Erving at that time wrote to his superior in Washington that he thought Pizarro had offered an intentionally unacceptable proposal in order to throw the affair into the mediation suggested as an alternative.[21] He told of a visit from Garay, the finance minister, who asked that Erving propose something to Pizarro. He added that Garay and the *secretario de estado* were conciliatory themselves, but seemed to be bound by opposition in the Cabinet. With respect to possibilities for the mediation, Erving thought that England and Russia were the Powers which Spain depended on chiefly, and that the latter was the more influential because of the strength of its minister Tatistcheff in the *camarilla* (inner council, or "kitchen cabinet").

HEREDIA'S GREAT STATE PAPER

How accurate Erving's suppositions were can be seen by studying briefly the thorough review of United States relations, written by Heredia, and presented by Pizarro in the meeting of the *Consejo de Estado* of June 10 and 11, 1817, and the decisions taken pursuant to that explanation. This paper (which is reproduced in Pizarro's memoirs, occupying 73 pages) included a long account of the negotiations, beginning with the independence of the United States, and outlined eight possible methods of procedure, with recommendations.[22]

With the *Exposición* were presented certain documents, and a map.[23] These were evidently the ones about which Pizzaro wrote Erving. The *Exposición* mentions that "the documents . . . just received from Mexico, in compliance with the order [of Charles IV] of 1805, came bound in thirty-one volumes,"[24] a description tallying with that in the letter of Viceroy Calleja previously quoted. It is thus apparent that a basic document in the preparation of Heredia's work was the historical memoir on the limits of Louisiana and Texas prepared by Padre Don Antonio José Pichardo. His name, however, was not mentioned. Presumably López de Haro had completed the copying of the accompanying map, upon which he had been working when the documents were forwarded. Pizarro secured for his own use, a few weeks after the presentation of the *Exposición*, the map prepared in Philadelphia in 1816 by John Melish, of which a later edition was cited in the Adams-Onís Treaty.

The *Exposición* discussed the five points at issue, namely, spoliations by the Spanish on United States commerce in the European war which ended in 1801; like spoliations by the French; damages caused by the suppression of the right of deposit at New Orleans without the substitution of another port, as stipulated in Pinckney's Treaty; the West Florida question; and the disputed western boundary of Louisiana. The last point was dealt with at great length, the Spanish claim to Texas being based generally on the historical outline as described in chapter ii of this study.

Strong opposition to the transfer of negotiations to Washington was expressed in Heredia's paper. It was thought that the affair could be more efficiently and advantageously handled if kept close to the reins of control in Madrid. But Erving's acrimonious and futile dealings with Cevallos, and later actions of Adams, had necessitated the removal of operations again to Washington. (It will be seen that in the ensuing negotiations Washington was the center of affairs until March, 1818, and again after July of that year.)

Of the eight possible programs discussed, there should be noted the first and second, both of which Pizarro favored; the third, which was adopted by the *Consejo;* and the eighth, which came nearest to the ultimate settlement achieved.

The first was a plan to offer the Floridas to England in exchange for her assistance in restoring Louisiana to Spain. The plan visualized a political balance in North America which would confine the ambitions of the United States and would give Spain and England the power of disciplining the United States in the west by shutting off the navigation of the Mississippi and the rivers flowing through the Floridas.

This plan, which admittedly was of questionable practicability because of Spain's weakness and England's apathy in the matter, showed the influence of Don José Alvarez de Toledo, the former Texas revolutionary leader. Toledo had made his peace with Onís, given valuable counsel, and been sent to Spain, where he was pardoned by the King. His advice was subsequently sought by the foreign office, and one of his opinions detailing the possible Spanish seizure of Louisiana was cited in this discussion.[25]

The second project, which likewise had the favor of Heredia and Pizarro, included the settlement of all issues through the mediation of one or more friendly Powers, on the basis of the *uti possidetis* of 1763 but recognizing the validity of the Louisiana Purchase. This arrangement was simultaneously suggested by Onís, the latter's despatch reaching Madrid after the presentation of the *Exposición.*[26]

The third, which became the basis of the offer made by Pizarro to Erving, was also much like one of Onís' alternatives. It was an exchange of the Floridas to the United States for all the territory west of the Mississippi. This indicates a confusion over whether or not Spain was to continue in the position that the purchase of Louisiana was invalid. For, whereas in the second plan the recognition of that transaction was to be given as something of a concession, here it must be considered to have been admitted. Without valid title to Louisiana the United States would have no territory west of the Mississippi to "exchange." But the question is largely one of words. After the failure of Labrador at Vienna it is clear that Spain never considered that she could effectively maintain her allegation that the United States did not own Louisiana.

In discussing this third plan, it was pointed out that the Spanish Interior Provinces would be safeguarded by placing the border of the United States far from their centers of population. The United States, besides gaining the valuable ports of the Floridas, would avoid the possible danger, if her population spread farther westward, of a dismemberment of the Union. However, it was pointed out that it would be difficult to obtain approval of such a plan at Washington because of the ambition of the United States to reach the Pacific and conduct commerce overland to the Columbia River.

This last point, like the opinion that expansion might so weaken the Union as to cause its dissolution, was based directly on the writings of Onís, and particularly upon his despatch of March 3, 1817.[27]

An important advantage which the third plan assertedly would give was the opportunity of sounding the possibilities of aid from England and France while the United States was studying the offer. In this respect, Erving's allegation concerning the Spanish desire for time was correct; but with respect to delay *per se*, the *Exposición* said:

in [this scheme] an admissible proposition is offered by Your Majesty, and the censure avoided that we have been tergiversating for many years and seeking evasions to prolong the discussion.[28]

Furthermore, it was pointed out that, in the event the United States did not accept the exchange proposed, Spain would then have a pretext for moving the center of negotiations back to Madrid, which, it was known, would please Erving as well as Pizarro. Both would play more important rôles in any settlement reached, and both sincerely thought more could be accomplished at Madrid than at Washington.

All the remaining plans comprised further concessions which, it was feared, might have to be made to the United States if none of the first three was acceptable. Some interest attaches to them in that they show the vague ideas of the writer on the geography of the country west of the Mississippi.

The fourth project provided for the recognition of the United States' ownership of West Florida in exchange for the establishment of a western line running from a point on the Gulf between the Calcasieu and Mermento rivers, between Los Adaes and Natchitoches, and then directly north. But the idea of a line drawn straight north on a map regardless of natural features was discouraged. The fifth plan would have seen the cession of both Floridas, and the establishment of a line beginning at the Bayou La Fourche (for all practical purposes a western mouth of the Mississippi), going up the Mississippi to the Missouri, and up that stream to its head. In this plan the lack of information on titles, accepted limits, and settlements on the North Pacific prevented the specification of a line beyond the headwaters of the Missouri. The sixth plan was much the same, but substituted the Arkansas for the Missouri; and further ignorance or confusion of geography was frankly expressed with respect to the location of the head of that river, and its probable proximity to New Mexico. The seventh scheme was simply one of settling the claims as satisfactorily as possible, leaving the boundaries undrawn, that being considered preferable to an unadvantageous treaty from which no appeal could be had.

The eighth plan, "that proposed by the Americans, who wish us to cede to them the two Floridas, leaving the limits of Louisiana at the Colorado river," was the one described by Pizarro in his *Memorias* as the one embodied in the treaty. It shows a geographical confusion that is easier for us today to understand the Spaniard's falling into than it was for Erving when the question arose in 1818. It is clear beyond doubt, from the *Exposición* and from marginal notes on Onís' treaty plan of April 8, 1817, that in referring to the "Colorado" River the writer had in mind the Red River of Natchitoches, which at times was designated by the other Spanish term of nearly the same meaning, "*colorado.*"[29] It is equally clear that in the negotiations of 1805, when Monroe and Pinckney proposed the "Colorado" as a boundary, they meant the Colorado of western Texas, flowing into Matagorda Bay. Until Onís and Adams discussed the matter in the winter of 1817 and 1818 the officials of the two countries apparently were unaware of the misunderstanding.

As has been stated, the third plan recommended in the *Exposi-*

ción was adopted, though Pizarro in his *Memorias* says he preferred the first and second. Accordingly, in his note of August 17, 1817, already referred to, that minister offered Erving the *projet* of a treaty. It was not accepted. Apparently Pizarro's design was not to submit an intentionally unacceptable plan, but he at least welcomed the resulting delay, which allowed him to sound out England and France.

ONÍS' NEW PROBLEMS

Immediately upon the failure of Pizarro's approach to Erving, a session of the *Consejo de Estado* was held, from which resulted new instructions for Onís. They became the basis of his first dealings with Adams when he met the new secretary of state in Washington in December of that year.

The *Consejo* agreed, on August 27, that Onís should be instructed to advance at Washington essentially the same proposal made to Erving, that is, he was to offer the cession of the Floridas (contingent upon approval of England in accordance with the Treaty of Utrecht) in exchange for acceptance of the Mississippi as the western limit of the United States.[30] Simultaneously he was to suggest as an alternative an appeal to the good offices or mediation of two or more friendly Powers.

Furthermore, a complete survey of the situation was made and a policy agreed upon which was to be followed if the United States rejected the plan. Onís was to advance as his own ideas the fourth, fifth, and sixth possible arrangements of the Heredia *Exposición*, but if any of them was agreed upon he must sign it *sub spe rati* only.[31] The all-important aim was to keep the negotiation open, trying by magnanimous dealings and by propaganda to dispel anti-Spanish sentiment in the United States. Onís was thus to ward off a breach of relations, or, what would be worse, open aid by the United States to the Spanish American insurgents, or perhaps even a declaration of war.

Special importance attaches to the date of these first instructions to Onís for the cession of the Floridas. After they were sent, Ferdinand made certain notorious land grants in that area which would seriously have embarrassed the United States. Their validity became a major issue later between the two countries. However, the chronology of Spanish diplomacy at this time appears to convict the King and his favorites of trying to dissipate what advantage the United States would acquire from the cession.

The new instructions reached Onís on October 31, 1817, in the hands of his secretary of legation, Luis Noeli, who had waited in Spain during the summer's deliberations. They arrived in time to enable Onís to begin his work in Washington as Congress convened, forestalling precipitate action by that body. But the efficacy of the instructions was menaced by new disturbing developments—intrigues in the Floridas, a plot to revolutionize Texas, and the threat of recognition of Buenos Aires by the United States.

In East Florida the famous General Gregor McGregor, veteran of the struggles of Miranda and Bolívar in Venezuela, had begun the operations by which he hoped to free both Floridas from Spanish dominion. With a commission from the agent in Philadelphia of the republic of Venezuela,[32] McGregor gathered a force numbering about a hundred fifty and from a rendezvous in Georgia captured Amelia Island in June, 1817, through a ruse which led the Spanish commander to overestimate the "patriot" forces. McGregor issued proclamations to some two hunderd "Anglo-Americans" who had set up a practically autonomous régime with the approval of the Spanish governor of East Florida, José Coppinger, in the region between the St. John's and the St. Mary's. Coppinger refused to welcome McGregor's "liberating" efforts, however, and when the latter's financial backers and purveyors despaired of his success he had to withdraw. Following a chaotic few weeks in which a Spanish force from St. Augustine was turned back, apparently because of the incompetence of its commander, the island was taken over by the notorious pirate Louis Aury, fresh from buccaneering operations at Galveston. Writers generally describe Aury as a pirate who was interested only in the lucrative business of bringing prizes in for condemnation in an outlaw port such as he controlled at Amelia. But it appears that he was also authorized by South American revolutionary governments to aid in the dismemberment of Spain's colonial empire.[33] He used the flag of the Mexican revolutionists.

Whatever Aury's motives were, surely piracy was among them, and the United States government, harassed by complaints of the illegal acts done at Amelia, so near its borders, and involving its citizens, determined to intervene. President Monroe in his opening message to Congress announced a decision to this effect, which was carried out in the occupation of the island by both land and naval forces on December 23, 1817.[34]

Onís had protested the original venture of McGregor, and now asked explanations of the President's intent regarding the invasion of Spanish territory by United States troops.[35] In the following month he protested the occupation, and Adams answered that if Spain could have protected her own territory the United States would not have had to do it for her, and that no conquest from Spain was intended.[36] The United States troops stayed until after the signing of the Adams-Onís Treaty, and throughout the negotiation it is evident that the Amelia affair was a source of serious irritation.

At the same time Onís relayed home reports of a menacing venture of certain French Bonapartists, who, after an attempt to form a colony on the Alabama River as an exile haven, proposed to capture Texas, eventually enlarging their scheme to include the crowning of Joseph Bonaparte as king of Mexico.[37] While their plot was brewing, a situation similar to that at Amelia developed at Galveston, where piracies led the United States government to occupy that island. This time the intervention was based on the claim that Galveston lay in United States territory.[38]

The third disturbing factor was the danger that the United States would recognize the insurgent Spanish colonies, having already given them a distinct status as belligerents by its neutrality legislation. That would of course end hopes of an accord between this country and Spain. Conspicuous as the leader of agitation for this step was Henry Clay, speaker of the House of Representatives. His arguments were based on the declaration of independence of the United Provinces of the La Plata at Tucumán in 1816, and the victories of San Martín over the Loyalists in Chile in the spring of 1817, which gave the independence movement definite momentum.

During 1817 plans were laid to send agents to investigate conditions in the insurgent countries. These plans finally materialized with the sailing of the frigate "Congress" on December 4, carrying Caesar A. Rodney, Theodorick Bland, and John Graham as commissioners appointed to report on the history and progress of affairs in South America. Onís had reported that in August, when the mission was in New York ready to leave on the sloop-of-war "Ontario," the commissioners had met John Quincy Adams, just returned from England. And Adams, who considered their journey premature, as a matter of policy, had persuaded Monroe to let the "Ontario" sail without them.[30]

Onís believed that the commissioners were to carry secret instructions authorizing them to recognize any of the new republics which they considered worthy. When the "Ontario" sailed in October, he supposed that its commander was empowered to carry on clandestine negotiations with the insurgents.[40] And when the commissioners finally left, in December, he referred to them as "ambassadors," although the government had not yet authorized recognition.[41]

Clay at the opening of Congress announced his determination to seek a decision in favor of recognition of the La Plata provinces.[42] Onís was aroused by this step, and more so by Clay's speech of March 24, 1818, in which he advocated the sending of an official minister to Buenos Aires. It will be seen that the prevention of recognition by the United States was a salient point in Spanish policy, and that efforts toward this end assumed increasing importance in Onís' maneuvers.

Troubled, then, by these three developments, as well as by his belief that the United States would never accept the proposals he was now authorized to make, the Spanish minister went to Washington, and arranged an appointment with the new secretary of state for December 1.

JOHN QUINCY ADAMS

John Quincy Adams began at this time to play a conspicuous part in the negotiation of the treaty which he later declared to be his greatest diplomatic accomplishment.[43] It is hardly necessary here to note the wealth of experience which he brought to the task. In addition to his background, his education, his proved abilities, and his many years in diplomatic posts, he had an intimate knowledge of the territorial and maritime problems of the United States, derived from his services at Ghent and as minister to England. His interest in the West had been shown at the time of the Louisiana Purchase, when, as Senator, he had favored the acquisition, though he sought a Constitutional amendment to make it legal.[44]

JOHN QUINCY ADAMS

Adams' adversary, nearly the same age, had almost as long a record of official service as he. But Onís' career in the foreign office at Madrid could not equal Adams' wider experience of travel, association, and observation. The new secretary, however, had great respect for the capabilities of the Spaniard.[45] He appraised his opponent, after considerable association, in such characteristic terms as these:

Cold, calculating, wily, always commanding his own temper, proud because he is a Spaniard, but supple and cunning, accommodating the tone of his pretensions precisely to the degree of endurance of his opponent, bold and overbearing to the utmost extent to which it is tolerated, careless of what he asserts or how grossly it is proved to be unfounded, his morality appears to be that of the Jesuits as exposed by Pascal. He is laborious, vigilant, and ever attentive to his duties; a man of business and of the world.[46]

The new secretary wrote to Erving on November 11, 1817, acknowledging receipt of the despatches from the latter brought by Luis Noeli,[47] who had left Madrid about August 31. Thus before opening negotiations with Onís, Adams had direct accounts of the Pizarro-Erving conversations in which Erving had rejected the Spanish proposal.

In due course Onís presented orally the propositions contained in his latest instructions. Adams rejected them, as had Erving a similar offer. Onís then resolved to enter upon a detailed discussion of limits, taking advantage of the time which must intervene before the arrival of information on the Spanish appeal to England and France for aid. On returning home the very day he had seen Adams, December 1, he found the letter he awaited. It was an instruction from Pizarro, saying that the British minister at Washington would suggest mediation, on the condition that it should be requested by both parties.[48] Onís in his reply declared emphatically that he hoped the negotiation might be moved back to Madrid, explaining the difficulty of diplomatic intercourse at Washington, where the executive had to refer to public opinion at every step, and where any correspondence which it suited the administration to reveal was promptly published on request from Congress.

In one of his frequent tirades on the dangers of United States expansion, Onís discussed Monroe's message of December 2, 1817,

regarding the situation on Amelia and Galveston islands. Concerning the President's speech, the Spaniard said:

> . . . you will see, finally, that [this government] does not attempt to hide
> the fact that it takes Indian lands and encourages [white] settlement in ac-
> cordance with its plan of extending the limits of this Republic toward the
> South, and then of realizing its great Project of reaching the Pacific Ocean.
> I confess to you that I cannot comprehend how the Powers of Europe fail to
> awaken from their lethargy on seeing the extraordinary steps of this Re-
> public, and how they can fail to see that it will be too late when they wish
> to place limits on it, if they allow it to take the flight on which its political
> actions are rapidly leading it.[49]

Inasmuch as a delay would still occur before the British suggestion of mediation could be made. Onís proceeded with plans for a
detailed discussion of the territorial claims of the two Powers. He
wrote asking for an appointment, and was requested to come to
the State Department on December 18.[50] In the interview the Spanish minister said to Adams that he thought the proper procedure
would be to discuss the respective titles to territory owned by the
two governments and then to define the indemnifications due, enabling them to decide what suitable equivalent Spain might accept
for the Floridas, which the King had decided to cede.[51] Adams
headed off Onís' efforts to argue the boundary questions by stating
that the United States had reached a decision in those matters, and
that he simply wished to know if Onís had the powers to make
further proposals. The Spanish minister then suggested that, since
Spain's propositions had already been advanced and rejected, the
United States should make a counteroffer. He hoped that the republic would propose to cede its own territory, not Spain's, in
exchange for the Floridas, alluding to previous projects advanced
by the United States concerning the region west of the Mississippi.

The two men then agreed that the spoliations and claims for
damages growing out of the suspension of the right of deposit at
New Orleans could be left to a claims commission. In this they
evidenced their willingness to exclude those matters from the negotiations and to devote all the attention to the boundaries. And in
fact such was the course of their subsequent dealings. The claims
settlement was easily made, once an agreement was reached on
the difficult territorial questions.

Onís, in reporting this conversation, warned Pizarro of the

dangers inherent in the United States' projected seizure of Amelia and Galveston islands, and in Spain's lack of fortification of her frontiers. He mentioned the possibility of a cession of the Spanish part of Santo Domingo to the United States, a detail which had been discussed at Madrid. Onís thought that that concession would not be sufficient to persuade the United States to accept the Mississippi River as the limit, and that it would too greatly endanger the island of Cuba. Its one advantage lay in the possibility that it might arouse England to active interest in the affair because of her own Caribbean ambitions.

Onís knew by now that there was a possibility that the United States might seize East Florida, a move suggested by the threats to quell Seminole Indian disturbances; also that the republic might recognize the La Plata provinces. He told Pizarro that in either eventuality he would withdraw, leaving only Noeli in Washington as chargé.

The Spanish minister followed up his conversation by letters to Adams, the first one presenting in detail the arguments for the Spanish title to West Florida, the second doing the same for Texas, the third dealing with the various claims of the United States against Spain, and the fourth protesting the finally effected United States occupation of Amelia Island.[52] In regard to claims, Onís admitted that the claims for damages by Spanish ships should be adjudicated, but minimized the damages suffered from the suspension of the right of deposit at New Orleans. He declared that Spain's only obligation with respect to damages by French cruisers was to use her good offices in helping the United States collect from France.

For some days Onís received no replies to these notes. But they were days not without interesting developments. On January 5 he reported receipt of word of a mutiny among the few Spanish troops at Pensacola, weakening its defense to such a degree that the commander was requesting fresh troops.[53] At the same time news came that the officials of the province of West Florida were disturbed by the settlement on the Alabama River of about a thousand persons led by French Bonapartist generals. Furthermore, reports were received that General Jackson had been authorized to take in hand the Seminole Indian troubles, giving the Spanish grounds to fear the seizure of both Floridas. Adding to the despair of Onís,

Governor Coppinger of East Florida had written a pathetic letter predicting difficulty in defending that province because he was in a "lamentable condition, for lack of stores, money, and other aids."[54]

On the same day, January 5, Onís wrote asking for a leave or a recall in view of these dangers and of his inability, through lack of instructions, to offer further concessions to the United States. He also cited as a reason for wishing to leave Washington the continued illness of his younger daughter, to which was now added his own indisposition due to "the rigors of this climate."[55] Citing his thirty-eight years in the service of the Spanish monarchy, he said that he felt entitled at least to permission to go to Spain for the spring.

His plea was not granted. But that Pizarro was cognizant of the dangers which Onís described is evident in a note from him to the war office relaying the description. The vital relation of border conflict to diplomacy appears in Pizarro's declaration that, if steps were not taken for defense, "the difficult negotiation based on the cession of the Floridas will be useless, as we shall not have them to cede."[56]

In Washington the Spanish representative again talked to Adams before receiving a reply to his notes. On January 10, 1818, the secretary told Onís that the delay was due to the length of the letters. With what Onís described as impatience, Adams remarked that the whole affair could have been settled in the time it had taken to translate the notes.[57] Onís refused to accede to Adams' request that he make a definite treaty proposal unless it be on the basis of the *uti possidetis* of 1809, the date of Onís' arrival. He in turn asked suggestions from Adams.

On January 14, however, before any further projects were launched, the more definite instructions which Onís was awaiting reached him. They had been sent in November, before Pizarro knew of the menacing determinations of the United States government regarding Amelia, Galveston, and the insurgent colonies. He did know, though, that further concessions must be made, a fact indicated in the *Exposición* of the preceding June and the instructions sent to Onís in August.

Spain's appeals to the Powers had resulted in nothing more than England's promise to make a qualified suggestion of mediation. No opposition to the cession of the Floridas was expressed; nor did

England assume any responsibility for guarding Spanish domain under the out-dated Treaty of Utrecht. Accordingly, after another session of the *Consejo de Estado* on October 2, the conditioning of the Florida cession upon the approval of England was eliminated from the new instructions to Onís.[58] Ratification of the Claims Convention of 1802 was to be offered on condition that Spain should not be held liable for the damages by French corsairs, and that spoliations committed since 1802 be left open to discussion. The plan promised no real settlement of the difficulties, since ratifying the old convention under these circumstances would be almost the same as carrying through the arrangement proposed by Pizarro to Erving. Thus little can be said to have been added to the possibilities of agreement. At the time the instructions were sent to Onís, the various ministers of the Spanish government were notified to instruct their officials in America to prepare for a possible war with the United States.[59]

DISTURBING FACTORS

The most likely source of irritation sufficient to lead to war loomed in the projected expedition of Andrew Jackson to discipline the Seminoles. Jackson had been ordered to supersede Major General Edmund P. Gaines in charge of the United States forces on the border. On January 6, 1818, he wrote a now-famous letter suggesting that if he should receive confidential, roundabout authorization from the President he could in sixty days realize one of his long-standing ambitions, the occupation of all of the Floridas. In conference ten days later, Adams opportunely warned Onís that if Spanish officials did not protect the Floridas from the Seminoles and from a threatened second invasion by McGregor the United States would be forced to occupy the region, under the provisions of the treaty of 1795.[60] Article 5 of that agreement had stipulated that the two parties should

... by all means in their power maintain peace and harmony among the several Indian nations who inhabit the country adjacent to the lines and rivers, which, by the preceding articles, form the boundaries of the two Floridas. And the better to obtain this effect, both parties oblige themselves expressly to restrain by force all hostilities on the part of the Indian nations living within their boundaries; so that Spain will not suffer her Indians to attack the citizens of the United States, nor the Indians inhabiting their territory; nor will the United States permit these last mentioned Indians to commence hostilities against the subjects of His Catholic Majesty or his Indians in any manner whatever.[61]

In the autumn of 1817, quarrels among the settlers and Indians about Fowltown, on the Apalachicola just above the Florida border, had led to the destruction of that town by United States troops under the command of Gaines. This had been followed on November 30 by a Seminole attack on a military supply boat on the Apalachicola just below the Spanish border.[62] Of a load of forty men, seven women, and four children, all were killed but one woman, who was made captive, and four men, who escaped. Reinforcements went down the river to protect further supply boats. In the midst of this critical situation Gaines was transferred to Amelia Island, and Jackson, by an order of December 26, was instructed to handle the Seminoles, and to "take the necessary measures to terminate . . . [the] conflict."[63]

The second McGregor threat mentioned by Adams lay in the plans of that general for an invasion of Florida, with the point of entry at Tampa Bay. In this venture he was backed by Captain George Woodbine, a former British officer, who had worked up the scheme from his base at New Providence in the Bahamas. By two days after Christmas, when McGregor left for England, the plan had proceeded as far as the naming of one Robert Christie Ambrister (later to become notorious) to lead the activities at Tampa.[64] But it was not until some months later that he arrived there.

In the face of these complications the diplomats went on with their efforts at agreement. Adams finally discussed the subjects of Onís' various notes in a reply dated January 16, for which President Monroe had given him suggestions the preceding day.[65] The note directed attention to the President's explanation of the Amelia Island affair given in his message of three days before; revived the boundary proposal of 1805 in nearly the same terms, offering to set the Colorado River as the limit, with Spain ceding all its territory east of the Mississippi; and suggested that the claims be submitted to a commission. Payment of the claims would be guaranteed by proceeds from the government's projected sale of lands in the Floridas, and in order to make this possible all grants of land to private individuals made by the Spanish crown since August 11, 1802, would be held canceled.

Onís replied to this note with a characteristically pompous flourish. After berating Adams for what he considered the latter's impatience in declining to discuss the history of the boundary claims, he burst out with the declaration:

Truth is of all times; and reason and justice are founded on immutable principles. It is on these principles that the rights of the Crown of Spain are founded to the territories eastward and westward of Louisiana, claimed by your Government as making part of that province. . . . There does not appear to be a single incident to give the smallest support to the pretensions of your Government.[66]

The Spanish minister went on to object to Adams' apparent disregard of the spoliations on Spanish commerce, and to the inclusion of the French spoliations with those of the Spanish on United States shipping. He also opposed the date of 1802 as the last for valid land grants, pointing out that Spain had full sovereignty and right of land dispensation long after that time.

One other sentence in this note is of interest in view of the later dispute over the names of the Texas rivers. Onís said:

I presume it is the river Colorado of Natchitoches [the Red, or Roxo] you speak of, and not of another bearing the same name, and which is still farther within the limits of the Spanish provinces.

From a despatch which he sent home four days later, before any further discussion with Adams, it would appear that this "presumption" was merely a suggestion thrown out to indicate the completeness of Spain's belief in her title to Texas, and that, truthfully, Onís had no such presumption at all. He explained to Pizarro the extent of Adams' claims by lamenting:

Of Spain is asked the cession of the Floridas, and of the province of Texas up to the Bay of San Bernardo into which flows the river of San Saba, which in the maps of this country is known as the Río Colorado del Norte, and it is proposed by way of generosity that we conserve the short space of that province between the Bay of San Bernardo and the Río Brabo or del Norte, which they have also talked of taking away from us. Such is, your excellency, the idea which has been formed here of our weakness, on seeing that we have not managed in six months to eject a band of adventurers from Amelia island.[67]

Further evidence that Onís must have known perfectly well what was meant appears in Adams' next rejoinder. He named over the long sequence of incidents on which the United States based its Texas claim, including the expedition of La Salle which gave rise to the idea of the Colorado River limit, and said plainly that the United States believed

that LaSalle, a Frenchman, with a commission and authority from Louis XIV, discovered the Bay of St. Bernard, and formed a settlement there on the western side of the river Colorado, in the year 1685, and that the possession thus taken of in the Bay of St. Bernard, in connexion with that on the Mississippi, had always been understood, as of right it ought, to extend to the Rio Bravo.[68]

This response of Adams was made only after weeks of preparation. It had been discussed at two Cabinet meetings, on January 31 and March 3, 1818, and submitted to the individual criticism, at other times, at least of the President, Secretary of War John C. Calhoun, and Secretary of the Treasury William H. Crawford.[69] It was also made subsequent to the administration's decision to stand on its own feet in the Spanish negotiation, rejecting the possibility of mediation by England.

Adams in this note replied to Onís' declaration concerning the omnipresence of truth in language matching the Spaniard's own, a passage as frequently quoted as that of Onís:

The observation, that truth is of all times, and that reason and justice are founded upon immutable principles, has never been contested by the United States; but neither truth, reason nor justice consists in stubbornness of assertion, nor in the multiplied repetition of error.[70]

Adams then went on to review at length the whole territorial argument, attempting to justify the claims based on French expeditions and accounts, and deprecating the rights acquired by Spain through her various settlements in Texas. On La Salle's venture Adams was particularly eloquent, saying that his undertaking "has every characteristic of sublime genius, magnanimous enterprise, and heroic execution." The secretary repeated the arguments in favor of including the French spoliations for the settlement of which Spain was liable, trying to appeal to Spanish resentment of the manner in which Napoleon toyed with the government of Charles IV. But no new propositions were made.

Onís replied soon after, on March 23, with the comment:

I wish not to rob La Salle of the glory you are disposed to allow him for his brilliant enterprises and sublime philanthropy. But what I have alleged, and can prove by the fullest evidence of which facts of this nature are susceptible, is, that La Salle did nothing more than traverse . . . through territories which, although included in the dominions of the Crown of Spain, were still desert, and without forts or garrisons to check the incursions of that French adventurer; that nothing resulted from them.

He continued by deprecating one of Adams' authorities on the subject of La Salle, Father Hennepin, reminding his adversary that

on the testimony of the Swedish naturalist Kahn, the opinion entertained of Hennepin, in Canada, is expressed in the following words: "The name of honor they give him there is *the great liar;* he writes of what he saw in places *where he never was.*"[71]

But the real purpose of Onís' voluminous note was to urge upon the secretary the idea of mediation by a Power or Powers, and, most important, to state that, lacking authority to consider Adams' demands, he must send a courier to Madrid for further instructions. In making this statement he evidently took the confusion of the rivers as a pretext to await instructions.

The basis of this decision as stated by Onís is directly contradictory to the evidence in an earlier cited despatch to Pizarro, that he knew well which Texas river the United States had in mind. For he said to Adams in the same note :

You must be aware, sir, that [the powers] I am already furnished with cannot extend to the case presented by the proposals contained in your note of the 16th January, since Spain never imagined that the Rio Colorado, hitherto spoken of by the minister of this republic, could be any other than that of Natchitoches; and I did not even think that you meant to speak of any other in your note, until I was more exactly informed by you; the river which you wished to designate being known by the name of San Marcos, or de las Canas. This circumstance . . . produces an infinite difference in the view to be taken of the first proposals made on the part of your Government to that of His Catholic Majesty; and I am unable to stipulate such sacrifices . . . until I have previously consulted my court.

Erving at Madrid evidently was irritated by this juggling of river names. He wrote Adams, when news came to him of Onís' declaration, that

The motive alleged by Mr Onis for requiring further instructions, or more extensive powers, is indeed the most extraordinary plea for delay that could have been hit on; it is to be hoped that it is the expiring struggle of procrastination, as it is the very apex of shuffling diplomacy, or the dregs of a worn out capacity: whatever *he* may have understood to have been meant by the "Colorado,"—it is not true that his government ever fell into the absurdity of taking it to mean "Red River."[72]

Erving's error was not in accusing Onís of using a subterfuge, which the latter undoubtedly employed, but in assuming the accuracy of the court's knowledge. As has been stated, Heredia and Pizarro in the summer of 1817 did confuse the Red and the Colorado.

In spite of Adams' statement that "we know of no maps which call the Red River of Natchitoches the Colorado,"[73] there was real reason for confusion in the documents employed in the negotiation. The Pichardo map, while employing the term "Roxo" for what we know as the Red, did not use the name "Colorado" at all, calling the river of that name in western Texas the "Segundo Brazo de Dios."[74] Professor Hackett points out that the padre was confused on the terminology of several Texas rivers. His failure to use the term "Colorado" might easily have caused the Spaniards to apply that name, on hearing it, to the river at Natchitoches, the names of the two being sometimes interchangeable in meaning. The French maps called the river at Natchitoches the "Rouge," a name which might easily have been translated "Colorado" instead of "Roxo."[75] The Melish map, used in the State Department at Washington, employed the terms as we now use them.[76] But the one prepared by Zebulon Pike, and published at Philadelphia in 1810, calls both rivers by the disputed term, the eastern of the two being labeled "Río Colorado de Natchitoches."[77] This might easily have represented current usage in Texas, from where Pike had just returned.

The uncertainty was removed, however, by the conversations and despatches, and for the first time the two countries began really to understand each other's views and determinations. Onís was not authorized to agree upon the Colorado River of the Bay of St. Bernard as the limit until the final stages of the negotiation.

While Onís awaited further instructions (the note bringing them was passing en route his despatch requesting them), further disturbing circumstances lowered his hopes of success. Chief among them were the famous Meade case, the increasing trouble over the Spanish American insurgents, and menacing developments in the Floridas.

Richard W. Meade was a citizen of the United States who had been a merchant in Cádiz since 1803. Becoming involved in 1816 in a lawsuit over a matter of some fifty thousand dollars, he had been peremptorily imprisoned by the Spanish authorities.

In February, 1818, Onís complained to Adams on behalf of the Spanish vice-consul at New Orleans, Diego Morphy, who had been assaulted by a French resident there. The Washington government told Onís orders had been sent for the arrest of the culprit, but at the same time demanded of the minister an explanation of the Meade affair. Indignation over the latter ran high in this country. Onís had then to send home for information in that case, of which he pleaded ignorance.[78]

Enough news of the Meade affair had been received in this country for the Senate Committee on Foreign Relations to resolve that Meade deserved the protection of his government, and "that whatever intentional injury may be done him should be retaliated by the employment, if necessary, of the force of the nation."[79] The Meade case was later to cause a serious complication in the claims settlement provided in the Adams-Onís Treaty.

Objects seemingly as far remote from diplomacy as a door lamp and a dead chicken added to Onís' anxieties. He complained to Adams in February, 1818, that Spanish American revolutionary agents had become insulting to him and to his government. First, he said, they threw stones and broke his windows. Then they broke the lamp outside his door. And finally they hung a dead fowl to the bell-cord, in mockery, as Onís interpreted it, of the debility of the Spanish monarchy. Not only diplomatic protection but personal and national honor he felt were involved in these affronts. He refused to be satisfied with Adams' explanation that these were but the pranks of children, and wrote that some night the plotters might set his house on fire, "or commit some other offence to which Foreign Ministers accredited to civilized Powers are never exposed."[80]

Meanwhile, in heights of oratory, Clay had carried on the fight for recognition of the insurgent colonies—at the same time carrying terror to Onís. His appeal in the House of Representatives on March 24 for funds for a diplomatic mission to Buenos Aires was a forensic exhibition. The measure lost, however, by the wide margin of 115 votes to 45, presumably because of the influence of the administration. It was with real relief, but still with anxiety, that Onís reported the adjournment of Congress in April. He warned his chief that if affairs were not settled before the opening of the next session, set for November 13, 1818, that meeting would see the recognition of the La Plata provinces, authorization of open aid to the insurgents, and a declaration of war on Spain.[81]

Andrew Jackson, whom Onís had described as a *"caudillo,"*[82] had meanwhile assumed command of some seventeen hundred men at Fort Scott on the Apalachicola just above the Florida border. There he was preparing to avenge the Indian depredations, which were blamed in part on Spain. In an effort to ward off trouble in that sector, Onís sent to Adams a letter on March 27, accompanied by documents describing the relations between Governor Coppinger and the Seminole leader, Bowlegs. These papers were intended to support the Spanish allegations that Florida officials had endeavored to keep the Indians peaceful, and that the troubles were originally due to cattle raids by the frontiersmen of Georgia and Alabama and to the government's ruthless Indian policy. Amelia Island was still occupied, and now Jackson was openly preparing to enter Florida. Onís accordingly lodged vehement protests against invasions of Spanish territory.

In Texas a band of Bonapartist exile plotters was organizing an attempt to invade Mexico through that province. And in New Mexico the detention of the Chouteau-De Mun party and eventual seizure of the goods of these United States traders by Spanish officials had occasioned protest by Adams to Onís.[83] Small wonder that the spring of 1818 was a trying time for the minister of His Catholic Majesty!

NOTES TO CHAPTER IV

[1] Rafael Altamira, "Spain, 1815–1845," *Cambridge Modern History* (London, 1902–1912), X:212.

[2] José García de León y Pizarro, *Memorias* (Madrid, 1894–1897), I, *passim*.

[3] *Ibid.*, p. 201.

[4] *Ibid.*, III:209–382.

[5] Erving to Monroe, December 15, 1816, in D.S., Despatches, Spain, XIII.

[6] Heredia had served the foreign office since 1798 with the exception of a period during the Peninsular War. He had been secretary of the legation in the United States from 1801 to 1803, and his younger brother, José, held the same position under Onís (besides being the latter's son-in-law). Heredia was forty-two years of age in 1817. He was the accepted authority on affairs with the United States until the autumn of 1818, and again in 1820. After that he became, as the Conde de Ofalia, ambassador to France, then to England, and eventually foreign minister.

[7] Pizarro to Onís, July 3–30, 1817, in A.M.E., 223. An order had been given to limit each letter to a single topic, but it was not strictly observed.

[8] Viceroy Felix Calleja to the *secretario de estado*, March 15, 1813, in A.G.I., Est., 31.

[9] Calleja to the *secretario de estado*, September 30, 1816, *ibid.*

[10] "*Bosquejo de las relaciones de la España con los Estados Unidos*," November 6, 1816, in A.H.N., Est., 5559, Expediente 5.

[11] Monroe to Onís, January 14, 1817, in *A.S.P., F.R.*, IV:437.

[12] Onís to Monroe, January 16, 1817, *ibid.*, p. 438.

[13] Luis de Onís, *Memoria sobre las negociaciones* (Madrid, 1820), II:211.

[14] Onís to Pizarro, February 3, 1817, in A.H.N., Est., 5642.

[15] Onís to Pizarro (private), April 6, 1817; published in Pizarro, *Memorias*, III:346–354.

[16] Pizarro to Erving, July 16, 1817, in *A.S.P., F.R.*, IV:442–443.

[17] Erving to Pizarro, July 19, 1817, *ibid.*, p. 443.

[18] Pizarro to Erving, August 17, 1817, *ibid.*, pp. 445–459. He no doubt referred to the work of Fathers Talamantes and Pichardo. Boundaries were clearly the major issue by this time. The chief obstacle to agreement lay in the disputed title to Texas, especially to that part lying between the Colorado River, which flows into Matagorda Bay, and the Red River of Natchitoches.

[19] The British disavowed any such obligation. See *infra*, chap. v, p. 105.

[20] Erving to Pizarro, August 19, 1817, in *A.S.P., F.R.*, IV:449–450.

[21] Erving to Adams (private), August 27, 1817, in D.S., Despatches, Spain, XIV.

[22] Narciso de Heredia, "*Exposición hecha al rey ... sobre nuestras relaciones políticas y diferencias actuales con el gobierno de los Estados Unidos de América*"; published in Pizarro, *Memorias*, III:225–298.

[23] Conde de Castañeda de Lemos (secretary of the *Consejo*) to the Marqués de las Hormazas (an absent member), June 25, 1817, in A.H.N., Est., 5661. A list of treaties, from Utrecht to the Convention of 1802, and other documents submitted to the *Consejo* appears in A.H.N., Est., 5660.

[24] Heredia, *op. cit.*, p. 272. Pichardo's treatise and the accompanying documents were sent in thirty-one volumes, according to the report of Viceroy Calleja to the *secretario de estado*, September 30, 1816, in A.G.I., Est., 31.

[25] An account of Toledo's activities and four of his writings on Spanish affairs in America are to be found in Pizarro, *Memorias*, III:209–224, 311–346. A discussion of his relations with Onís, setting forth his motives, appears in Joseph B. Lockey, "The Florida Intrigues of José Alvarez de Toledo," Florida Historical Society, *Quarterly*, XII (1934):145–178.

[26] Onís submitted with his despatch of April 8, 1817, a verbose treaty project, largely copied from Pinckney's Treaty of 1795. It was evidently intended chiefly as a basis for diplomatic bargaining, because he said emphatically that the United States would not accept such a settlement, and that the matter could be solved only by mediation. His plan did not include the cession of the Floridas, but left most of the Louisiana region to the United States, drawing the limit along the Red River to the Thirty-sixth Parallel and leaving the rest of the definition to a commission. He also submitted alternative suggestions closely similar to Heredia's third and fourth. See A.H.N., Est., 5660.

[27] Onís to Pizarro, March 3, 1817, *ibid.*, 5642.

[28] Heredia, *op. cit.*, p. 285.

[29] Annotations on treaty project, with Onís to Pizarro, April 8, 1817, in A.H.N., Est., 5660. See *infra*, p. 97.

[30] *Minuta* of the *Consejo*, August 27, 1817, and Castañeda de Lemos to Pizarro, August 29, 1817, in A.H.N., Est., 5660; Jerónimo Bécker, *Historia de las relaciones exteriores de España durante el siglo XIX* (Madrid, 1924–1927), I:463–464. Cf. footnote 18.

[31] Onís of course had "full powers." But the King would not be obliged to ratify his actions unless the minister stayed within the limits of his instructions.

[32] The commission is printed in T. Frederick Davis, "McGregor's Invasion of Florida," Florida Historical Society, *Quarterly*, VII (1928):4–5. Material on the authorization of McGregor and Aury by the revolutionary governments, and a detailed contemporary outline of McGregor's plan, are given in Francisco José Urrutia, *Los Estados Unidos de América y las repúblicas Hispano-Americanas de 1810 á 1830* (Madrid, 1918), pp. 99, 105–143.

[33] *Ibid.*, pp. 99, 105.

[34] James Monroe, Message of December 2, 1817, in *A.S.P.*, *F.R.*, IV:130.

[35] Onís to Adams, July 9 and December 6, 1817, *ibid.*, pp. 442, 450.

[36] Onís to Adams, January 8, 1818, and Adams to Onís, January 16, 1818, *ibid.*, pp. 463–464.

[37] Onís to Pizarro, October 26 and November 29, 1817, in A.H.N., Est., 5642.

[38] Adams to Erving, November 11, 1817, in D.S., United States Ministers, Instructions, VIII.

[39] Onís to Pizarro, August 29, 1817, in A.H.N., Est., 5642.

[40] Onís to Pizarro, October 29, 1817, *ibid.*

[41] Onís to Pizarro, December 2, 1817, *ibid.* The instructions actually given to the commissioners appear in William R. Manning (ed.), *Diplomatic Correspondence of the United States concerning the Independence of the Latin-American Nations* (New York, 1925), I:47–49.

[42] Carl Schurz, *Henry Clay* (Boston and New York, 1887), I:146–150.

[43] John Quincy Adams, *Memoirs* (Philadelphia, 1874–1877), XII:78. Adams arrived from Quincy just before Congress convened and took up his headquarters in the Department of State. Onís, who had previously spent his winters in Philadelphia, reached Washington at about the same time. He established himself in the house formerly occupied by Monroe and later by

the British ministers, at 2017 I Street, N.W., now the headquarters of the Washington Arts Club. For entertaining remarks on the "Onís House" and on life in the capital, see S. E. Morison (ed.), "Charles Bagot's Notes on Housekeeping and Entertaining at Washington, 1819," in Colonial Society of Massachusetts, *Publications*, XXVI (1927):438–446.

⁴⁴ Adams, *op. cit.*, I:266–268.

⁴⁵ In view of the fact that this negotiation, which Adams called his greatest accomplishment, was carried on with a suave Spaniard of keen abilities, it is interesting to note the prevailing supposition regarding the Adams family, as set forth in the statement of James Truslow Adams that "each generation [of Adamses] was to score a great diplomatic triumph, and it is not a little singular that in each case it was to be against Englishmen. . . . John Quincy, in the second generation, and Charles Francis, in the third, would have to meet as antagonists only the disliked but understandable British. . . . For three generations, the family's diplomatic successes were to be solely against the English. They were never, after Vergennes, pitted against the subtler brains of the Latin."—James Truslow Adams, *The Adams Family* (Boston, 1930), pp. 62, 63, 70.

⁴⁶ John T. Morse, *John Quincy Adams* (Boston, 1882), p. 112.

⁴⁷ Adams to Erving, November 11, 1817, in D.S., United States Ministers, Instructions, VIII. The messengers of each government frequently carried confidential correspondence between the officials of the other, as a courtesy, saving the expense of duplicate journeys.

⁴⁸ Pizarro to Onís, September 28, 1817, in A.H.N., Est., 5660.

⁴⁹ Onís to Pizarro, December 2, 1817, *ibid.*, 5642.

⁵⁰ Adams' office was then in a building on Seventeenth at G Street, N.W., on the site of the present State, War, and Navy Building. See Gaillard Hunt, *The Department of State* (Washington, 1914), p. 201.

⁵¹ Onís to Pizarro, December 18, 1817, in A.H.N., Est., 5642.

⁵² Onís to Adams, December 29, 1817, and January 5 and two of January 8, 1818, in *A.S.P., F.R.*, IV:452–463.

⁵³ Onís to Pizarro, January 5, 1818, and enclosed letter from Consul Felipe Fatio to Onís, New Orleans, November 26, 1817, in A.H.N., Est., 5643.

⁵⁴ José Coppinger to Onís, November 17, 1817, *ibid.*, 5644.

⁵⁵ Onís to Pizarro, January 5, 1818, *ibid.*

⁵⁶ Pizarro to the *secretario de guerra*, February 26, 1818, *ibid.*, 5643.

⁵⁷ Onís to Pizarro, January 11, 1818, *ibid.*

⁵⁸ *Exposición* and *minuta* of the *Consejo*, October 2, 1817, *ibid.*, 5660; Pizarro to Onís, November 3, 1817 (with Pizarro to Onís, February 25, 1818), in A.M.E., 224.

⁵⁹ Pizarro to the *secretario de gracia y justicia*, November 3, 1817, in A.G.I., Est., 88.

⁶⁰ Onís to Pizarro, January 16, 1818, in A.H.N., Est., 5661.

⁶¹ "Treaty of Friendship, Limits, and Navigation Signed at San Lorenzo el Real October 27, 1795," in D. Hunter Miller, *Treaties and Other International Acts of the United States of America* (Washington, 1931—), II:322.

⁶² General Gaines to the secretary of war, December 2, 1817, in *A.S.P., F.R.*, IV:598.

⁶³ Marquis James, *Andrew Jackson, the Border Captain* (Indianapolis, 1933), p. 307; John S. Bassett, *Life of Andrew Jackson* (New York, 1916), I:245.

⁶⁴ Davis, *op. cit.*, p. 42.

[65] Adams, *Memoirs*, IV:42; Adams to Onís, January 16, 1818, in *A.S.P.*, *F.R.*, IV:463–464.

[66] Onís to Adams, January 24, 1818, *ibid.*, pp. 464–467. The date of this note later became important as that on which the validity of land grants in Florida was to be based.

[67] Onís to Pizarro, January 28, 1818, in A.H.N., Est., 5643.

[68] Adams to Onís, March 12, 1818, in *A.S.P.*, *F.R.*, IV:470.

[69] Adams, *Memoirs*, IV:51–61.

[70] Adams to Onís, March 12, 1818, in *A.S.P.*, *F.R.*, IV:468.

[71] Onís to Adams, March 23, 1818, *ibid.*, pp. 483–484. On the point to which Adams referred, Father Hennepin appears to have been correct, though historians have disproved some of his statements.

[72] Erving to Adams, June 12, 1818, in D.S., Despatches, Spain, XV.

[73] Adams to Erving, April 20, 1818, in D.S., United States Ministers, Instructions, VIII. Presumably Adams overlooked Pike's map, which bears such a name, and which had been published in 1810.

[74] *"El nuevo Mexico y tierras adyacentes, mapa levantado ... por el P. D. José Pichardo,"* section printed in José A. Pichardo, *Pichardo's Treatise on the Limits of Louisiana and Texas*, Charles W. Hackett, ed. (Austin, Texas, 1931—), I:474.

[75] For example, Alexandre de Humboldt, *Carte du Mexique* (Paris, 1811).

[76] John Melish, *Map of the United States* (Philadelphia, 1816).

[77] Zebulon M. Pike, *Map of the Internal Provinces of New Spain* (Philadelphia, 1810).

[78] Onís to Pizarro, March 11, 1818, in A.H.N., Est., 5644.

[79] Resolution of Senate Committee on Foreign Relations, March 24, 1818, in *A.S.P.*, *F.R.*, IV:153–154.

[80] Onís to Pizarro, February 27, 1818, in A.H.N., Est., 5644.

[81] Onís to Pizarro, April 21, 1818, *ibid.*, 5643.

[82] Onís to San Carlos, January 3, 1815, *ibid.*, 5640.

[83] Adams to Onís, April 11, 1818, in D.S., Notes to Foreign Legations, II.

CHAPTER V

SPAIN APPEALS TO THE POWERS, 1814–1819

British Influence in Spain

"IF ALL EUROPE or its principal governments do not take steps in time against the scandalous ambition of this Republic when they perceive the need of doing so and of obstructing the well established scheme of conquest which she has set for herself it may well be too late; and she may be master of Cuba and of the New Kingdom of Mexico or whatever other region suits her."[1]

The fears of Spain and her constant tendency to depend upon neighbors, who at the time had little respect for her, are clearly indicated in this warning sent by Onís to the Spanish ambassador in London. Indeed for some time the Madrid foreign office had earnestly tried to enlist outside aid in restraining the United States, and to obtain diplomatic assistance in negotiations with her. The desire of the Powers to recoup their fortunes in peace prevented the fulfillment of the first aim, and the second was only partially successful.

It was to England that Spain turned first and most urgently. In view of England's well-known isolation policy during the post-Napoleonic period it is not surprising to find that her rôle in the Adams-Onís negotiations was almost wholly negative. Spain asked England to protest to the United States against the latter's encroachments on Spanish territory. This England did, but only as a communicating agent, and only during the War of 1812. Later Spain wanted England to assume responsibility for maintaining the integrity of the Spanish Empire, and to mediate directly in the affairs of Spain with the United States. These things the British did not do.

Between the United States and England there were too many diplomatic bargainings in process, and there was too little harmony in public sentiment, to allow the interposition of an added complication. Negotiations were in progress concerning the various problems growing out of the Treaty of Ghent: fisheries, the boundaries of Canada, and disarmament on the Great Lakes. Fur-

---

[1] For notes to chap. v, see pp. 128–130.

thermore, the commercial interests of the two countries competed in Spanish America. The United States feared that England might acquire territory there, or at least gain a large share of the trade. At the same time the administration was cautiously sounding the degree of agreement between the two rivals in their political attitude toward the insurgent Spanish colonies, a process which led to the enunciation of the Monroe Doctrine.

Great distrust of the late enemy was evidenced in the public opinion of each nation.[2] Any intervention of England in non-English affairs would be resented both at Washington and throughout the country. The United States, opposed to the reactionary monarchical trend in Europe, was beginning to feel the pride which later developed into the spirit of "Manifest Destiny," and felt fully able to stand on her own feet diplomatically. This sentiment boded ill for any attempted interference on the part of England.

His Britannic Majesty's government did, however, play an active part at Madrid. One can find in the mass of correspondence a narrative of rivalry between the British and the Russians for controlling influence. Though the latter held the lead for most of the period with which this study is concerned, the British ambassador, Henry Wellesley, conducted highly important negotiations.

The close association between Spain and England had naturally grown out of their alliance against Napoleon. After his defeat and the return of the old régime at Madrid, the intimacy suffered because of Ferdinand's intrigues and because of British policies. There was, nevertheless, an important treaty of alliance signed in 1814, on which Spain later was to base its appeals for English aid. In that agreement, the two Powers promised "to endeavour to forward, by all possible means, their respective interests," though the alliance was not directed ostensibly against any other Power.[3]

One of the first means suggested for profiting by the alliance, and one favored by some Spaniards, including for a time Onís, was a plan of provoking the United States to an attack upon Spanish territory. In such an event, England might be drawn to the defense of Spain. An alternative scheme was to cede the Floridas to England, which would inevitably antagonize the United States toward the latter. These dangerously ingenious ideas were largely developed by José Alvarez de Toledo, the former rebel who had become Onís' confidant.[4] More cautious heads governed at Madrid,

London, and Washington, however, for none of the administrations wanted war. No suggestion of starting one appears in the outlines of Spanish policies drawn up by Heredia, nor was such a move seriously considered by the *Consejo*.

Still, Spain realized the advantage which might be gained from the active assistance of the greatest naval Power, especially since that country had widespread commercial interests in the Americas. She looked to England, therefore, for mediation, if not positive support, in three controversies: her colonial rebellions, her dispute with Portugal, and the negotiation with the United States.

Volumes of correspondence went back and forth all over Europe and America concerning the first problem, the colonies.[5] England was the controlling Power throughout. During the Napoleonic Wars, the Spanish Regency had declined the mediation offer of England because the latter Power proposed to make too great concessions to the colonies. Later, Ferdinand caused delay by debating endlessly over foreign intervention. He considered strongly the plan of Russia for a general mediation of the Powers, in connection with the aims of the Holy Alliance. Disagreement between England and Spain on the extent of political and economic privileges to be given the colonials frustrated this plan. But the issue remained a live one throughout the period covered by this study. It indirectly influenced the Adams-Onís negotiations inasmuch as the threat of European intervention in Hispanic America was the greatest obstacle to recognition of the insurgents by the United States. Government caution both in this country and in England was constantly attacked by blatant popular sympathy for the colonials.

Portugal, Britain's traditional ally, presented the second problem on which Spain sought English aid. The Braganza court, then at Rio de Janeiro, was naturally intimately interested in the progress of the Spanish colonial revolutions. Carlota, wife of King João VI of Portugal and sister of Ferdinand VII, was anxious to assume the latter's authority over Spain's colonies while he was in captivity. Accordingly, Brazil had begun an expansionist program by the seizure of the Spanish colony of the Banda Oriental (now the republic of Uruguay). Despite the recent marriages of Ferdinand and his brother Charles with their nieces, the princesses of Portugal, little cordiality existed between the two courts. Spain appealed to England and the other Powers to force the return of the Banda Oriental. England took some part in this dispute as a mediator, but the territory remained Brazilian until after the end of all Spanish control in South America.

The thought of asking aid in negotiations with the United States, Spain's third problem, was not a new one when the formal request was made in 1817. It followed naturally from the attempt of Spain to be considered in the Treaty of Ghent. Since that vain effort, though, developments had taken place which made the assistance of England even less probable than before.

Castlereagh's well-known desire for a balance of power in Europe, and for a workable accord with the United States, led him to subordinate minor claims in his effort to arrive at an amicable settlement of difficulties. With a widespread scorn for Spain and distrust of the United States evident in public opinion and even in the Cabinet, Castlereagh often found it hard to hold public indignation in check and to calm troubled waters.

Castlereagh's program was difficult to achieve at Madrid. There the emphasis was placed on favoring the establishment of a firm absolutist government, on securing the abolition of the slave trade, and on combating the intrigues of Russia. The whole pattern of foreign machinations must be viewed against the background of British commercial ambitions and Alexander's vision of a Holy Alliance.

The effort to guide the actions of Ferdinand's government was entrusted to Henry Wellesley, brother of the Iron Duke and, in 1817, a veteran of seven years' service in Spain. He was having trouble at the time in protecting the interests of English merchants in Spain, who were suffering under severe and at times seemingly unduly arbitrary commercial regulations and legal processes. Further embarrassment was caused Wellesley by members of the Opposition party in England, who frequently berated Spain violently in the Parliament.

Meanwhile, with lavish exchange of decorations and compliments, Dmitri Pavlovitch Tatistcheff, Russian ambassador at Madrid, was building up his influence. He supported a more liberal policy than that indicated in the counsels of England with respect to Spanish internal policy, and in this had the coöperation of the Queen.[6] He is said to have been responsible for the appointment of

Pizarro, but Wellesley reported a growing coolness between the Russian and the *secretario*.[7] One of Tatistcheff's most notorious intrigues was carried on through the *camarilla*, without Pizarro's knowledge.[8] That was the sale to Spain, in the winter of 1817–1818, of a fleet of ships to transport troops to America. The condition of the ships, which proved unseaworthy, and the unsavory circumstances surrounding the negotiation, made this a major scandal in a scandalous régime.

Erving was in a position to observe the rivalry of Wellesley and Tatistcheff, and recorded the following opinions:

The english embassy here keeps its secrets very well, but it is not difficult to perceive that affairs do not go to their liking ... there is some collision between the cabinet politicks of St Petersburg & those of St James, & the influence of the former prevails here, & seems still to be gaining ground; —this of itself is sufficient cause of dissatisfaction . . . Mr Tertischeff [*sic*] the Russian minister . . . is bitterly hostile to England & every thing english; —by his arts & intrigues he has gained the entire confidence of the king, & does not fail to use his influence to withdraw Spain entirely from her connexion with England; —at the same time he promotes objects of major importance . . . Mr Tertischeff is adroit, & the king in his weakness imagines that if he has the great Emperor Alexander for his friend, he has nothing to fear; —there is an under cabinet here called by contempt "camarilla" (little chamber) composed of individuals neither great nor wise, but very servile: —these inferior persons the king delights to talk with, & to put confidence in . . . here Mr Tertischeff has established his authority, & there is no saying how far by this influence he may be able to lead his majesty.[9]

Nevertheless, Wellesley did manage to put through a treaty for the abolition by Spain of the slave trade, giving the British fleet the right of search to enforce the abolition, and involving the payment of £400,000 to Spain. This achievement was followed shortly by Tatistcheff's victory in the ship sale, and for a time Wellesley had to yield to the Russian the close and intimate influence over the court. Tatistcheff's preëminence was gained through ruse and intrigue. In background and personal qualities the advantage appears to have been with the Englishman, whose despatches and activities convey the impression that he was a man above most of his associates in ability and integrity.

During the slave trade negotiation, in the summer of 1817, the matter of intervention in the affairs of Spain and the United States came up for discussion. Intervention had been suggested in the

Bosquejo on relations with the United States, written in 1816. But in that paper mediation by Russia was favored. By the summer following, when Heredia prepared the *Exposición* which was submitted to the *Consejo de Estado* by Pizarro, it appeared best to ask England to intervene. Immediately after the *Consejo* had decided on the course to be pursued, a lengthy note was addressed to Wellesley, in which were summarized the five major points of contention between Spain and the United States, and the bases for Spain's assertion that England should assist in curbing the republic's ambitions, both from the standpoint of self-interest and from a sense of duty.[10]

BASES OF SPANISH PERSUASION

Pizarro's note went into great detail concerning the background of the American problem, even covering the whole history of the Spanish and French colonization of Texas. It then cited the responsibility of England, under the Treaty of Utrecht, to assist in maintaining Spain's domains as they stood at the death of Charles II.[11] The Spaniard painted a disturbing picture of the dangers to British commercial interests on the Pacific from the possible establishment of the United States on that ocean. He asserted that Spain's withdrawal of her claim that the Louisiana Purchase was illegal was an indication of Ferdinand's conciliatory policy, as contrasted with his opponent's unreasonable demands. Then with purposeful compliment he told the British ambassador that simply the knowledge that England was to intervene would no doubt be sufficient to moderate the stand of the United States.

Another interesting basis for asking England's assistance appeared in the Spanish interpretation of a conversation which took place between Castlereagh and Adams, while the latter was still in London. Count Fernán Núñez (Spanish ambassador to England until March, 1817) had reported the conversation to Pizarro. The British official said, according to Fernán Núñez, that, inasmuch as England had told Spain that she would not allow any cession of the latter's territory, she must also tell the United States that she would not approve any extension of the limits of the United States, and that in the event such were attempted the whole procedure of the British Cabinet would be changed. England then "would take the course she considered fitting, with respect to the interests of her ally Spain, and to her own."[12] The last allusion was to the alliance between England and Spain arranged in the treaty of 1814 (rendered ineffective, however, by the Russo-Spanish concord).

That Castlereagh's warning to Adams was less menacing than the Spaniard reported it to be, is seen in a letter of the British foreign minister to Wellesley:

Spain cannot be too Cautious in avoiding by every possible Means a Quarrel with that Power [the United States], and don't let her falsely calculate upon Embarking Great Britain in her Cause. . . . I make this remark the rather, because, I observed in the Note presented in Oct.ʳ by Fernan Nunez, but which was prepared at Madrid, an assertion that we Had pledg'd ourselves to resist by War any Encroachment on the part of America in the Dominions of Spain, not being conscious of any such Declaration, I asked Fernan Nunez to what this referr'd, and found as I supposed that it was attempted most inaccurately to be built upon a Confidential Conversation of mine with Mr Adams, the American Minister in London, in which in reply to a question from Him as to the Rumour of our being in Treaty with Spain for the Purchase of Certain of her American Territories, I disclaimed any views of Settlement or Aggrandizement in that Quarter, stating that I could Venture to assure Him that such would be our firm policy, so long as the United States observed the like principle, but that *in the Event* which I deprecated, and which he altogether disclaim'd of attempts on their part at Extention, that it would then become a New Question for Gt. Britain to consider, what course it became Her to adopt.[13]

Adams' account to Monroe corroborates Lord Castlereagh's report of the conversation (which was held on January 25, 1816), though in somewhat less sedate terms. Castlereagh had told him, according to Adams:

If it is supposed that we have any little trickish policy of thrusting ourselves in there between you and Spain, we are very much misunderstood indeed. You shall find nothing little or shabby in our policy. . . . There is not a spot of ground on the globe that I would annex to our territories, if it were offered to us tomorrow. . . . Do you only observe the same moderation. If we shall find you hereafter pursuing a system of encroachment upon your neighbors, what we might do *defensively* is another consideration.[14]

Still another basis for alleging that England was obliged to assist Spain was given in a note written by the Spanish chargé in London, Campuzano, to Castlereagh in August, 1817. Campuzano stated that the Floridas had been guaranteed to His Catholic Majesty by England in the treaty of 1783, when the latter Power returned them to Spain after twenty years' domination, and that that stipulation still held.[15]

England did not feel greatly bound by any of these "obligations," nor did she even consider them to be such. In April, 1817, when Castlereagh knew that Spain might request mediation, he told Wellesley that he thought there was "no claim that we should ... entangle ourselves ... with a New and Complicated Mediation with the United States in favor of Spain."[16] A month later his attitude toward Spain was more vehemently expressed:

I have not attempted in my official answer to Enter into any reasoning in Reply to Pizarro's Note [on the slave trade negotiation], in truth there is something so ludicrously extravagant in the Manner a Spanish Minister Endeavors to persuade you to place yourself at his disposal, that it defies all reply—One might infer from this Singular Specimen of Spanish Logic that Spain was the most accommodating Ally, and the most liberal protectress of British Commerce in the World. In short it is too bad, and too absurd, and it would be difficult to find any rational Motive, except the Obligations of Treaty, and Habits of Friendship growing out of the late Struggle, for keeping on any Terms with so perverse and so shortsighted a Government ... with respect to the Intervention with the United States, you will, without giving too peremptory a Negative discourage Spain from looking to our Entangling ourselves in New difficulties, whilst we have so many of our own to adjust with that State. We may possibly find an occasion of being of some Use to them in that Quarter by our Influence, but there is nothing in our recent relations with Spain or the United States which would justify us in Undertaking a formal Intervention.[17]

In spite of such a cold reception to its sounding of British policy, however, Spain did make the formal request. Wellesley suggested that some attention be paid to it, rather for use in diplomatic bargaining than as a piece of altruism, when he wrote:

... I think it might be useful to our Negociations here if Your Lordship were to authorize me to state that His Majesty's Minister in America would be instructed to use his good offices in favor of Spain, if he should be of opinion that he could do so with any effect.[18]

Owing partly no doubt to Wellesley's suggestion, the British yielded to the point of making a halfhearted offer. It was handled through Charles Bagot, the minister to the United States. He had taken that post with reluctance and misgivings, but had made himself remarkably popular in Washington and contributed notably to good feeling between the United States and England. Onís thought Bagot unduly friendly to the United States, and the despatches show little association or accord between the two.

Bagot was primarily engrossed in other dealings with the United States. He was actively engaged in negotiations over the fisheries problem, disarmament on the Great Lakes, the boundary problems left over from the Treaty of Ghent, and in various conversations relating to the respective policies of the two countries toward Spanish America. Amicable compromises were eventually reached on all issues. The one of particular interest in this study was the delineation, in October, 1818, of the northern boundary along the Forty-ninth Parallel to the Rockies, the territory west of the mountains being left for joint occupation. This agreement prevented the Adams-Onís Treaty from having the distinction of being the first specific territorial delimitation involving the regions west of the Mississippi.

Bagot received instructions in January, 1818, which were calculated at once to appease Spain and to avoid complications with the United States. They were accompanied by a copy of, and in fact were based upon, Castlereagh's letter to Wellesley of August 28, 1817, in which it was stated that the Prince Regent would be glad to interpose his influence

if He could flatter Himself that He could do so with a reasonable prospect of success, but to justify this expectation, His Royal Highness is of opinion that the Mediation should be desired by both the Parties interested, and that it should be undertaken at their joint instance . . . the British Government, being in possession of the Wishes of His Catholick Majesty, might, through their Minister in America, ascertain how far the United States would be disposed to listen to such an intervention, professedly directed to a friendly and impartial settlement of the points in dispute.[19]

Bagot was instructed to show that letter to Adams, and accordingly "to sound the Government of the United States upon its disposition to accept such a Mediation."[20]

The exact nature of the British approach has been subjected to various definitions, but it can hardly be called an out-and-out intervention proposal. Pizarro knew perfectly well that England did not mean to intervene unless it should be at the request of the United States; he also knew that the latter country would probably not be willing to make such a request.[21] But he thought that some sign of sympathetic interest from England would help. Onís, before learning of Pizarro's opinion, accused Adams of having rejected a direct offer of mediation.[22] Adams promptly set him straight with a denial. Most historians refer briefly to the whole affair as the rejection of a direct offer on the part of England. Yet I believe it should be clear that Castlereagh, in urging Bagot to discuss affairs very frankly with Adams, meant him simply to state that Spain wanted mediation, and that England would offer it if the United States would join Spain in the request. From the correspondence, and from the rapidity with which the matter was dropped, the fact is obvious that it was no disappointment to Britain when the suggestion was rejected.

THE UNITED STATES STANDS ON ITS OWN

Rejection of the mediation suggestion came during a conference between Adams and Bagot, following a Cabinet meeting, on February 3. Adams reminded the British minister that England had at times showed a desire to aid Spain in the issues at stake, referring, as Bagot supposed, to the Morier and Foster letters of 1810 and 1811.[23] But after Bagot had assured the secretary of his government's disinterestedness, Adams stated as the reason for the decision the administration's fear that such a mediation would jeopardize the friendly relations between the two countries; that public opinion was none too generously inclined toward Britain, and that the people at large would presume that England was entering the negotiation to guide it in Spain's favor.

Adams, in his memoirs, confirms Bagot's account of that conversation.[24] When Onís expressed Spain's disappointment to Adams, the secretary spoke of the affair as an offer by Spain to submit the disputes to mediation, in which England simply served as a messenger. He gave as the reason for rejecting the offer this country's policy of keeping aloof from "the labyrinth of European politics."[25] Onís countered with the reminder that in 1813 Monroe had been very glad to accept a European mediation; but there was no changing Adams' mind.

That there was some mistrust of England's motives, and some rancor at Spain's method of dealing, is evident in Adams' account of the affair to Erving. He noted that Pizarro must have made the request to England, without Erving's knowledge, at the time that he was ostensibly trying to draw up a treaty with Erving.[26] Onís had explained this duplicity of Spain, falsely, by saying that England really offered the mediation to Spain, of her own volition, at the time Spain asked England's view on the cession of the Floridas. Madison, now retired, expressed the prevailing dislike for Spain's maneuvers when he wrote to Monroe that "it proves, as all of us suspected, that the sauciness of Spain proceeded from her expectation of being powerfully backed in Europe."[27]

News of the refusal of the United States to request mediation was in due course transmitted from London to Madrid. It arrived there in time to cause the adoption of a more conciliatory tone in the instructions to Onís which were then being prepared and which were forwarded on April 25, 1818. Faced by the failure of plans for British aid, Pizarro, as will be seen, was obliged to make additional concessions to the United States, and accordingly he gave Onís authority, for the first time, to consider a boundary line west of the Mississippi.

One effect of the British mediation incident seems to have been a diminution in Spanish anxiety for an immediate settlement. Erving wrote in July, 1818, that Spanish fears of a rupture with the United States had lessened.[28] He was no doubt right, until further news from the Floridas arrived. And the easing of Spanish worries may well have come from Wellesley's report to Pizarro of the conversation at Washington. For Castlereagh had told Wellesley that

The two most prominent points in the Language of the President and his Secretary of State may be stated to be: 1st—That the subsisting differences between Spain and the United States are not of a description to lead to war, and—2ndly, A studied attempt to establish a Coincidence of Policy between the Proceedings of the British and the American Govts with respect to the Spanish American Provinces in Revolt.[29]

The foreign minister explained that the administration at Washington knew of the proposed plan for a European mediation in the colonial revolt, and that, in the event of such a mediation, Spain might expect the United States to refrain from recognition.

Spain continued to assert one of her claims for English intervention by professing to delay the offer of the Floridas to the United States until it was seen whether or not England would object under the terms of the Treaty of Utrecht. This was certainly one of the weakest bases Ferdinand's government could have found, and the Spanish officials could hardly have expected it to be accepted. Nevertheless, the gesture was made; it was officially rejected when England stated simply and definitely that the article of the Treaty of Utrecht which Spain would invoke was no longer considered in force.[30]

At about the time of that rebuff, in the spring of 1818, another serious irritation arose—encroachments by the United States upon the Floridas. As she had done in previous invasions or border disputes, Spain turned again to the Powers for sympathy and assistance. Onís kept the Spanish ambassador at London, the Duke of San Carlos, informed of the events at Amelia Island and on the Apalachicola in order that he might protest to the English government. In June, Pizarro directed a vigorous note to Wellesley, justifying Spain's attitude in the whole negotiation, and urging that England take some action in repressing United States aggression.[31]

The British reply was given in a conversation between Castlereagh and San Carlos, in which the former stated that Pizarro's note had been read to the Cabinet. The Spanish minister was told that his country had reason for complaint, but, as he relates it, "that England following the system which it had adopted, could do nothing; that Spain could from then on adopt whatever means it considered fitting." San Carlos, still anxious to break down the British aloofness, went over some of the reasons why the ambitions of the United States were considered a menace to England, including the rumored threat of an attack on Canada. But he met rejection when Castlereagh "replied that the English ministry was very sorry, that they could not remedy it; that England after the expenses and sacrifices which it had incurred in the last war, could only think of its own recovery."[32] In this statement Castlereagh was voicing not only the thought of England's own welfare, but the prevailing British opinion that Spain did not appreciate Wellington's services in the Peninsular War.

When two British subjects were executed by Andrew Jackson in East Florida, the problem came closer home, but still brought no action. British popular opinion was aroused to a dangerous point, and Castlereagh had to exercise his best efforts to achieve a tactful settlement. He said later that "such was the temper of Parliament and such the feeling of the country, he believed war might have been produced by holding up a finger; and he even thought an address to the Crown might have been carried for one, by nearly an unanimous vote."[33] Alexander Arbuthnot, a British trader whom

Jackson had found at St. Marks and sentenced to death for inciting the Indians to hostilities, had written to Bagot a few months before, describing the sufferings of the Indians from alleged encroachments of "Anglo-American" frontier settlers. But Bagot had paid no attention to the communication, apparently being influenced by the current suspicion that "Arbuthnot" was a pseudonym of Captain George Woodbine, promoter of a plot to capture the Floridas.[34] That suspicion proved false, but Arbuthnot and Robert C. Ambrister, the latter a plotter who turned out to be an agent of Woodbine, went to their deaths without protest from the British government. Castlereagh, after reading the certified minutes of the courts-martial which sentenced the two Indian traders, wrote to Bagot:

I have . . . stated to Mr Rush [the United States minister at London] that . . . as it is impossible not to admit, that the unfortunate Sufferers whatever their intentions, had been engaged in unauthorized practices of such a description as to have deprived them of any Claim on their own Govt. for interference on their behalf, it has not been deemed fit, under all the Circumstances of this Case, to instruct you to take any further step in this business.[35]

Castlereagh added some unfavorable comments on the harshness of the army courts-martial in this country, and berated Jackson for changing the announced sentence of Ambrister from fifty lashes and a year's confinement to death. But in spite of a pronounced British dislike for the victor of New Orleans, the punishments were not officially protested.

The foreign minister, with great restraint, curbed not only resentment over Jackson's escapade, but also opposition to the signs of expansionist sentiment in the United States. Still an important Caribbean power, England, as a matter of sound policy, looked askance at any advance of the ambitious republic toward that sea.[36] Official opinion toward the Floridas is clearly expressed in Castlereagh's statement to Bagot that

Were Great Britain to look to its own interests alone, & were that interest worth asserting at the present moment, at the hazard of being embroiled with the United States there can be no question that we have an obvious motive for desiring that the Spaniards should continue to be our neighbours in East Florida, rather than that our West Indian Possessions should be so closely approached by the Territory of the United States—but this is a consideration, that we are not prepared to bring forward in the discussion at the present moment, in bar to a settlement between Spain & North America. . . . The

avowed & true Policy of Great Britain being in the existing state of the
World, to appease controversy, & to secure if possible for all states a long
interval of Repose, the first object to be desired, is a settlement of these
differences upon reasonable terms.[87]

RUSSIAN EVASION

Spain meanwhile had appealed to all the major Powers of the
Continent for sympathy and aid in the matter of encroachments
by the United States and had received polite but largely evasive
answers from all. To Russia, an urgent plea was made for diplomatic aid at Washington, although the idea of a definite mediation,
and of a cession of either Florida or Texas to the Czar, never went
beyond the stage of discussion.

Russia's attitude toward the Spanish negotiations with the
United States does not appear to have been one of great concern.
The change in Tatistcheff's relationship with Pizarro, from friend-
liness to antagonism, which is said to have cost the latter his office
eventually, affected likewise the Russian view on the treaty plan,
a favorite project of Pizarro's. The reply of the St. Petersburg
government to the request for aid was of no value to Spain. The
Spanish minister, Francisco de Zea Bermúdez, wrote from St.
Petersburg in May, 1818, that His Imperial Majesty regretted the
hostile conduct of the United States, and had instructed the new
Russian minister in Washington to use his good offices to avoid
a break between that country and Spain.[88] Count Capodistrias,
Russian foreign minister, had sent word to Zea Bermúdez that the
influence of his government might be "more efficacious," and its
language "more firm and pronounced," if the United States were
bound to the Powers by the treaties of Vienna and Paris. And,
evidently glad enough to keep clear of the affair, the Russian minister said that his government would not object to the use by Spain
"of the good offices and even the mediation of any other power
which may have more active political relations than [has] Russia."

How inactive Russia was, and how ineffectual her influence at
that time, can be seen in the facts that André de Daschkoff, Russian minister to the United States, had broken off diplomatic relations with the State Department in 1816, not to resume them
again until he presented his recall in March, 1819; and that his
successor, Pierre de Polética, who carried the instructions men-

tioned in Zea Bermúdez' letter, did not reach Washington until after the signature of the Adams-Onís Treaty.[89]

There is no evidence of Russian pressure on Spain concerning the drawing of the boundary line to the Pacific Coast. Inasmuch as that question did not reach the stage of specific negotiation until a few months previous to the signing of the treaty, possibly the Russians were not aware of the threat of recognition of the United States' claim to land on that shore. But rumors of the republic's ambitions in that direction had been current in Madrid for some time, and Tatistcheff must have been aware of them. Even though he was, after the possibility of United States extension to the Pacific became apparent at Madrid there was not time to report back to St. Petersburg and receive more instructions before the signature of the Adams-Onís Treaty. A consideration of the Russian view toward its ratification must be left for a concluding chapter dealing with that problem.

FRANCE AND THE LOUISIANA FRONTIERS

That France should be concerned in the affairs of Spain and the United States was natural in view of her recent ownership of Louisiana, the dispute over damages by French corsairs in the Napoleonic Wars, Napoleon's interference in Spain, and the widespread activity of Bonapartist plotters after 1814.

French testimony concerning the limits of Louisiana varied in different periods, though in general the Restoration government of France usually avoided backing the claims of the United States. It has been noted that the instructions of Napoleon to General Victor in 1802 tended to support the broadest interpretation of the western limits of Louisiana; but that, outside of vaguely encouraging statements made by French officials to Livingston, the inclusion of West Florida in Louisiana was not generally conceded in Paris. Talleyrand, in letters which the Spaniards claimed to have received from him, contradicted his statements to Livingston by declaring that West Florida was excluded.

The Duke of Richelieu, foreign minister under Louis XVIII, held the opinion that West Florida was not a part of Louisiana after 1763, inasmuch as at that time both Floridas were ceded to England, and therefore that the region east of the Iberville could not have been included in either the Treaty of San Ildefonso or the

Louisiana Purchase. A statement to this effect was transmitted both to the United States and to Spain.⁴⁰ Concerning the western boundary no specific declaration was made. Roth, the French chargé in Washington in 1816, told Monroe that France did not feel concerned in that question, and simply considered the Louisiana-Texas limit as undefined.⁴¹ Onís later reported, though, that he knew positively Napoleon had once described Louisiana as extending to the Bay of San Bernardo, and that the government of Louis XVIII would be willing to declare the same.⁴² Whatever the truth of this may have been, no such statement was officially made at any time during the Adams-Onís treaty negotiations.

The rôle that France did play was carried out chiefly by her minister to the United States, Baron Guillaume Hyde de Neuville. He came to that position in 1816, but had previously lived for some years in this country as an exile, owned property in New Jersey, and liked the "Anglo-Americans." His basic instructions defined the part he was to enact throughout the affair between the United States and Spain.⁴³ In them he was told to cultivate friendly relations, and to distinguish clearly between the governments of France before and after August 30, 1814, clearing the latter of responsibility for the acts of the former. He was to remember that the relations of France and Spain made his government desirous that the Spanish Empire should not be further weakened. But, inasmuch as the insurgent colonies might become so strong that their independence would be inevitable, he was not to oppose them openly and thereby deprive France of commercial opportunities should they become free. And he was to bear in mind that the chief necessities of France were to maintain peace and build up her commerce.

Among other instructions, Hyde de Neuville received a warning to watch the activities of the Bonapartist exiles. That duty consumed much of his time and caused him no little anxiety. For not only was Napoleon's older brother living in the United States, but a group of his military officers were developing colonization schemes, planning attacks on Spanish American territory, and plotting liberation of the former emperor.

Joseph Bonaparte, once the "intruder king" of Spain, had come to the United States in 1815, and soon settled down in New Jersey, where he lived until 1832. He did not actively engage in any expeditions himself, but maintained cordial relations with other

Napoleonic exiles, giving them counsel and even providing money for some of their attempts to find themselves homes. The activities of the Bonapartists were the subject of great discussion and controversy in this country. Naturally the most scornful were the British sympathizers, and particularly British Minister Charles Bagot, who wrote in 1816 that "all the ragamuffins of the earth are in the United States—more especially the French ragamuffins, as I have been telling Lyttelton in the following nervous lines:

> "Joseph the Just, Iberia's King,
> Lefevres Desnouettes,
> Grouchy, Clausel, St. Angely,
> And all the patriot set,

> "Who 'scaped from Louis' iron sway,
> Have reached this happy shore,
> And live upon Tobacco Quay
> In Lower Baltimore."[44]

Ostensibly no more than a colonizing venture was the organization called the "Society for the Cultivation of the Vine and Olive," which obtained four townships on the Tombigbee River in 1817. Under a plan by which each settler was to pay a small price for his land, and receive title after certain conditions of development had been met, some hundred and fifty persons went to Alabama in December of that year. A majority of the prominent exiles were shareholders in the enterprise, the leading settler in the group being General Lefebvre Desnouettes. His large establishment proved to be the only successful one in the colony. In a few months the whole scheme collapsed, and the lands were mostly abandoned, including Desnouettes'.

At about the same time the more adventurous of the exiles were working out a plan which would have led to an invasion of Mexico through Texas. Generals Charles and Henri Lallemand headed this enterprise, which was to some extent financed by money borrowed on the members' land holdings in the Tombigbee River tract. As a result of the expedition, it was hoped that Joseph Bonaparte would be established on the throne of Mexico. Such success might enable his men to achieve the dream of all the Bonapartists—the release of Napoleon from St. Helena. It has not been proved, however, that Joseph Bonaparte gave his sanction to the Lallemand scheme, friendly as he may have been at times with the two generals.

In November, 1817, General Charles Lallemand had an interview with Adams in Washington, in which he professed the peaceful intentions of his group. He disclaimed knowledge of still a third exile plot which had stirred the diplomats of three countries, but which resulted in no actual operations. That was the scheme of one Joseph Lakanal, a former French professor, to establish a "Napoleonic confederation," an independent state which was to include the Mississippi and Ohio valley regions. A letter, alleged to have been written by Lakanal to Joseph Bonaparte, was intercepted and delivered to Hyde de Neuville. He became greatly perturbed over the affair and caused Onís and the United States government also to become aroused.[45]

Although the Lakanal scare eventually proved to be nothing more than a visionary scheme, the Lallemand Texas enterprise actually got under way. General Rigaud, another veteran of Napoleon's campaigns, led a band of about a hundred and fifty from Philadelphia in December, 1817, to Galveston, where they were joined by the Lallemands. They were welcomed by the pirate Jean Lafitte, who gave them supplies and lent them some small boats. In these the four hundred would-be colonists, well supplied with arms and with equipment to establish a settlement, moved up the Trinity River. After a difficult journey, they reached "Champ d'Asile," as they called it, a spot thirty miles up the river which had been selected by their leaders.

Although the Lallemand party professed peaceable intentions, they went armed for emergencies, and the scope of their ambitions is now fairly clear. They would have based their crowning of Joseph as king of Mexico on his rights to domain over the colonies derived from his reign as king of Spain, to which position they considered him still entitled. They were in fact obviously conducting an unauthorized invasion of territory which was claimed by both the United States and Spain.

Both Powers took steps to curb the enterprise. Spain moved first and her efforts were more effective. Troops from San Antonio under Captain Juan de Castañeda marched overland to eject the intruders. But the French learned of their approach. Short of supplies and presumably outnumbered, the colonists decided to retreat. When Castañeda arrived at the Trinity encampment site on October 12, 1818, he found the place abandoned.[46] When the Spanish moved down the river, some officers were sent to Galveston Island, where they found the refugees barely surviving through the generosity of Lafitte. Thus was the French menace in Texas completely removed.

President Monroe, at the instance of the French and Spanish ministers, had sent an investigator, George Graham, to Galveston. Graham left Washington in June, 1818, and returned four months later, with the report that he had found the French refugees at Lafitte's island and that their threatening enterprise had been completely foiled.

No sooner had the Bonapartist adventure come to an end than a crisis arose in another border episode, causing complaints against the United States to be sent to France from Madrid. This was the invasion of the Floridas by Jackson. Appeals by Spain to England and Russia regarding actions of the United States at Amelia Island and on the Apalachicola have already been discussed. There only remains here to note what response France gave to Spain's appeals.

Spain's most urgent protest was in the form of a circular letter addressed by Onís to the various foreign ministers in Washington, July 7, 1818.[47] Hyde de Neuville's reply to that note was a refusal to write to Adams in support of Onís' complaints. His grounds were that, although he did not wish to condone an outrage, his major purpose was to work for peace between the two countries, and not to further irritating exchanges of demands.[48] Although Hyde de Neuville did not, accordingly, officially support Onís' protests, he was active in the negotiation from that time until its conclusion.

The French minister's activity derived from the pleas of Spain to France, not for mediation, but for diplomatic assistance. Nearly a year before, in pursuance of the policy determined upon by the *Consejo de Estado* at Madrid after the reading of Pizarro's *Exposición*, Ambassador Fernán Núñez had written two notes to Richelieu.[49] The first was largely a restatement of the five major points of contention with the United States, and a complaint at the injustice of the United States' demands. The second explained Spain's claims on France.

Fernán Núñez in the second note enclosed a copy of Pizarro's *projet*, which had been presented to Erving on August 17. He asked in connection with it the following actions by France: a declaration that the United States had no legitimate claim to damages for the spoliations by French cruisers, on the ground that they had been settled in the Franco-American Convention of 1800; a declaration to the United States that neither West Florida nor Texas beyond the "Colorado river near Natchitoches" was part of the Louisiana Purchase; and instructions to the French minister at Washington to aid Onís in the conclusion of a favorable treaty.

French Conciliation

Richelieu replied to Fernán Núñez by pleading a lack of detailed and legal information regarding the French spoliations, and reiterating that his government did not hold itself responsible for the acts of the Napoleonic régime.[50] According to Fernán Núñez' account, Richelieu considered that the United States had settled that debt with the same French government which had contracted it, and therefore that it should be considered extinct. He said that he did not know whether or not Spain might be liable for any "special obligations." Therefore he could not make such a declaration as Fernán Núñez asked, a declaration which would completely clear Spain. In other words, Richelieu tried to free France from responsibility, but would not undertake to do the same for France's neighbor.

With respect to the territorial questions, Richelieu said that the French government would be glad to make the declarations desired whenever the King of Spain so wished. The French foreign minister in a letter to Hyde de Neuville written shortly before[51] had again stated his position that West Florida should be excluded from Louisiana. It does not appear, though, that any specific declaration was ever made to the United States on the western limit. Hyde de Neuville's desire to promote peace at any cost dissuaded him from making any firm declarations opposing the United States' claims.

In his reply to Fernán Núñez, Richelieu stated that Hyde de Neuville's original instructions would be renewed, authorizing him to "act in the rôle of conciliator, the only one which the Minister of a Power friendly to both the two countries can be called upon to fulfill."[52]

The Spaniards, however, were disappointed. In a report to the *Consejo de Estado,* Pizarro spoke of the French evasion of responsibility, and said that he supposed that Spain must be satisfied with only the effort to conciliate. The value of that, he noted, must depend on the influence, character, and aptitude of Hyde de Neuville.[53]

An interesting proposal appeared later in the winter, when Pizarro wrote Fernán Núñez to ask for further French coöperation. He relayed the opinion of Onís that Hyde de Neuville's instructions had not been sufficiently amplified to make him of great use to Spain.[54] Accordingly the ambassador was instructed to offer to France the Spanish portion of Santo Domingo in exchange for assistance "adequate to the great object and intentions" of Ferdinand. The proposition was to be made confidentially, and as an idea originating with Fernán Núñez to which he thought his government might accede.

It is hardly surprising to find that the French agent who was assigned to confer with Fernán Núñez rejected the possible acquisition of unstable, war-torn Santo Domingo, saying that it would be a liability rather than an asset. He suggested an alternative, according to Fernán Núñez, who reported that

if we could cede them Puerto Rico, the question would be changed . . . and for that acquisition they would give us ships of war . . . and four or five thousand men . . . to be sent with our officers wherever we wished . . .[55]

That sly French counterplan, however, did not fit in with the prevailing Spanish program, which was to cede useless lands the better to protect other territory which was of value. Puerto Rico was not to be relinquished for many decades.

Onís was growing more and more disgusted because of the lack of effective support from the French minister. Although Onís' diatribes were chiefly directed at the French government, it was apparent that the close understanding which had prevailed between Onís and Hyde de Neuville was gradually disappearing. In 1817, at least two incidents had evidenced their accord. The first was a complex and rather amusing debate among the diplomatic corps over their order of procession at Monroe's inauguration. In preliminary discussions Onís had claimed the right to head the diplomatic corps, and the French minister had argued in his favor. Bagot and others denied Onís' seniority on the ground that his residence should be counted only from his recognition as minister, rather than from his arrival in the country. As it happened, the corps did not receive formal invitations, and stayed away en masse. But Hyde de Neuville's support of Onís' claim is notable.

Soon after that, when Onís' wife died, Hyde de Neuville as an intimate friend took over the management of the funeral, and Mme Hyde de Neuville comforted and cared for Onís' daughters in her home. Onís' account of these kindnesses resulted in official thanks being tendered to the French government from Madrid.[56] At that period the French minister was described as being favorable to Spanish interests.

The following winter, however, the Spanish minister began to be perturbed when he was informed that the French government had supposedly given Hyde de Neuville instructions to aid him. Onís wrote that no matter what efforts he put forth, and no matter what personal requests he made of Hyde de Neuville, not a single document that he asked for in support of Spanish interests had been forthcoming.

By the next July, when Hyde de Neuville was so convinced of the urgent need for settlement on any terms that he advised Onís to accept the proposals suggested by Adams, the Spaniard's disgust reached great heights. He said then to Pizarro:

I can assure you with positive knowledge that the French Cabinet proceeds now with the same duplicity with which it proceeded under Napoleon, in this matter, and that it works definitely to avoid anything which might compromise it with the United States. . . . The French Cabinet acts with the most firm and decided machiavellism if it states . . . that orders have been given to its minister that he should act in accord with me and support my claims.[57]

He added that if France were to decide all the issues its judgment would be more unfavorable to Spain than that of any other Power. Hyde de Neuville's attendance, contrary to the practice of the diplomatic corps, at a Fourth of July dinner, and his toast to the "perpetuity of the assured blessings of the United States," was taken by Onís as an indication of the bad faith of the French toward Spain.[58]

In the discussion of the later negotiations, the active part played by Hyde de Neuville will be described. His services assumed major importance just at the time of the complaints of Onís quoted above. For, during the dispute over Jackson's maneuvers, Adams used Hyde de Neuville as a go-between to transmit his propositions to

Onís, then at Bristol.[59] What worried the Spaniard was that the messenger not only brought the notes, but zealously argued for the acceptance of Adams' plans.

A valuable service was performed by Hyde de Neuville in acting as the agent for continuing negotiations, because of the desire of Adams and Onís to reach a conclusion while intercourse was officially severed pending the outcome of the Florida affair. On receipt of word (through Hyde de Neuville, as it happened) of a tense situation in Washington in July, 1818, Pizarro wrote to Fernán Núñez, as well as to Duke Montmorency Laval, French ambassador at Madrid, urging just that course of action. He said that in that way without loss of dignity Onís would have a means of continuing the negotiation.[60]

Before that exhortation reached Paris, however, final instructions had been sent to Hyde de Neuville, upon receipt of his report of the July crisis. Richelieu wrote:

The King has approved the wisdom of your conduct; and you should, Monsieur, continue to follow the same system. You cannot present yourself as a mediator, still less as arbiter; but, as the American government and the legation of Spain have had recourse to you, as a conciliator, you have done well to charge yourself with that honorable rôle.[61]

It will become evident that Hyde de Neuville followed rather closely the fine distinctions made in that instruction.

NOTES TO CHAPTER V

[1] Onís to the Duke of San Carlos (Spanish ambassador at London), July 18, 1818, in A.G.S., Est., 2675 moderno. A similar note was sent to the Duke of Fernán Núñez (then ambassador at Paris), June 18, 1818; see A.H.N., Est., 6797.

[2] Antagonism between England and the United States is treated as a controlling factor in their diplomacy in Edward H. Tatum, Jr., *The United States and Europe, 1815–1823* (Berkeley, 1936). In reviewing that book, I have differed to the extent of pointing out that the exigencies of diplomacy brought about coöperation despite popular feeling. See *Hispanic American Historical Review*, XVII (1937) :70–72. T. R. Schellenberg has kindly permitted me to see portions of his manuscript, "The European Background of the Monroe Doctrine, 1818–1822," now in process of revision. It analyzes both European policies and public opinion in this country and portrays the latter as an intense nationalism, antagonistic toward the Quadruple Alliance as a whole.

[3] Treaty signed at Madrid, July 5, 1814, in *British and Foreign State Papers* (London, 1841—), I :273–276.

[4] Onís to Cevallos, August 11, 1816, in A.H.N., Est., 5554, Expediente 30. The arguments of Toledo and Onís for the second plan, advanced in 1816, are discussed in J. B. Lockey, "The Florida Intrigues of José Alvarez de Toledo," Florida Historical Society, *Quarterly*, XII (1934) :145–178.

[5] Much evidence on these negotiations, showing the overconfidence of Spain toward a reconquest of her colonies, appears in the bundles marked "*Pacificación*," in A.G.I., Est., 86–90 inclusive. A fine summary of the international aspects of this problem appears in Charles K. Webster, *Foreign Policy of Castlereagh, 1815–1822* (London, 1925), pp. 405–436.

[6] Rafael Altamira, "Spain, 1815–1845," in *Cambridge Modern History* (London, 1902–1912), X :211–212. Tatistcheff served in Madrid from 1815 to 1819, and was later ambassador at Vienna for fifteen years. See *Russkii biograficheskii slovar'* (St. Petersburg, 1896–1913), XX :347–349.

[7] Wellesley to Castlereagh, July 29, 1817, in Public Record Office (London), Foreign Office Papers, series 72, volume 199.

[8] Pedro Aguado Bleye, *Manual de historia de España* (5th ed., Bilbao, 1927–1931), II :560–561.

[9] Erving to Adams, April 6, 1817, in D.S., Despatches, Spain, XIV.

[10] Pizarro to Wellesley, June 22, 1817, in P.R.O., F.O., 72/199; Pizarro, *Memorias* (Madrid, 1894–1897), III :299–309. Attention is given to the Anglo-Spanish relations concerning the United States in J. Fred Rippy, *Rivalry of the United States and Great Britain over Latin America (1808–1830)* (Baltimore, 1929), pp. 32–70.

[11] The eighth article of the Anglo-Spanish Treaty of Utrecht, July 13, 1713, stated "that neither the Catholic King, nor any of his Heirs and Successors whatsoever, shall sell, yield, pawn, transfer, or by any means, or under any name, alienate from them and the Crown of Spain, to the French or to any other Nations whatever, any Lands, Dominions, or Territories, or any part thereof belonging to Spain in America. On the contrary, that the Spanish Dominions in the West Indies may be preserved whole and entire, the Queen of Britain engages, that she will endeavour, and give assistance to the Spaniards, that the ancient limits of their Dominions be restored, and settled as they stood in the time of the abovesaid Catholic King, Charles IInd. . . ." That

treaty had been specifically renewed, so far as subsequent treaties did not replace it, as late as 1783, but was not incorporated in the alliances of 1809 and 1814. See *British and Foreign State Papers*, I:273–276, 612–613, 648–649, 667–672.

[12] Fernán Núñez to Cevallos, April 16, 1816, in A.G.S., Est., 2675 moderno.

[13] Castlereagh to Wellesley (private), January 10, 1817, in P.R.O., F.O., 185/66.

[14] Adams to Monroe, February 8, 1816, in Adams, *Writings* (New York, 1913–1917), V:502–503.

[15] Campuzano to Castlereagh, August 13, 1817, in A.H.N., Est. 5643. Article 5 of the treaty signed at Versailles, September 3, 1783, began: "His Britannic Majesty likewise cedes and guarantees, in full right to His Catholic Majesty, East Florida as also West Florida"; as published by authority, *Annual Register*, 26 (for 1783, London, 1785):334. All copies of the treaty were in French, the original text of this portion being: "Sa Majesté Britannique cedè en outre, & garantit, en toute propriété, à Sa Majesté Catholique, la Floride Orientale, ainsi que la Floride Occidentale." See George F. von Martens, *Recueil des principaux traités* (Göttingen, 1791–1801), II:487–488.

[16] Castlereagh to Wellesley (private), April 14, 1817, in P.R.O., F.O., 185/66.

[17] Castlereagh to Wellesley (private), May 27, 1817, *ibid*.

[18] Wellesley to Castlereagh, July 14, 1817, *ibid.*, 72/199.

[19] Castlereagh to Wellesley, August 28, 1817, *ibid.*, 185/66.

[20] Castlereagh to Bagot, November 10, 1817, *ibid.*, 115/29.

[21] Pizarro to Onís, February 20, 1818, in A.H.N., Est., 5643.

[22] Onís to Adams, February 10, 1818, in *A.S.P., F.R.*, IV:467.

[23] Bagot to Castlereagh, February 8, 1818, in P.R.O., F.O., 5/130. Morier and Foster, chargé and minister, respectively, had relayed Spanish protests to the United States while Onís was still unrecognized.

[24] Adams, *Memoirs*, IV:52.

[25] Adams to Onís, March 12, 1818, in *A.S.P., F.R.*, IV:478.

[26] Adams to Erving, April 20, 1818, in D.S., United States Ministers, Instructions, VIII.

[27] Madison to Monroe, October 2, 1818, in Gaillard Hunt (ed.), *The Writings of James Madison* (New York, 1900–1910), VIII:415.

[28] Erving to Adams, July 22, 1818, in D.S., Despatches, Spain, XVI.

[29] Castlereagh to Wellesley, March 27, 1818, in P.R.O., F.O., 72/209.

[30] Castlereagh to San Carlos, April 28, 1818, *ibid.*, 72/216.

[31] Pizarro to Wellesley, June 28, 1818, in A.H.N., Est., 5643.

[32] San Carlos to Pizarro, August 1, 1818, *ibid.*

[33] Richard Rush, *Memoranda of a Residence at the Court of London* (2 ser., Philadelphia, 1845), pp. 151–153.

[34] Bagot to Castlereagh, April 7, 1818, in P.R.O., F.O., 5/131.

[35] Castlereagh to Bagot, January 2, 1819, *ibid.*, 115/34.

[36] An interesting presentation of rivalries in plantation enterprise of this period is given in Thomas P. Martin, "Some International Aspects of the Antislavery Movement, 1818–1823," *Journal of Economic and Business History*, I(1928):137–148.

[37] Castlereagh to Bagot (most secret and confidential), November 10, 1817, in P.R.O., F.O., 115/29.

[38] Zea Bermúdez to Pizarro, May 4–16, 1818, in A.H.N., Est., 5643.

[39] John C. Hildt, *Early Diplomatic Negotiations of the United States with Russia* (Johns Hopkins Studies in History and Political Science, Ser. XXIV [1906], nos. 5–6), p. 127.

[40] Reported in Monroe to Gallatin, June 1, 1816, in D.S., United States Ministers, Instructions, VIII; Richelieu to Montmorency (French ambassador at Madrid), February 24, 1818, in A.H.N., Est., 5643.

[41] Monroe to Gallatin, June 1, 1816, in D.S., United States Ministers, Instructions, VIII.

[42] Onís to Pizarro, April 24, 1818, in A.H.N., Est., 5644.

[43] Richelieu to Hyde de Neuville, January 26, 1816, in Archives du Ministère des Affaires Etrangères (Paris), Correspondance politique, Etats Unis, vol. 72. See also Elizabeth Brett White, *American Opinion of France, Lafayette to Poincaré* (New York, 1927).

[44] Bagot to Rev. John Sneyd, June 12, 1816, in Josceline Bagot (ed.), *George Canning and His Friends* (London, 1909), II:24. Bagot's comments on the city of "Squashington," and on "John Squintz Adams," quoted in the work are also entertaining. My discussion of the Bonapartist ventures is largely taken from Jesse S. Reeves, *Napoleonic Exiles in America* (Johns Hopkins Studies in History and Political Science, Ser. XXIII [1905], nos. 9–10).

[45] Hyde de Neuville to Richelieu, September 14, 1817, in A.M.A.E., Corr. Pol., E.U., 73.

[46] Viceroy Conde de Venadito (Juan Ruiz de Apodaca) to *secretario de estado*, January 31, 1819, in A.G.I., Est., 33.

[47] Onís to Hyde de Neuville, July 7, 1818, in A.M.A.E., Corr. Pol., E.U., Supplément 8.

[48] Hyde de Neuville to Onís, July 14, 1818, in A.H.N., Est., 5643, and in A.M.A.E., Corr. Pol., E.U., Suppl. 8.

[49] Fernán Núñez to Richelieu, August 12 and September 1, 1817, *ibid.*

[50] Richelieu to Fernán Núñez, September 11, 1817, *ibid.*

[51] Richelieu to Hyde de Neuville, July 31, 1817, *ibid.*

[52] Richelieu to Fernán Núñez, September 11, 1817, *ibid.*

[53] Pizarro's *memoria* presented to the *Consejo de Estado*, October 2, 1817, in A.H.N., Est., 5661.

[54] Pizarro to Fernán Núñez, February 11, 1818 (with Pizarro to Onís, February 25, 1818), in A.M.E., 224.

[55] Fernán Núñez to Pizarro, March 16, 1818, in A.H.N., Est., 5643.

[56] Onís to Pizarro, March 6 and May 24, 1817 (with marginal notes of the latter), *ibid.*, 5642.

[57] Onís to Pizarro, July 12, 1818, *ibid.*, 5644.

[58] Onís to Pizarro, July 18, 1818, *ibid.*

[59] Adams, *Memoirs*, IV:110–115; Hyde de Neuville, *Mémoires et souvenirs* (Paris, 1890–1892), II:375. The Frenchman's memoirs are not full for this period, and give much less information than his despatches. The fact that he mentions Onís only briefly and formally might indicate that little cordiality between them survived to the time the memoirs were written.

[60] Pizarro to Fernán Núñez, and Pizarro to Montmorency, September 6, 1818, in A.H.N., Est., 5643.

[61] Richelieu to Hyde de Neuville, September 1, 1818, in A.M.A.E., Corr. Pol., E.U., 76.

CHAPTER VI

FINAL WRANGLES AND AGREEMENT, 1818–1819

FEARS OF A COLLISION

"OLD 1817, JUST PAST, but already consigned to the heap of eternity, was not very productive of great events in any part of the world, so far as we are informed of its concerns. Suffering *Europe*, borne down with the crafts and crimes of princes and priests, has vainly endeavored to raise herself up, and assume an erect attitude—but her people, exhausted in the fruitless exertion, despondingly look for new homes. . . . Nor in *America*, where things change so suddenly, has any matter of material importance occurred: the great republic of the north steadily, and prosperously, pursues her course to population, wealth, and power; and the new republics of the south are yet contending with their enemies with various success, but generally in favor of the cause of freedom. . . . Spain will, perhaps, make a last desperate effort to recover her colonies, and questions of interest may separate those the 'holy alliance' has unnaturally joined. And how we ourselves are to be affected by these things, no man knoweth—but we must expect collision, though we may avoid war. . . . Our southern border has been disturbed by an Indian war, which, probably, had its origin in the vile intrigues of pretended British agents located in the *Floridas,* and against which we can never be secured until we obtain possession of the country. The territory is of no value to Spain, but to us it is very important; and have it we must, if the state of things is not immediately changed. . . . The possession of the Floridas, by treaty or force, will probably be among the interesting events of the new year."[1]

In such manner did the well-known and respected *Niles' Weekly Register* greet the year 1818. The discussion of European diplomacy in the preceding chapter, revealing Spain's desperate but futile effort to rally the Powers to her aid, tends to bear out Niles' impression of conditions on that continent. Hispanic America is seen as a favorite toast of the freedom lovers of this country. One "great event" had certainly transpired there, when José de

---

[1] For notes to chap. vi, see pp. 166–169.

San Martín crossed the Andes to conquer Chile. And the progress of the revolutions was reflected in the United States' attitude, not only toward Hispanic America, but toward Spain herself.

It was indeed inevitable that "collision" would occur during the year, both in the borderlands and on the diplomatic front. Small wonder, though, in view of boundary disputes, claims controversies, anxiety over Spanish America, and Jackson's raid, that a peaceable acquisition of the Floridas did not materialize during the year. Possession of most of those provinces by force did develop, as Niles had predicted, but the seizures were returned to await transfer by diplomatic methods.

Before such an end could be accomplished, it was essential that Onís should have wider latitude for bargaining. The authority which permitted him to offer unconditionally the cession of the Floridas and the ratification of the old Claims Convention, forwarded by Pizarro in November, 1817, had proved too limited. Onís had accordingly written in the following March asking for more authority. But before that request reached Spain, further instructions had been sent, and Pizarro had engaged in another series of disputes with Erving. A review of events at Madrid must precede any study of the final series of Adams-Onís negotiations.

Pizarro believed that the latitude he had given would enable Onís to make real progress. On February 20 he wrote that he had sent all the advice he could, and that he did not understand what further instructions Onís expected.[2] At the same time he advocated negotiating and settling matters as soon as possible, without any reliance on foreign Powers. He was confident that the United States would not request British mediation, and he knew that without such a request England would take no part in the affair.

By this time there had been many conferences and much correspondence about the long-projected European mediation in the Spanish American revolutions. Pizarro told Onís to let the United States understand that arrangements for the mediation were nearly complete. This optimistic report would naturally lead to the conclusion that England, France, Austria, Russia, and Prussia were about to come to the aid of Spain against her colonies; in the face of such a movement the United States would not dare recognize the insurgents. Whatever effect Onís' statements may have had, Adams continued to be always alert to the situation of the insurgents, and frequently requested direct information from his subordinates in European capitals on the progress of the mediation scheme.

Hardly had Pizarro's instructions left for Washington when a despatch from Onís reached Madrid telling of his dealings with Adams in December, and warning of the dangers of United States recognition of the insurgents and invasion of the Floridas. Immediately Pizarro wrote that Onís should take all possible steps to prevent the recognition, and repeated his statements concerning the probability of European mediation.[3] The best policy, he said, would be to strive for a prompt settlement of pending disputes on the basis of the authority Onís then possessed, so that the United States would not be encouraged to use the threat of possible recognition as a diplomatic weapon. It did in fact serve as such, for it appears to have been one of the major factors finally influencing Spain to make the concessions on the western boundary which were incorporated in the Adams-Onís Treaty.

Onís was told that if the United States recognized any insurgent nation he was to break off the negotiation immediately and leave for Madrid; and that if Adams declined to agree to Onís' boundary offers the negotiation should be transferred back to Madrid. Onís had in fact chosen the latter course, apparently through subterfuge, long before receiving this instruction. It will be remembered that in his note to Adams on March 23, 1818, Onís said that he must refer to his government for instructions because of the confusion in river names.

On the receipt early in April of Onís' account of his futile conversation with Adams on January 10, Pizarro sent more advice. Although he showed his own understanding of the situation, he was not authorized by the *Consejo* to give the minister much more latitude.[4] He left to Onís' judgment, based on circumstances at Washington, such questions as whether or not that minister should avoid making proposals to Adams. He noted three great dangers— war, recognition of the insurgents, and further invasion of the Floridas—and ranked them in that order of importance.

Much as he wished to settle affairs amicably in order to ward off dire consequences, Pizarro could not yet authorize sufficient compromises on the western limits. Onís had said that he thought Adams would offer two million dollars for the Floridas, leaving the western boundary unsettled, and providing no assurance against further United States aid to the insurgents. Pizarro suggested enlarging such an agreement if possible to include a promise of nonrecognition. He further explained:

I know that my instructions are very limited. . . . I have had to bind myself by the deliberations of the Councils of State, whatever my intimate experience of affairs indicates, as [is proved by the fact that] you will have seen in my memoir [the *Exposición* of June, 1817] other means for reaching the great object. . . . You and I see this affair alike. We see that we must yield as a last resort, but it is not possible to give you more latitude than that.stated.

The additional means suggested in those portions of the *Exposición* which Pizarro mentioned had to do chiefly with compromises in the matter of the western boundary.[5] So far, Pizarro had been unable to obtain approval of any concessions on the original demand of Cevallos that the limit be the Mississippi.

Significant extensions of Spanish policy were made necessary by the failure of the British mediation scheme. Pizarro wrote on April 25, 1818, that in order to avoid the dangers so greatly feared and to provide a permanent settlement of the western boundary Onís should offer the cession of the Floridas and the mutual cancellation of all claims for indemnification. In addition, he was to suggest a line drawn up either the Calcasieu River or the Mermento, then between Natchitoches and Los Adaes, straight north across the Red River and the Arkansas to the Missouri, up that stream to its source, and from there directly north.[6] The United States was to promise not to recognize or to aid the insurgents, and in return would receive most-favored-nation privileges in the ports of the colonies when they were pacified.

In this letter Pizarro took up the most notorious, though not the most important, phase of the entire situation. This was the apparent scheme of the Spanish court favorites to deflect the intended course of the arrangements regarding land grants in Florida. The concentration of the sparse population of the Floridas into a few towns has been indicated in an earlier chapter. It had long been understood that the plan of the United States government on taking over the provinces would be to sell what land was usable and unclaimed in the unoccupied areas, using the profits to meet the cost of claims settlements. Obviously in a treaty of cession a clear statement on the legal status of private lands must be made, and

Adams had proposed that all grants made by the Spanish king subsequent to August 11, 1802, be declared invalid, those of earlier date to be maintained.

Before Pizarro could comment on Adams' proposal, however, he learned that Ferdinand had issued to three favorites, the Duke of Alagón, the Count of Puñonrostro, and Pedro de Vargas, grants embracing almost all the unoccupied lands in the Floridas! Such a procedure, if upheld, would seriously jeopardize the agreement to a treaty by disrupting the plans of Adams for the sale of the lands. Erving learned that the grants had been made and accordingly warned Adams in February. Later he transmitted copies of the grants. A despatch sent in September indicated that the Puñonrostro grant had been made as early as mid-December of the preceding year.[7]

Erving had taken up the matter with Pizarro, and "brought him to consent that these grants *might be* cancelled." Erving reported that Pizarro "said enough to convince me that there will be no difficulty on this head."[8] But Pizarro did not and could not promise any satisfaction; nor could he be certain, as he suggested, that the grants would be withdrawn and the favorites recompensed with land in other parts of New Spain. Pizarro had himself been duped, as we know from the words of his aide, Heredia. The latter declared that the grants were made without the knowledge of the foreign office, and that, although Pizarro protested against them with determination before the *Consejo*, he had slight success.[9] An order was issued, indeed, that the grantees should not sell any of their land for the present, but that did not eliminate the difficulty.[10]

In his note to Onís on April 25, Pizarro showed that he was worried by this complication. He could offer no solution; but in commenting upon Adams' proposal that 1802 be the determining date he said that that concession might be made. Pizarro certainly would rather have given up these grants specifically than yield further on the western boundary. It does not appear that he gave Onís the dates of the grants—he may not even have known them!

Pizarro concluded this important despatch by warning Onís not to let the Floridas go without providing a definite settlement of limits on the west. He advanced at this time the first step in that delineation as finally embodied in the treaty. If it were absolutely necessary, in order to avoid a break in the negotiations or recognition of the insurgent colonies, he said, the limit might be set at the Sabine River, *sub spe rati.* This was in truth no innovation, since the Sabine had been the effective line for many years, and the official boundary of Louisiana since its admission to statehood in 1812. The diplomats were forced, under the circumstances, simply to acknowledge existing conditions of occupation.

ERVING'S LAST EFFORTS

Before Onís had a chance to act upon his latest instructions, there was a further exchange of views between Pizarro and Erving at Madrid. The discussion was futile but is of interest in showing the gradual wearing down of the Spanish diplomatic defense. It will be remembered that Onís in March, 1818, had transferred the center of negotiation to the Spanish capital. Pizarro conferred with Erving immediately upon the receipt of Onís' despatch. Pizarro began the discussion with Erving by saying that the two chief obstacles to the negotiation were the United States' insistence upon the line of the Colorado River, and the demand for indemnity from Spain for the spoliations by French vessels in Spanish ports.[11] The subsequent debate, however, was primarily upon the first of these problems. Much futile conversation ensued as the two men argued the relative merits of the territories concerned, in the southwest and the southeast. Erving deprecated the value of the Floridas, whereas Pizarro magnified the munificence of the King in offering to cede them.

Erving firmly maintained his insistence on the Colorado River limit, and soon added the request that Spain ratify the Claims Convention of 1802. At the end of June the Spanish *secretario* informed his adversary that his government had finally determined not to accept the Colorado River limit, and that it would not approve the convention unless the claim for indemnification for the French spoliations be definitely abandoned by the United States.

In such an impasse the negotiation lapsed for a time, and Erving lost all hope of reaching a settlement.[12] He was anxious to leave Madrid, both because of his health and because of his dislike for his mission. Like Onís, he coupled his complaint of illness with a denunciation of the climate. The Madrid summers troubled him as much as the Washington winters did Onís.

The delay was not long. On July 3 Pizarro reopened the discussion by offering unqualified ratification of the Convention of 1802.[13] That agreement, it will be remembered, stipulated that claims for spoliations by French cruisers should be subject to further negotiation, thus not relieving Spain of her obligation in the eyes of the United States. Erving declined to accept Spain's ratification, not having that of the United States to exchange for it. Pizarro accordingly sent it to his subordinate in Washington to be exchanged there.

The *secretario* at the same time brought up the question of the territorial guaranty of Spanish dominions beyond the Mississippi which had been offered by Charles Pinckney in 1803. Erving discountenanced the idea completely, declaring that the guaranty had been intended to apply only to Louisiana and that, since Louisiana had passed to the United States, it was entirely irrelevant now.

In reporting these conversations to Adams, Erving astutely expressed the belief that the ratification of the Convention of 1802 had been made simply to permit its use as a bargaining point. Its acceptance would remove one motive for the occupation of Florida, inasmuch as the United States had at times claimed that region as indemnity for spoliations.[14] He also believed that Pizarro, for the benefit of other European Powers, sought to strengthen the impression of Spain's conciliatory attitude, and that with this concession to his credit Pizarro would feel greater assurance in the matter of the western limits.

The most interesting view expressed by Erving, however, is his opinion that Spain's hand was being forced (as it undoubtedly was) by Jackson's expedition into East Florida. Word of that invasion had just been received in Madrid. In the long run, Jackson's maneuver was indeed one factor in causing Spain to come to an agreement. But at the moment it was to prove a stumbling block, as it caused an inevitable breach in diplomatic relations.

Pizarro was reluctant to break off negotiations when he had such urgent reasons for wanting a settlement. Conferences and correspondence continued for a few weeks.[15] Pizarro added more arguments on the guaranty of Spanish territory which had been offered by Pinckney, maintaining that it applied to all of America and should be revived. Erving resisted the plan for any guaranty at all, and offered instead the security of a thirty-league desert area along the boundary, another scheme which had been discussed many years before. Pizarro accepted the plan of a no-man's land, but controversy ensued over its location.

In July Erving became worried by reports that the prohibition on the sale of the lands granted to the court favorites had been removed. He wrote Pizarro warning him that the supposition might be made that, having mollified the United States by ratification of the convention, Spain felt free to proceed with alienation of the lands. He restated the expectation which his country naturally held of being able to sell the unoccupied lands in order to meet the claims as adjudicated. Pizarro replied in a manner tending to reassure Erving, but he did not state specifically whether or not the prohibition remained in force.[16]

These futile negotiations ended when further news of Jackson's enterprise reached Madrid. On August 6 Pizarro wrote Erving of the capture of St. Marks, a Spanish post, by United States troops, who charged that its officials had aided the Indians. Five days later, Pizarro vehemently protested Jackson's seizure of the capital of West Florida, Pensacola. The *secretario* demanded restitution, and conditioned any agreement with Erving on a previous restoration of the seized territory. On the twenty-ninth the American minister received a note suspending negotiations until satisfaction should be had for the peacetime invasion of the Floridas.[17] Copies of the letter were sent to the leading governments of Europe.

Erving replied with a withdrawal of his offer of a thirty-league desert on the boundary, and with that note he ended direct negotiations at Madrid on the whole affair. Erving's only subsequent contributions to the Adams-Onís Treaty were bits of information on developments at the Spanish capital. He was recalled before the argument over ratification arose. But the remarks which he made to Adams on his dealings with Pizarro in 1818 merit attention.

Erving believed that the pressure applied by such events as Jackson's maneuver would provide the only means of forcing Spain to come to an agreement.[18] In his estimation it would have been possible to reach a settlement which included the Colorado as a boundary had the decision been left to Pizarro. This opinion is supported in Pizarro's letter to Onís emphasizing the need for concessions. But Erving realized, as Pizarro himself stated, that the *secretario* was overruled in the councils of state.

Two other weapons of diplomatic pressure were mentioned in Erving's letter. One, the menace of a recognition of the Spanish American republics, had been rendered innocuous by the telling defeat (115 votes to 45) of Clay's measure for sending a diplomatic representative to Buenos Aires. The second, a threat to break off relations, Erving had discarded as too hazardous unless he should have instructions from Washington to use it.

In the same despatch Erving gave Adams his opinion of the man with whom the latter was to arrange the treaty:

... tho Mr Onis was a much better minister to treat with than Mr Cevallos, with whom it woud [*sic*] have been impossible ever to have settled any one point, yet he is much inferior to Mr Pizarro, for this last has a cool head, more forecast, & the best dispositions; besides that his influence is daily augmenting so that what he may not be able to do to day, he might effect a week hence: —whereas Mr Onis besides being tied down to his instructions, is unaccommodating from temper, his views are limited, he is in a state of constant irritation, & is living as you say in the time of Ferdinand the Catholick [the patron of Columbus] & not in that of Ferdinand the 7th; add to this he does not touch & feel as Mr Pizarro does the affairs of Europe, so that I fear that you will have a great deal of further trouble before you can come to an accord with him.

Erving was no doubt well qualified to speak on Onís' character, having known him in the foreign office prior to 1810 and in Washington in 1815. The Spaniard would appear to a less biased observer, though, "unaccommodating" not from temper but from conscience.

EXCITING MIDSUMMER DAYS IN WASHINGTON

It has been seen that by the time Onís appealed for further instructions in March the irritating Florida venture was becoming a serious international incident. Until the arrival of the awaited orders from Spain, his work was largely to study, report on, and protest the events on the border.

Onís went to his country place at Bristol in mid-June. His first act there was to transmit a protest (not the first) to Adams, as well as a despatch to Pizarro, on Jackson's seizure of St. Marks. His account of the report sent by the Spanish governor of West Florida from Pensacola indicates the state of affairs in that province and explains why Jackson advanced so easily:

Governor Mazot concludes his report by telling me that that city has been since the cession of Louisiana to the United States so completely ruined that the inhabitants have not the means to subsist; that from the three thousand inhabitants it had in 1800, it is reduced to less than four hundred, that he is without money, with a small garrison, with stores for only fifteen days, and that from this I can understand why it is impossible for him to defend the city, unless aid is sent him from Havana.[19]

Three days after writing that despatch, Onís received word that Pensacola had fallen before the fiery general on May 24.

With what he considered to be tacit approval from Monroe of his notorious ambition to seize the Floridas,[20] Jackson in March had led his troops over the Spanish border. Hearing that the Seminoles were gathered at St. Marks, he hastened overland to that post. The small Spanish garrison, greatly outnumbered, surrendered to the invaders. Among his prisoners Jackson found a seventy-year-old Scotchman, Alexander Arbuthnot, who had lived with the Indians and had carried on what was evidently an honest trade with them, becoming their friend and confidant.

The Indians had fled eastward, and the United States forces set out after them, penetrating some hundred miles farther into Spanish territory to the village of Chief Bowlegs on the Suwanee. Again the soldiers found no Indians, but they did capture another British subject, Robert C. Ambrister (mentioned earlier as Woodbine's agent for his plan of an invasion through Tampa Bay). Ambrister had reached Tampa Bay in March, appropriating stores which belonged to Arbuthnot, and then had come northward to work among the Seminoles.[21] Jackson found at Bowlegs' village a letter from Arbuthnot, advising the Indians not to resist Jackson's greater force (about 3,000), and asking his son to move his property to a safer place.

Jackson destroyed Indian settlements and property all along the way, wreaking vengeance on the natives, who had successfully eluded his men. Then, late in April, he returned to St. Marks and set about the disposition of his various prisoners. Two captives, the Indian chiefs Francis and Himollimico, had already been hanged. Now there occurred the famous courts-martial in which officers of Jackson's army decided that both Arbuthnot and Ambrister were guilty of inciting the Indians to hostilities. The case against the former was not clear, although evidently he had warned the Indians, permitting them to escape. The disappointment of the soldiers at not catching the Indians prejudiced them against him.

The hostility of other whites in Florida, particularly the agents of John Forbes and Company, also worked to his disadvantage. He was sentenced to be hanged.

Ambrister plead guilty of leading the Indians in war against the United States, and was sentenced to be shot. In Ambrister's case, which has been considered the more definite, one of the officers sitting on the court-martial reconsidered his vote, which changed the sentence from death to fifty lashes. Jackson, who approved of both original sentences, discountenanced the reconsideration. On April 29, Ambrister was shot and Arbuthnot was hanged.

Not wishing to return to the United States, and having heard that a body of Indians had gathered at Pensacola, some 275 miles away, Jackson marched westward from St. Marks. He accused the Spanish governor at Pensacola of having aided the Indians, and demanded the surrender of the town. The basis for his accusation was so weak that the venture had best be explained as simply a part of his plan for seizing the provinces, and holding them for indemnity.[22] Whatever the real motive, on May 24 he occupied Pensacola, and three days later Fort Barrancas, to which the governor and garrison had fled, and which they defended briskly but briefly. The Spaniards were allowed to go to Havana, and a guard of United States troops was left in charge of the fort. Jackson had meanwhile ordered General Gaines to seize St. Augustine, but such a drastic step was discountenanced by the War Department and the orders were revoked. The general then retired to his home in Tennessee, leaving the diplomats with an embarrassing *fait accompli*.

Onís' sojourn at Bristol was disturbed, as has been explained, by increasingly dire reports from the Floridas. While he awaited their confirmation, he received the instructions of April 6 and April 25, the latter of which gave him his first authority to place the boundary limit as far west as the Sabine. From this date it was the constant effort of both Onís and Adams to push the negotiation as fast as propriety would permit, in the hope of bringing their diplomatic positions into accord before frontier collisions should make a peaceable settlement impossible. Thus each will be seen with one hand brandishing violent protests because of insulted national pride, but with the other reaching for some sort of a conclusive agreement.

"I was roused from bed," wrote Adams in his diary on July 7, "by a servant from the Spanish Minister Onis, who brought me a note from him . . . asking for an interview as soon as possible upon objects of the highest importance to Spain and to the United States."[23] Onís had come posthaste from Bristol on receipt of definite reports that Pensacola had fallen to the "Napoleon of the woods" (as Hyde de Neuville once characterized Jackson).[24] In the conference, as well as in a note written the following day, he vehemently protested the seizure and demanded the restitution of the Spanish towns.[25] The Spaniard stayed in Washington six days, long enough for three conversations with Adams, and long enough to send complaining notes on the affair to all the other foreign representatives.

Despite the border complications, the two principals endeavored to work out treaty provisions. In discussing possible boundary delineations, they used the map of the United States prepared by John Melish. Onís at the time called it "a map prepared at the order of this Government to sustain its pretensions."[26] The charge seems to have been groundless. Melish was a Scotch geographer and commercial map maker, who had made his home in the United States and won repute as a fair, unbiased, and reasonably accurate authority. His map showed physical features as completely as any then available, and the fact that it was accepted as a basis for a treaty might well be interpreted as one indication of its merit. In long conferences over it, Onís urged the Arroyo Hondo as the proper Louisiana-Texas limit, whereas Adams pointed to the Colorado River as the last concession which the United States would make.

When Adams suggested the innovation of drawing a boundary to the Pacific Ocean from the head of the Missouri, Onís evaded the issue by opening a verbose discussion of titles on that coast, based on vague information. But the conversation is highly significant as marking the first pronouncement of the idea which was Adams' most original contribution to what he termed his greatest diplomatic accomplishment—the idea of a *transcontinental* boundary agreement.

The Spanish minister was sufficiently worried at this time to advise his government that it would be wise to come to a settlement on any basis obtainable. He declared that it would be impossible to head off the United States in her ambitions to reach the Pacific, and that an article promising nonrecognition of the insurgent colonies would be "absolutely inadmissible" at Washington.

At the moment, though, neither boundaries nor the insurgents comprised the chief problem for the administration. Monroe, who had just returned to Washington from his Virginia farm, immediately called his Cabinet together to discuss Jackson's venture and Onís' protests.[27] In seven days six Cabinet meetings were held. Adams, who was determined to maintain the authority of executive action by upholding Jackson, was convinced of the weight of the Florida occupation as a diplomatic lever. He vigorously advocated that opinion against the judgment of the President and all the other Cabinet members. Secretary of War John C. Calhoun was particularly censorious of his subordinate's action.

The compromise reached was that an offer should be made to return the seized posts; that Monroe should write Jackson a mildly reprimanding letter; and that Attorney General William Wirt should write a communication designed to gain public approval which should appear in the administration organ, the *National Intelligencer*.

Hyde de Neuville now reëntered the negotiations as a messenger and counselor. In his anxiety to effect a peaceful settlement he had been actively endeavoring to persuade Adams to agree to the Sabine River as a boundary. He succeeded in obtaining the secretary's consent to a withdrawal only as far as the Trinity.[28]

Hyde de Neuville then turned to deal with Onís. Following the Cabinet's decision on Jackson, the French minister took Adams' note of July 23 to the Spanish minister at Bristol. He spent two days there urging the latter to accede to the demands of the United States. When Onís declined to consider the Trinity, Hyde de Neuville took it upon himself to say that he thought the Washington government could be brought to agree on the Sabine if Onís would yield on the other points at issue.[29] This prediction of the agreement which was finally reached shows how clearly the Frenchman knew the situation.

The Spaniard refused to declare himself further, however, saying that he was determined to await the outcome of the Pizarro-Erving dealings at Madrid. He wrote accordingly to Adams, enclosing documents from the Florida officials to combat any justification of Jackson's acts. Onís indicated that he was perfectly aware that Jackson had no specific orders to seize the Spanish posts. Late in August Adams replied, again defending Jackson. He repeated the declaration that St. Marks would be returned to any Spanish forces strong enough to protect it, and that Pensacola would be restored to any authorized officials.[30] Onís transmitted this information to Spain and to Cuba in order that steps might be taken to reclaim the seized properties.

After several weeks of waiting, Onís received on October 3 new instructions, which added two important diplomatic weapons to those already at his disposal.[31] These were the Spanish act of ratification of the Convention of 1802 and the authority to offer the Sabine as an unqualified limit, not *sub spe rati* as specified in the directions sent him in April. At the same time Onís received a number of documents from Sevilla, and one of the volumes of manuscripts which came with Padre Pichardo's report on the Louisiana-Texas boundary.

New Proposals

Adams agreed to Onís' proposal to withhold exchanging ratifications of the Claims Convention until it should be seen whether ratification could be included in a treaty settlement, and on October 25 he received the new Spanish proposals. These included the cession of the two Floridas (admitting all land grants to date as valid); the renunciation of all spoliation claims, with the declaration that the United States had received nothing from France and thus that Spain was entitled to collect the amounts due for damages by French cruisers; and a strengthening of the neutrality laws of the United States.[32]

Onís considered the western limits to be the most important problem of all.[33] He proposed a boundary beginning on the Gulf between the Calcasieu and Mermento rivers, following the old Arroyo Hondo line, thence going north across the Red at latitude 32° north, thence to the Missouri, and up that stream to its source.

Onís' wording of his propositions to Adams is characteristic and somewhat amusing. Instead of being in simple, clear, legal phraseology, the articles he drafted usually included wordy confessions of evil for the United States' negotiator to sign and boasts of generosity on the part of His Catholic Majesty. Thus, he would have had the article of cession begin: "The United States declare that they deeply regret the violation of Spanish territory . . ." Such a meticulous diplomat as John Quincy Adams frequently was irritated by this method of procedure, but just as frequently, according to Onís' own testimony, he laughed at it.

Onís wisely took upon himself the important responsibility of omitting from the proposals two details included in his instructions. One was the plan for a neutral ground along the border, which he believed would only provide a sanctuary for lawless adventurers. The second was the demand that the United States promise not to recognize the insurgent colonies as independent, a request which he knew would be futile.

In reporting these steps to Pizarro, he expressed worry lest the Alagón, Puñonrostro, and Vargas grants in Florida cause trouble. John Forsyth, chairman of the House Committee on Foreign Relations, had visited Onís and explained the United States' view that the granting of these lands just before the probable cession of the provinces was an act of bad faith. Onís had to put him off with reassuring vagueness, not being able to say definitely that the grants would be rescinded.

In view of what I believe to be the unfounded charge that Onís deliberately misrepresented facts to Adams in order to protect these grants, it is important to note the words of his despatch of October 31:

You can see . . . that these concessions will be one of the greatest obstacles to success, and that it is to be feared that one must subscribe to the means that you have indicated of annulling them [excluding all grants made after 1803], although it is unjust and indecorous, in order not to lose the essential [advantage] which is to establish the limits to the west of the Mississippi.[34]

Onís at no time expressed either desire or intent to save the land grants in Florida at the expense of other stipulations. He knew that the Spanish government was not sure of its policy in regard to them when on October 3 he received the repetition of the order that no land in the three grants mentioned was to be alienated, particularly to foreigners.[35]

Adams now countered Onís' proposals with what he called the United States' ultimatum. This was a set of proposals which was to remain the basis of contention for many weeks. Besides the cession of the Floridas, Adams proposed that all land grants made since 1802 be canceled; that both parties renounce all claims, including those of the Convention of 1802 and those for spoliation by French cruisers; and that the United States undertake to settle those against it to the amount of five million dollars.[36]

The western boundary would be along the Sabine River from the Gulf to latitude 32° north, thence north to the Red, up that river to its head, along the crest of the "Snow mountains" [the Rockies] to the Forty-first Parallel, and west on that line to the "South sea." This was truly meant as an "ultimatum," inasmuch as President Monroe was not now anxious to settle with Spain promptly, and Adams (besides being discouraged in regard to a probable settlement) believed that this country had nothing to lose and much to gain by a delay. Thus they were willing to state their desires in firm terms even at the risk that the negotiation might be suspended.

There was one man in Washington, however, besides Onís who did not care to see the possibility of a break arise. Hyde de Neuville came to see the secretary on November 4, seeking a way to make possible some agreement. Adams dealt with him readily, though he did not trust him completely, having written three months previously:

His avowed instructions are to do everything in his power to preserve peace between the United States and Spain, and his secret instructions are to support the cause of Spain to the utmost of his power. . . .[37]

He told Adams that he had tried to persuade Onís to be conciliatory, but that he feared the negotiation must fail.[38] Onís' account of that conversation was a bitter denunciation of Hyde de Neuville, who came to him in an "arrogant" mood and urged that he accept the United States' proposals, even backing this country's claims to Texas as far as the Colorado River.[39] Thankless indeed is the task of a conciliator!

Onís in fact was soon authorized to accept the Colorado if that should prove to be necessary. Before he answered Adams' ultimatum, he received more instructions, the last of importance to be sent by Pizarro. These included the important authority to go beyond the Sabine if necessary in order to avoid a break. At the same time Onís was informed of the cessation of negotiations in Madrid, due to the Florida invasion. He was told, however, to continue his negotiations, through some foreign minister if need be. It is interesting to note that, as on several previous occasions, in this last suggestion Onís was being directed to do what he had already begun on his own initiative before the instructions arrived. The instructions did not enable him to continue negotiations much farther, however, because they did not authorize him to draw the boundary to the Pacific Coast.[40]

On the basis of those instructions, Onís submitted a counterplan to Adams on November 16. Concealing his authority to yield on the Texas limit, Onís proposed a boundary along the Sabine, thence across the Red to the Missouri, and up that river to its source. From there it was to be left to a boundary commission.[41] As before, he insisted on restitution of the Floridas, making that contingent to a cession. Furthermore, he now suggested for the first time that January 24, 1818 (the date on which he had written Adams definitely announcing Ferdinand's decision to cede the Floridas), be established as the deadline for the validity of the land grants. That date was to be the crux of bitter controversy four months later.

Unless Onís had some secret instructions which are not now available in the public archives, there is apparent no intent on his part to deceive in the matter of the land grants. In reporting his latest offer to Pizarro he implied that he meant to exclude the then recent large grants:

I have overcome the point of the grants made by His Majesty in the Floridas ... declaring that I will agree that the grants made by the authorities of His Majesty since the twenty-fourth of January last be considered annulled, [that being] the day in which I stated the will of His Majesty to cede to this Republic the Floridas, not because His Majesty no longer has the indisputable right to make such cessions, but because as they were made with the sole object that said lands should be populated, they have been annulled in fact by the concessionnaires' not having fulfilled the conditions.[42]

Onís did not expect his propositions to be accepted, because they lacked provisions for drawing the boundary to the Pacific, a point on which he truthfully protested lack of authority. Almost simultaneously, Monroe issued a message to Congress, on November 17, which was distinctly unfriendly to Spanish interests. The negotiation was officially brought to a standstill at the end of the month in an exchange of notes mutually withdrawing the unaccepted offers.

Two projects which were already under way were consummated, however. The ratifications of the Claims Convention of 1802 were exchanged on December 21, 1818; and the restoration of the Floridas to Spain was finally effected on February 8, 1819, two weeks before the signing of the treaty.[43]

Inasmuch as there was to be a change of ministry in Spain before the resumption of negotiations, it is interesting to note what had been accomplished during Pizarro's régime. The cession of the Floridas had been taken for granted. Although a definite agreement had not been formulated, the suggestion of Onís that January 24, 1818, be the date for determining the validity of land grants proved to be the plan adopted. The restoration of the Floridas had been ordered. Although the Convention of 1802 provided for the withholding of the claims for spoliation by French cruisers in Spanish ports, Adams' ultimatum of October 31 had proposed the decision which was finally reached, namely, that the United States should renounce those claims, leaving to Spain the privilege of trying to collect them from France. Adams had also stipulated to what amount the United States would assume the claims of its own citizens against Spain for other damages (Onís was to protest this point and to argue over its phrasing, but to no avail). A statement of the extent to which the maritime provisions of Pinckney's Treaty should remain in force likewise had been agreed upon.

Although discussion of some of these points did recur intermittently, the western boundary remained as the only important question on which the ultimate agreement had not been essentially conceded. In regard to that, the Sabine, already the effective line on the frontier, had been mentioned in the latest proposals of both parties. The rest of the delineation was highly conjectural. Onís did find one other difficulty, that of strengthening the neutrality laws of the United States. His demands on that point had been refused, and they continued to be consistently rejected.

ADAMS DEFENDS JACKSON

Adams, who had received word from Erving that negotiations had ceased at Madrid three months before, set out to answer the complaints that had stopped them. Pizarro not only had demanded the restitution of the Florida posts, but had asked indemnity for property damaged and the official censure of General Jackson. Adams noted that the restitution had already been ordered, and then took up the gauntlet on Pizarro's other demands, the payment of damages and the castigation of Jackson. The result was one of Adams' most notable state papers, one which has been described in many ways, from a masterly document to obvious special pleading. It was in the form of instructions to Erving."

Because Pizarro had stressed the execution in Spanish territory of two subjects of a Power at peace with Spain, Adams' "narrative of dark and complicated depravity" consisted largely of an account of the activities and connections of Arbuthnot with Nicholls and of Ambrister with Woodbine and McGregor. He had something to say besides concerning the "disposition of enmity to the United States, and . . . utter disregard to the obligations of the treaty [of 1795]" shown by the Florida officials. Carrying his refutation of Pizarro's charges to the extreme, he said that it was the Spanish officials of the Floridas who should be summoned for inquiry rather than Jackson, whom he praised." Accompanying the letter were seventy-two documents to substantiate its arguments.

Shorter communications of the same purport were sent by the secretary to Onís, and to Richard Rush and other ministers abroad, in order that the official position of the United States might be generally understood. This was done in an effort to combat the effect of Pizarro's argumentative note to Erving of August 29, which had been sent to all the courts of Europe and published in numerous newspapers before it had been received at Washington.

Adams' defense of Jackson also met the test of battle in Congress and in the press of this country. Monroe on December 3 submitted to Congress many of the documents on the "Seminole War"; and in the *National Intelligencer* of December 28 were published the famous instructions to Erving of November 28 and a continuation addressed to him on December 2.

Nearly all the other important governmental officials hesitated to approve Jackson. Calhoun and Crawford in the Cabinet, John Forsyth in the Senate, and William Henry Harrison and Joseph Hopkinson in the House were especially opposed to the popular hero. Onís wrote that Adams favored the General in order to gain popular support for his own presidential ambitions. That opinion was perhaps exaggerated because of the irritations of a long and difficult negotiation. But Onís was not alone in this view. Bagot was somewhat astonished at Adams' position, and commented:

> Although I was pretty well aware of the nature of this answer, I confess to your Lordship that I was not prepared for the direct and high handed defense of General Jackson. . . . There is however a Key which will explain this, and always will explain every measure of this Government viz:—Elections.[46]

With the rivalries which culminated in 1824 already splitting the Cabinet, such suspicions may have had some foundation. But anyone who has read Adams' diplomatic correspondence and has seen his conscience unfold in his diary must feel that a sense of national pride and a desire to bolster his diplomatic strategy were the dominant motives in this notable exposition.

Debate on the proposed censure of Jackson continued in Congress and in the press until two weeks before the signing of the treaty, giving the diplomats many anxious moments. Finally, on February 8, 1819, the House, in a session which set a record for attendance, defeated resolutions intended to express official disapproval of the trials of Arbuthnot and Ambrister.[47]

THE COLUMBIA RIVER

During the time that negotiations were suspended, the word Onís most anxiously awaited was authorization to negotiate concerning the Northwest. It has been seen that most of the other issues had been clarified. Along the frontier, Texas no longer was the source of worry that it had been previously, now that the Sabine had been settled upon as the limit and the French adventurers had been driven from the Trinity. Farther west, the problem of keeping the United States border a safe distance from Santa Fé had presented itself when Adams demanded that the Red River form the boundary line, and various trading and exploring parties had learned that the New Mexico frontier was not to be a peaceful one. But the greatest uncertainty centered in the region beyond the "Snow mountains."

The area actually in controversy lay between the Columbia and the Forty-first Parallel. The only settlements to be found there were Fort George (Astoria), Fort Nez Percés near the mouth of the Walla Walla, and such temporary posts as fur trappers and traders might set up seasonally. The first-named place had remained under the control of the Northwest Company since its transfer to the firm in 1813. So far as the active fur trade (the one great reason for interest in the territory) was concerned, the region continued to be dominated by the British even after Special Commissioner John B. Prevost, on October 6, 1818, received at Fort George the official British act of surrender in accordance with the terms of the Treaty of Ghent.

Nothing appears in the documents to explain definitely why Adams was led to propose in July, 1818, the inclusion of the Oregon country in the treaty negotiations. He later claimed with pride that the initial suggestion was his own. Perhaps the current boundary negotiation with England caused him to meditate upon the desirability of a treaty title to the region. But with economic interest in the area so dominated by one industry it is only natural to wonder if there might not have been at that time something comparable to the present-day "lobbies" of private interests in Washington.

Such a speculation must center about John Jacob Astor, the one outstanding figure in the United States in the fur-trapping and fur-carrying trade. Considering his intimate connection with Astoria, he may very possibly have guided Adams' attention toward the Northwest. Surely he was in frequent touch with the State Department during the Adams-Onís negotiation. One of his ships which was engaged in the Pacific trade, the "Beaver," had been detained at Talcahuano, Chile, on charges of violating Spanish colonial maritime regulations by carrying contraband goods destined for Valparaiso, then in the hands of the insurgents. The matter became the subject of a diplomatic complaint and worried Onís because he feared that an offense to such a rich and prominent citizen might arouse adverse public opinion throughout the United States.[48]

Furthermore, Astor did believe that title should be obtained to the Northwest Coast. It is said that he greeted Albert Gallatin on the latter's return from Ghent with the remark that there was one thing the commissioners should not have left undone. "You should have settled more definitely the question of the Columbia territory," said Astor; and when Gallatin suggested that their great-grandchildren would be the ones to talk about that, Astor answered,

"If we live, Mr. Gallatin, we shall see trouble about it in less than forty years."[49] Gallatin did live to see the final Oregon settlement.

In 1816 Astor wrote to Monroe, then secretary of state, asking permission to send an agent to the Columbia if the long-anticipated reoccupation of Astoria took place. He even offered to furnish a ship to carry out the mission, saying:

> I see the Russians are doing greathings in that country I have observed in a Late London paper the arrival a the Russian Ship Suwarro [Suworow?] from the north Pacific with a Cargo of furs Sayd to be worth not Less than £200.000 Stg with which she was proceeding to St. Petersbourgh this Shows something of what the trade is in the north Pacific.[50]

A year later Astor was instrumental in assembling a dinner party of a hundred persons to welcome Adams home from England.[51] Did he greet the new secretary of state with the same admonitions which he had made to Gallatin? There is no record available. In the same year, however, official recognition was given to Astor's interest in the region. The President, when the "Ontario" was sent out, stated his desire that the fur magnate be notified of the intention finally to reoccupy Astoria.[52]

The continued attention which the United States gave to the Northwest, and the prevailing vagueness with respect to claims therein, are indicated in the negotiations of Richard Rush and Gallatin with Henry Goulbourn and Frederick John Robinson at London, which resulted in the Convention of October 20, 1818. By that agreement England and this country set the boundary at latitude 49° north, from the Lake of the Woods to the Rockies, leaving the region west of the mountains, to which both laid claim, for joint occupation over a period of ten years.[53] It is important to emphasize here that the limits of the territory reserved for joint occupation were not defined either on the north or on the south.

The southern limits of that region, inasmuch as they would be virtually established by a definition of the United States' claim, rested on the outcome of the Adams-Onís negotiations. The proposal which Adams had made for a line along the Forty-first Parallel would have taken from Spain the region now included in all or parts of seven northern counties of California, three counties of Nevada, seven of Utah, and four of Wyoming. Had his plan been effected, it is probable that quite a different delineation of state boundaries might appear today.

On the other hand, had Adams followed the urging of Hyde de Neuville in the winter of 1818–1819 and accepted the Columbia as a limit, the United States would have had to wait some time longer before obtaining the whole of the present state of Oregon, most of Idaho, and a good share of Wyoming. But Onís was convinced that concessions would have to be made at least liberal enough to allow the United States free access to the Columbia. The departure of an expedition of three hundred men and six boats on a journey up the Missouri (the Long-Atkinson scientific and military parties), and the sailing of the frigate "Macedonian" presumably for the Columbia, appeared to Onís to be developments so menacing as to make advisable a prompt boundary agreement.[54]

Among Onís' statements regarding the Northwest Coast is a reference to two possibly useful ports in the region lying between the extreme demands of the two countries. They were Trinidad Head, in latitude 41° 02' north, of which Heçeta had taken possession in 1775; and Point St. George, in latitude 41° 46' north, sighted and named by Vancouver in 1792.[55] Neither was occupied, however, and it appears that Onís was simply exaggerating the value of the territory saved for Spain in the final agreement.

More remarkable, however ineffective, was his idea of fortifying the mouth of the Columbia, a spot over which Spain had never exercised actual control. Onís wrote to Pizarro in the spring of 1818 that,

there being at a very short distance from the mouth of the River Columbia on the Pacific ocean an island situated in the middle of said river which offers an excellent position for a military establishment, it is of the highest importance that it be occupied as soon as possible, with the purpose of protecting the possessions and the commerce of the Monarchy in that region, as the United States will not delay in carrying out its project of opening a route by that river to the South Sea.[56]

The plan was well received in Madrid, and the war office sent to the viceroy of Mexico an order to put the island in a state of defense "without giving the slightest motive of complaint to the United States; it being your responsibility to justify this project as you find it most convenient."[57]

The viceroy, long troubled in trying to pacify Mexico itself, considered the plan not at all feasible. He replied that, although such a fortification might be desirable, it would necessitate a naval force on the Pacific to maintain it; and that at the time he could count on only one brigantine, and that in bad condition.[58] Onís meanwhile had decided that it was too late to head off the ambitions of the United States in that vicinity.

IRUJO TAKES THE REINS

In the meantime, the apparent failure of Pizarro's negotiations with Erving and the collapse of Garay's financial reorganization, combined with court intrigue, caused the peremptory dismissal of the two ministers. Tatistcheff, who had turned against them, seems to have contributed to their downfall, which culminated in their banishment from the capital. On the day of their removal from office, September 14, 1818, the Marquis of Casa Irujo was appointed to succeed Pizarro. This was the same man who had had such a checkered career as minister to the United States in Jefferson's administration. He had once before been named *secretario de estado,* in 1812, but could not fill the post because he happened to be in Philadelphia at the time.

Erving's comments on the banishment of Pizarro reveal the high esteem in which that minister was held by foreign observers:

... the dismissal of Mr. Pizarro ... must needs weaken very much the confidence of foreign cabinets in this, it will be seen that no minister however estimable is certain of his place for a day. ... The intelligence and good sense,—the moderate and conciliatory temper, and the honor and good faith of Mr. Pizarro recommended him to every one;—no spanish Minister of late years has done so much to repair the disordered state of affairs as he has done, and none has received more marks of the satisfaction of the foreign Cabinets with whom he has treated.[59]

At the same time he said of the new official:

I expect no good from him in our affairs, and shall be very happy if I can only keep him from undoing whatever Mr. Pizarro has done favorable to an amicable adjustment of them.

Erving himself was replaced the following spring by John Forsyth, but before he left he had carried his feeling of antagonism toward Irujo to such an extreme that the latter returned one of his notes as too insulting to be received. The United States minister charged, and apparently with good reason, that Irujo did nothing except follow Pizarro's plan in regard to the negotiations at Washington. At least he did not "undo" that plan. He rather carried it to its logical conclusion, a move which Pizarro had advocated but had not been authorized to execute.

Pizarro left a long instruction for Onís on the table. His successor revised it in some minor details of wording and sent it along, dated October 10.[60] Irujo did make one important change, however, in telling Onís to set 1804 as the date after which the Florida land grants should be invalid, instead of 1803. Pizarro later charged that this was done in order to include some grants which Irujo had obtained in the region.[61] However that may be, the instruction was so worded as to convey the worthy idea that to insist on the validity of the very recent grants would be to favor the interests of individuals at the expense of obtaining a better bargain for the good of the nation. This contributes to the opinion that it was not the intention of the Spanish foreign office to deceive the United States in the matter of the land grants, whatever machinations the *camarilla* may have sponsored. The despatch emphasized two things: that Onís was to be not too particular over the satisfaction obtained for the Florida invasion, and that he was to achieve the best arrangement he could in the west. If the United States would agree to turn over the seized territory just long enough to permit the Spanish flag to be raised previous to the cession, for appearance' sake, further indemnification was not to be demanded. With respect to Texas, the minister was to obtain the Sabine as the boundary line if possible, but again he was told that he could go as far west as the Colorado if that were absolutely necessary to avoid a break, recognition of the insurgents, or an invasion of the Provincias Internas. North of the Red River, Onís was told simply to settle as best he could, preferably running the boundary along the Missouri to its source and thence to the ocean as far north as possible.

This letter reached Washington on January 4. Onís thought, however, that it would be of no help to him because it did not authorize him to treat on the basis of Adams' "ultimatum" of October 31. He indicated the importance of the boundary question at this time when he wrote:

I do not believe that [these instructions] will further matters, because they do not authorize me to take for limits the Red river to its source, from there the crest of the Snowy mountains to the 41st degree, and that line west to the Pacific, and it is doubtful if this government will yield an inch from these limits.[62]

Whether by turning about and offering to yield to the Colorado, as he was authorized, Onís could have obtained a diminution of the United States' pretensions in the Northwest sufficient to reach an agreement, one cannot say. He obviously considered the Texas question settled and therefore did not tender the concession that he had been empowered to make. Adams, consequently, did not know precisely to what extent Onís' instructions would permit him to compromise.[63] Adams regretted yielding the claim to Texas more than most of the Cabinet members, but considered the concession necessary to an agreement.

Despite the insufficiency of these instructions, Onís set out to negotiate further. On January 10 he called on Hyde de Neuville, only to become more than ever disgusted with that minister's efforts to make him agree to Adams' ultimatum and declaration that the United States would not concede a single point. Undaunted, however, the Spaniard wrote Adams on the next day, saying that he would be able to reopen the conversations with a view to further compromise.[64]

No sooner had Onís taken that step than he heard that Hyde de Neuville had new instructions which directed him to aid the Spaniard in reaching a suitable settlement of the affairs as promptly as possible. This was a distorted report of the Frenchman's instructions of September 1, 1818, quoted in the preceding chapter, telling him to act as a conciliator. Onís remarked, however, that he would not trust French aid far, for he believed that France's real aim was to ingratiate herself with the United States as a means of "combatting the ambition of England."[65]

Adams, in a conference on January 15, 1819, told Onís that the people generally thought that he had been too liberal, and that, far from making new propositions, he could only renew those of October 31. Onís, therefore, submitted his revised scheme the following day, acting on his own initiative regarding the northwest boundary because he believed that concessions were essential in order to avoid serious trouble. His note was short, inasmuch as he simply repeated his former proposal (that of November 16) and made the additional statement that he would accept the course of the Columbia as the line westward from the head of the Missouri.[66] Onís, in urging this solution, assumed a confidential tone with Adams, telling him of the stupidity of the men who made up the

Spanish *Consejo,* and relating the extreme difficulties he had had in persuading them to agree, as he said they had, on the Columbia line.[67] The statement that the *Consejo* had approved such a limit was at the time, as far as Onís knew, untrue; but the Spaniard was now determined to push a settlement even though he exceeded his instructions, hoping his government would realize that half a loaf was better than none.

Ten days later Onís was still waiting for an answer. His call on Adams to request a reply resulted in an acrimonious discussion, with the secretary saying that he was "so wearied out with the discussion it became nauseous" and that he had given it up in despair, and with Onís saying that he did not wish for any more discussion but simply wanted an answer.[68] One may question the statement that Adams had given up in despair, and be inclined to impute it more to an effort to force Onís to a conclusion than to a real surrender in a negotiation which the secretary was obviously anxious to conclude.

Adams sent Onís the desired answer on January 29, repeating the plan of October 31, 1818, as an ultimatum. At the same time he called in Hyde de Neuville, at the President's behest, asking him to ascertain if Onís would settle in the event the Red River line were adjusted in such a way as to keep it some distance away from Santa Fé.

Before the Frenchman could approach Onís on that question, the latter received new and vitally important instructions, on or about January 26. They were the last major set to reach Washington before the conclusion of the treaty, and gave the minister the latitude necessary to make the agreement.

Irujo, as he stated, had learned in mid-October, through Montmorency, the French minister at Madrid, of the United States' pretensions regarding the Red River and the Northwest Coast. On the basis of this information the *Consejo de Estado* authorized a broad extension of powers in regard to that phase of the controversy.

In these instructions, dated October 23, Irujo told Onís that he could accept a limit along the Red River to the head of navigation, but that the line must turn northward there to avoid Santa Fé.[69] Even that was made conditional on the necessities of the situation. He was to seek a line from the source of the Red, parallel to the mountains, to the head of the Missouri. Although the Spanish government did not relish the notion of yielding rights on the coast as far south as the Columbia, it was stated that, if the United States insisted upon an outlet to the sea by way of the Columbia, there would be no objection to continuing the line along that river. But the Spanish rights on the coast both below and above it were to remain intact! Without clearly formulating the idea, the *secretario* apparently visioned some sort of a corridor to the ocean with Spanish territory on either side. This would have been a futile proposal, for the British had long before effectively dissipated any Spanish hope of establishing dominion north of the Columbia.

Onís, who knew that even greater concessions would have to be made, relied during the remainder of the negotiation on the concluding paragraph of the instruction:

Finally His Majesty charges me to say, you are fully authorized to construct, discuss, and conclude the agreement according to the circumstances, without the necessity of further consultation [of your government] regarding the matter.

This statement constituted practically a *carte blanche* for Onís, and authorized him to make the settlement which he had already resolved to make on his own responsibility.

CONCESSIONS AND COMPROMISES

Onís on February 1 revised his treaty plan, offering a line up the Sabine to its source, thence north to the Red, along it to longitude 95° west, due north to the Arkansas, and along it to its source. From there the line was to be drawn directly west to the San Clemente, or Multnomah (now the Willamette), and along that river to the sea.⁷⁰ As it happens, the last-named river does not reach the sea, but Onís no doubt would have been equally satisfied in knowing that it flowed into the Columbia. The location of the source of the Arkansas was uncertain but was considered to be at about latitude 41° north, nearly two degrees north of its actual position.

On receipt of this proposal Adams consulted Monroe and Jackson. He was seriously perturbed over the imminent threat of trouble from Clay. But Monroe pointed out that Clay would be troublesome whether the treaty were signed or not and said that in his estimation the acquisition of the Floridas and the assurance of a title on the Pacific Coast would offset popular opposition to

the failure to obtain Texas. Jackson, so Adams testifies, expressed
the same opinion, although many years later the General de-
nounced that failure.[71] Other members of the Cabinet voiced their
opinions not only to Adams and Monroe, but, to the disgust of the
secretary, also directly to Onís and Hyde de Neuville.

Monroe, anxious to reach a settlement, would have accepted
Hyde de Neuville's proposal of turning the line from the Red
River at longitude 100° west, and running it to the Pacific along
the Forty-third Parallel.[72] Adams, on the other hand, was more
firm. He drafted a *projet* dated February 6, proposing a line between 101° and 102°, with the line to the ocean along the Forty-
first Parallel. He added the stipulation that Spain should make
no settlements on the Red or the Arkansas River, and that the
navigation of those streams should remain to the United States.

Onís, fearing as did Adams that the disgust shown in Congress
and in the press at the failure to obtain Texas might jeopardize the
whole arrangement, hastened to reach an agreement. He tried still
another counterproposal on the ninth, but wrote home that if he
could not obtain any further concessions he would sign on Adams'
terms.[73] He did in fact get an important concession on the limits,
for which Spain had to thank Onís' pertinacity alone.

The *projet* which he delivered differed from preceding ones in
no material way except regarding the boundary. He planned to
have it drawn along the Sabine from the Gulf to latitude 32°
north, thence directly north to the Red River, following that river
westward to longitude 100° west, north on that line to the Arkansas, up it to the Forty-second Parallel, west along that line to the
Multnomah, down it to the Forty-third Parallel, and thence west
to the Pacific.[74] Both this proposal and the treaty which was ultimately signed manifested current ignorance of the fact that the
Arkansas rises considerably below the Forty-second Parallel.

The Cabinet met on the eleventh and twelfth to discuss Onís'
projet. Adams noted that an agreement was so near that "the
President inclines to give up all that remains in contest." Monroe
would have accepted a line turning from the Red at longitude 100°
west and running to the Pacific from the Multnomah on the Forty-
third Parallel. The secretary of state "was convinced that we
should obtain more by adhering to our points," but maintained
that view almost alone.[75] Acceptance of the President's suggestion

was authorized by the Cabinet, however, as was Adams' plan to limit the assumption of claims liability by the United States to five million dollars.

Adams had again raised the question of claims, knowing that some arrangement would have to be made. It would be demanded not only by the claimants but by the public, which had been stirred by the Meade case, by the seizures of traders in New Mexico, and by other instances where private citizens had suffered. Adams knew further that no money could be had from Spain and that a mutual renunciation of obligations between the two governments would be included in the treaty. Onís realized that the claims would amount to more than the figure stipulated and was glad to have Spain relieved of the burden. Little had been said about this question in the negotiations, and at no time had it been mentioned in connection with the boundary. The two problems were debated and decided separately.

Onís knew well enough the views of different persons on the whole negotiation, and that it was not entirely in the hands of the secretary of state, however resolutely that official expressed his opinions. "You cannot imagine," he wrote to Irujo, "how many meetings and discussions have been held."[76] He recognized the danger of popular opposition to the line of the Sabine, especially when Erving was alleged to have written to a Congressman that he could have obtained the Colorado.

To bring Adams and Onís into closer agreement more activity was necessary on the part of Hyde de Neuville, who was evidently moved only by a desire to get them to reach some sort of peaceful settlement. Onís believed that the French minister had been sent to sound him on the possibility of setting the boundary at the Brazos de Dios, between the Colorado and the Sabine. Adams' own detailed account mentions no such proposal at this late date, although it does confirm the sending of Hyde de Neuville to ask a definite answer on Adams' proposal of the thirteenth.[77] Adams wished to have the line continue up the Red River as far as longitude 102° west, and he still endeavored to have it drawn from the head of the Arkansas to the Pacific on the Forty-first Parallel.[78] He and Hyde de Neuville conferred at length on these questions, as well as on two others which remained unsettled up to the last few days. One was whether the boundary should follow the center or the west and the south banks of the rivers along which it ran. The other question arose from the wording of the cession of the Floridas. Onís had phrased his *projet* in such a manner as to make the United States renounce its former pretensions to West Florida. Such a concession in theory was naturally unpalatable to Adams.

When Hyde de Neuville took up the latest proposal with Onís, the latter received Adams' demands with an intentional display of anger, desiring "to alarm him more than the government."[79] He believed that Adams depended on the French minister to put through the negotiation and that the latter had definite orders from Paris not to allow it to be suspended. Thus Onís thought he could be quite firm in talking to Hyde de Neuville. And for some days the Spaniard, pleading indisposition, did not see Adams.

He stated rather incidentally in his report to Madrid that he was incapacitated on account of chilblains. But he added, and this was the important fact, that he considered it more efficacious to carry on the negotiations through a third party, who could convey his firmness and his semblance of anger to Adams without the danger of a direct affront to the secretary. Onís told Hyde de Neuville that he would accept a boundary settlement of the Sabine, a line leaving the Red at longitude 100° west, and the Forty-second Parallel from the Arkansas to the sea. Those were the final terms, although Adams did endeavor to modify them further (Art. 3 of the treaty).

Hyde de Neuville wrote a memorandum in which he placed the Onís proposal of February 9 and that of Adams of February 13 in parallel columns, noting the agreements and differences which his conversations with the two men had revealed.[80] Among the lesser disputes which arose, after the major issues were so nearly agreed upon that Adams allowed himself for the first time to feel confident of a settlement,[81] were those over his opposition to the admission of Spanish ships in ports of the ceded territories on the same footing as those of the United States; over whether the boundary should be drawn in the center or along the west and the south banks of the rivers; and over Onís' objection to the limitation of United States liability for claims on Spain to five million dollars.

Upon the first point Adams yielded to the compromise of admitting Spanish ships, exclusively, for twelve years to St. Augustine and Pensacola under the same duties as United States ships (Art. 15 of the treaty).

Concerning the second point, heated dispute occurred among members of the Cabinet, and between Adams and the French minister, whose argument was largely over an incident which greatly offended Adams' dignity.

Onís' difficulty from chilblains had lessened sufficiently by February 17 for him to attend the President's last drawing room of the season. There he approached the executive on the subject of the navigation of the rivers along the boundary, and the ownership of the islands. The President was conciliatory, and after some conversation, according to Onís' report,

The President shook hands, and told me that he would do what I wished, that he could not refuse me anything, having had a personal esteem for me ever since the first day he had dealt with me, he offered to drink a glass of wine with me, and the matter was agreed, not without the great resentment of Mr. Adams, who could not forget the shame of having his ultimatum destroyed in all its points.[82]

Monroe's cordial words, if Onís reports them correctly, are reminiscent of his ingratiating manner toward the French in 1794. That time he incurred the wrath of the Federalists. On this occasion it was the sensitive and precise nature of Adams which was offended. He could not properly condemn his chief, but to Hyde de Neuville he poured out his anger at Onís. What right, he asked, had Onís to go directly to the executive over the head of the secretary of state, who had full powers to negotiate?[83] Eventually Adams got the better of the controversy, for it was agreed that the western bank of the Sabine and the southern banks of the Red and the Arkansas should form the boundary, but that the navigation of the rivers should be free to both countries (Art. 3).

The third dispute involved one of the most common misinterpretations which historians have made of the treaty. There was no "purchase" of the Floridas. The claims discussion, as has been stated, was kept quite separate during the whole course of the negotiations from that on the boundary. Adams always spoke of sacrifices in other sections of the frontier, particularly in Texas and the Northwest, as the price of the Floridas, and never mentioned the claims assumption in that connection. Secretary of the Treasury Crawford tried to influence Adams to keep the amount stipulated as low as possible. Onís, on the other hand, saw the possibility of misinterpretation and vehemently objected to the limitation to five million dollars. He wished to have the United States assume responsibility for all types of claims in order to relieve Spain of the litigation. Furthermore, he argued that the ignorant grandees of the Spanish court might think it was a purchase and consider the price too small, as the Floridas were worth far more than that sum. Onís feared, as Adams explained it, that, "if the limitation of five millions should be in the treaty, it might give them a handle to say that the interest and honor of Spain were both sacrificed by the bargain."[84] Adams remained firm, however, and five millions was the amount stated to which the United States would reimburse its own citizens for the several kinds of claims against Spain which were enumerated (Arts. 9 and 11).

Onís called on Adams on the eighteenth, and the drafts of the agreement were studied. A Cabinet meeting was held on the following day, but no important revisions resulted. In the final settlement, January 24, 1818, was set as the date up to which Spanish land grants in the ceded territories should be validated (Art. 8). Onís had suggested to Irujo that any Florida grants which might be ruled out by this provision could be replaced by lands in Texas, "which remain assured to the Crown, and which are of infinitely better quality, and in a better climate."[85] Such substitution, however, was never made.

The right of Spain to call on France for payment for spoliations by the French cruisers was allowed, and the declaration was made that the United States had received no recompense on that account and that it renounced any claim thereto (Arts. 9 and 14). Other renunciations of the United States included damages incurred in the suspension of the right of deposit at New Orleans in 1802, and all maritime claims on Spain. This country was released, on the other hand, from Spanish claims for damages resulting from the Pike and Miranda expeditions, and from unlawful seizures at sea (Art. 9). The Convention of 1802 was annulled and all claims included in it were renounced (Art. 10).

A nice distinction was made in the wording of the section of the treaty which pertained to the cession of the Floridas, with the result that the previous claims of the two governments were not defined, and the notorious West Florida controversy remained forever unsettled.

The King was to cede "all the territories which belong to him, situated to the Eastward of the Mississippi, known by the name of East and West Florida" (Art. 2). A comma after the word "territories" would have changed the whole sense by making the following clause a positive declaration. As it stands, the United States

[Translation of the despatch of Onís of February 22, 1819, in A.H.N., 5645.]

Most Excellent Sir.

Duplicate
No. 32.

My dear Sir: I have just this moment signed the definitive treaty concluded between His Majesty and this Republic designed to end all the differences between the two governments which have been pending for eighteen years. It was transmitted to the Senate at once for their approval, and as soon as this is received I will send it to Your Excellency by messenger on the first ship available.

I renew my respects to Your Excellency and pray God to guard your life many years. Washington 22 of February of 1819.

> Most Excellent Sir
> I kiss the hand of Your Excellency
> your most attentive servant
> Luis de Onís

His Excellency the Marquis of Casa Irujo

could interpret it as meaning that the only portion of West Florida which belonged to His Catholic Majesty was that east of the Perdido and the Apalachicola, never claimed as a part of Louisiana. Spain could consider it as a cession of the whole region west to the Mississippi, in the conviction that it was all legally Spanish until then. Adams wanted the statement to be concise and believed that a more specific explanation was unnecessary. Onís, on the other hand, had promised his government to avoid a specific recognition in the treaty of the United States' claims to West Florida west of the Perdido.[86]

It was agreed that the document should be signed on the following Monday, Washington's birthday. In the interim Adams' meticulous care in diplomatic form was revealed in the arguments over wording. The difficulties were finally settled, however, and on the appointed day Onís and Adams put their signatures to the treaty, thus ending the many years of demanding, waiting, threatening, and bargaining.[87] By its terms the United States received the Floridas, rounding out its domain east of the Mississippi; Spain was

Exmo Senor.

D°
N°32.

Muy S' mio: Acabo de firmar en este momento
el Tratado definitivo concluido entre S. M. y esta
Republica, para poner fin à todas las diferencias
pendientes de diez y ocho años à esta parte entre los
dos Gobiernos. Se pasó inmediatamente al Senado
para su aprobacion, y al instante que la reciba,
despacharé un Mensagero con èl à V.E. por el primer
barco que se presente.

Renuevo à V.E. mis respetos y pido à
Dios Gue su vida m.ª añ.ª Washington 22 de
Febrero de 1819.

Exmo S'
B.L.M. de V.E.
su m.ª at.º Serv.º
Luis de Onis

Exmo S'. Marques de Casa Yrujo.

DESPATCH OF ONÍS OF FEBRUARY 22, 1819

confirmed in her title to Texas; Santa Fé was protected by the bending of the line to leave 360 miles between that town and the border; and in the Northwest the ambitious republic acquired all of Spain's rights north of what is now the California-Oregon boundary, thus being for the first time assured of a transcontinental domain.

NOTES TO CHAPTER VI

[1] "The New Year," *Niles' Weekly Register* (Baltimore), XIII (January 3, 1818): 297–298.

[2] Pizarro to Onís, February 20, 1818, in A.H.N., Est. 5643.

[3] Pizarro to Onís, February 25, 1818, in A.M.E., 224.

[4] Pizarro to Onís, April 6, 1818, *ibid.*

[5] The draft of Pizarro's letter includes these words: "the question of western limits (the most important) . . ." In the final copy sent to Onís the phrase in parentheses was omitted, but the draft no doubt shows Heredia's and Pizarro's own evaluation.

[6] Pizarro to Onís, April 25, 1818, in A.H.N., Est., 5643.

[7] Erving to Adams (private), February 10, February 26, April 5, and September 20, 1818, in D.S., Despatches, Spain, XV–XVI. A map showing the extent of the land grants appears in D. Hunter Miller, *Treaties and Other International Acts of the United States of America* (Washington, 1931—), III:41.

[8] Erving to Adams, April 26, 1818, in D.S., Despatches, Spain, XV.

[9] Narciso de Heredia, *Escritos del Conde de Ofalia* (Bilbao, 1894), pp. 273–275.

[10] Erving to Adams, May 14, 1818, in D.S., Despatches, Spain, XV.

[11] Erving to Adams, June 12, 1818, *ibid.*

[12] Erving to Adams, June 30, 1818, *ibid.*

[13] Erving to Adams, July 13, 1818, *ibid.*, XVI.

[14] *Ibid.*

[15] These negotiations are described in Erving's despatches to Adams of July 13, 14, and 22, and August 7, 13, and 31, 1818, *ibid.*

[16] Pizarro to Erving, July 19, 1818, in *A.S.P.*, *F.R.*, IV:516.

[17] Pizarro to Erving, August 6, 11, and 29, 1818, *ibid.*, pp. 519–523.

[18] Erving to Adams, July 22, 1818, in D.S., Despatches, Spain, XVI.

[19] Onís to Pizarro, June 17, 1818, in A.H.N., Est., 5643.

[20] John S. Bassett, *Life of Andrew Jackson* (New York, 1916), I:246–248.

[21] T. Frederick Davis, "McGregor's Invasion of Florida," Florida Historical Society, *Quarterly*, VII (1928):3–71.

[22] Bassett, *op. cit.*, I:260–262.

[23] John Quincy Adams, *Memoirs* (Philadelphia, 1874–1877), IV:104.

[24] Hyde de Neuville to Richelieu, January 14, 1819, in A.M.A.E., Corr. Pol., E.U., Suppl. 10.

[25] Onís to Adams, July 8, 1818, in *A.S.P.*, *F.R.*, IV:496–497; Onís to Pizarro, July 18, 1818, in A.H.N., Est., 5643.

[26] John Melish, *Map of the United States* (Philadelphia, 1818); Onís to Pizarro, July 18, 1818, in A.H.N., Est., 5643 (see "The Melish Map," *infra*, Appendix II).

[27] Adams, *Memoirs*, IV:108–115.

[28] *Ibid.*, p. 110.

[29] Onís to Pizarro, August 4, 1818, in A.H.N., Est., 5644.

[30] Onís to Adams, August 5, 1818, and Adams to Onís, August 24, 1818, in *A.S.P.*, *F.R.*, IV:504–509.

[31] Pizarro to Onís, July 9 and 15, 1818, in A.H.N., Est., 5643.

[32] Onís to Adams, October 24, 1818, in *A.S.P.*, *F.R.*, IV:526–530.

[33] Onís to Pizarro, October 31, 1818, in A.H.N., Est., 5643.

[34] *Ibid.*

[35] Onís to Pizarro, November 1, 1818, *ibid.*, 5644.

[36] Adams to Onís, October 31, 1818, in *A.S.P., F.R.*, IV:530–531.

[37] Adams, *Memoirs*, IV:126.

[38] *Ibid.*, p. 161.

[39] Onís to Pizarro, November 12, 1818, in A.H.N., Est., 5643.

[40] Pizarro to Onís, August 30, 1818, and *memoria* of Heredia read by Pizarro before the *Consejo* on August 26, which was the basis of these instructions; both in A.H.N., Est., 5643. This authorization to go beyond the Sabine if it were absolutely necessary did not enter into the negotiations between Erving and Pizarro at Madrid. The Spanish government preferred to take the chance of having Onís reach a more favorable agreement at Washington, rather than offer such a concession directly to Erving. The United States minister had said in July, 1818, that he could obtain the Colorado limit if Pizarro were not overruled in the *Consejo*. See Erving to Adams, July 22, 1818, in D.S., Despatches, Spain, XVI. Pizarro was so overruled, however. Erving overlooked that fact when in 1844 he asserted that he could have obtained Texas had not Adams' pride caused the latter to keep the negotiation at Washington. Adams refuted the charge in a bitter diatribe against Erving and Andrew Jackson during the Texas annexation controversy. See "Address before the Boston Young Men's Whig Club," *Advertiser and Patriot* (Boston), October 10 and 11, 1844. At no time, in fact, did Erving have Adams' complete confidence.

[41] Onís to Adams, November 16, 1818, in *A.S.P., F.R.*, IV:531–533. The version in the *American State Papers* is in error in naming the Mississippi in place of the Missouri.

[42] Onís to Pizarro, November 23, 1818, in A.H.N., Est., 5643. Onís' intention to have the three disputed grants excluded is indicated also in Adams, *Memoirs*, IV:265.

[43] Felipe Fatio (consul at New Orleans) to Onís, February 18, 1819, in A.H.N., Est., 5645.

[44] Adams to Erving, November 28 and December 2, 1818 (with enclosures), in *A.S.P., F.R.*, IV:539–545, 546–612.

[45] An example of the errors into which able historians may fall by making one-sided studies of diplomatic history is found in Bassett's statement in regard to this letter that "the force of this argument was not lost on Pizarro," giving this as an explanation of Spain's final agreement to sign the treaty (see Bassett, *op. cit.*, 1:270). But Pizarro had been out of office for two months when the letter was written, and it could not possibly have reached Spain in time for return instructions to reach Onís before he decided to sign the treaty.

[46] Bagot to Castlereagh (private), January 4, 1819, in Public Archives of Canada (Ottawa), Bagot, American Correspondence, II.

[47] *National Intelligencer* (Washington), February 9 and 10, 1819.

[48] Onís to Pizarro, May 6, 1818, in A.H.N., Est., 5644.

[49] Charles A. Bristed, *A Letter to the Hon. Horace Mann* (New York, 1850), pp. 15–16. During the negotiation of the Treaty of Ghent, Astor's son-in-law called on the United States delegation and informed them that Astor intended to reoccupy Astoria as soon as possible after the war. See Adams, *Memoirs*, III:90.

[50] Astor to Monroe, September 5, 1816, in D.S., Miscellaneous Letters, August–September, 1816.

[51] Adams, *Memoirs*, IV:4. Information on the relations between Astor and Adams is only one of many valuable finds which would be revealed to the historian if the Adams family papers were open.

[52] Memorandum of Richard Rush, September 25, 1817, in D.S., Special Agents, VI.

[53] Miller, *Treaties*, II:658–662.

[54] Onís to Pizarro, October 31, 1818, in A.H.N., Est., 5643.

[55] Onís to Pizarro, February 16, 1819, *ibid.*, 5661.

[56] Onís to Pizarro, March 3, 1818, *ibid.*, 5562, Expediente 11.

[57] Quoted in Francisco Eguía (minister of war) to Pizarro, July 6, 1818, *ibid.*

[58] Viceroy Conde de Venadito to *ministro de guerra*, December 31, 1818, *ibid.*

[59] Erving to Adams, September 20, 1818, in D.S., Despatches, Spain, XVI.

[60] Irujo to Onís, October 10, 1818, in A.H.N., Est., 5643.

[61] José García de León y Pizarro, *Memorias* (Madrid, 1894–1897), II:85.

[62] Onís to Irujo, January 4, 1819, in A.H.N., Est., 5645.

[63] That Adams yielded Texas knowing that Onís' instructions authorized the latter to give it up is an unreasonable supposition. Yet it was suggested in debates at the time, in 1844, and recently in Richard Stenberg, "The Boundaries of the Louisiana Purchase," *Hispanic American Historical Review*, XIV (1934):54. Authorities cited by Stenberg include Adams' instruction to Forsyth of August 18, 1819, in *A.S.P., F.R.*, IV:245–250 [error for 658], and Adams' speech to the Young Men's Whig Club of Boston on October 7, 1844. To Forsyth, Adams said he knew that "both in relation to the grants of land in Florida, and to the western boundary, the terms which he [Onís] obtained were far within the limits of his instructions." He did not apply that specifically to the Texas question, however. In a part (not quoted by Stenberg) of the Boston speech, which was given when Texas was definitely the focus of attention, Adams said the letter to Forsyth did not refer to the western boundary. This conflicts with the wording of the letter if one takes it to mean the western boundary in general. An analysis of all Adams' statements on the matter, however, indicates that, although he knew that Onís could have accepted a different arrangement on the line north of the Red River, he did not know that the Spaniard was authorized to take any limit west of the Sabine, which appeared to have been definitely settled late in 1818.

[64] Onís to Irujo, January 11, 1819, in A.H.N., Est., 5645; Onís to Adams, January 11, 1819, in *A.S.P., F.R.*, IV:615.

[65] Onís to Irujo, January 12, 1819, in A.H.N., Est., 5645.

[66] Onís to Adams, January 16, 1819, in *A.S.P., F.R.*, IV:615–616.

[67] Adams, *Memoirs*, IV:219. In his despatch to Irujo of January 16, 1819, Onís explains his determination to proceed on his own initiative; see A.H.N., Est., 5661.

[68] Adams, *Memoirs*, IV:231.

[69] Irujo to Onís, October 23, 1818, in A.H.N., Est., 5643.

[70] Onís to Adams, February 1, 1819, in *A.S.P., F.R.*, IV:616–617.

[71] Adams, *Memoirs*, IV:238–239.

[72] *Ibid.*, p. 244. A map illustrating the various boundary proposals appears in Thomas M. Marshall, *History of the Western Boundary of the Louisiana Purchase* (Berkeley, 1914), facing p. 66. See also Charles O. Paullin, *Atlas of the Historical Geography of the United States* (Washington and New York, 1932), pp. 66–68 and plate 95A.

[73] Onís to Irujo, February 8, 1819, in A.H.N., Est., 5661.

[74] Onís to Adams, February 9, 1819, in *A.S.P., F.R.,* IV:617–619.

[75] Adams, *Memoirs,* IV:250.

[76] Onís to Irujo, February 16, 1819, in A.H.N., Est., 5661.

[77] Adams, *Memoirs,* IV:253.

[78] Adams to Onís, February 13, 1819, in *A.S.P., F.R.,* IV:619–621.

[79] Onís to Irujo, February 16, 1819, in A.H.N., Est., 5661.

[80] Hyde de Neuville to Adams, February 16, 1819, in *A.S.P., F.R.,* IV:621–622.

[81] Adams, *Memoirs,* IV:261.

[82] Onís to Irujo, February 19, 1819, in A.H.N., Est., 5661.

[83] Adams, *Memoirs,* IV:269.

[84] *Ibid.,* pp. 258–259.

[85] Onís to Irujo, February 19, 1819, in A.H.N., Est., 5661.

[86] Adams, *Memoirs,* IV:255; Onís to Irujo, January 23, 1819, in A.H.N., Est., 5661.
Note that in 1933 Dr. Frederick Merk and Dr. Charles O. Paullin disagreed on this point, but both assumed that there was a definite clarification, in Charles O. Paullin, *op. cit.,* Frederick Merk, Review of same, in *New England Quarterly,* VI (1933) :620–625; and correspondence regarding the review, *ibid.,* pp. 847–852.

[87] "Treaty of Amity, Settlement, and Limits, Signed at Washington, February 22, 1819," in D.S., Treaties. See also Miller, *Treaties,* III:3–64, for the most reliable published edition, with excellent explanatory notes.

CHAPTER VII

RATIFICATION AND EXECUTION, 1819–1821

JUBILANT REACTIONS

THE UNITED STATES SENATE unanimously approved the Adams-Onís Treaty on February 24, 1819.[1] It was welcomed by nearly all political groups throughout this country, a fact which in all fairness should be emphasized in view of the acrimonious controversy of twenty-five years later over the relinquishment of Texas.

Adams, unwittingly suggesting the disheartening wrangles that were to follow while Spain delayed ratification for two years, wrote in his diary on the day of signing:

It was, perhaps, the most important day of my life. What the consequences may be of the compact this day signed with Spain is known only to the all-wise and all-beneficent Disposer of events, who has brought it about in a manner utterly unexpected and by means the most extraordinary and unforeseen. Its prospects are propitious and flattering in an eminent degree. May they be realized by the same superintending bounty that produced them! May no disappointment embitter the hope which this event warrants us in cherishing, and may its future influence on the destinies of my country be as extensive and as favorable as our warmest anticipations can paint! Let no idle and unfounded exultation take possession of my mind, as if I could ascribe to my own foresight or exertions any portion of the event. It is the work of an intelligent and all-embracing Cause. . . . The acquisition of the Floridas has long been an object of earnest desire to this country. The acknowledgment of a definite line of boundary to the South Sea forms a great epocha in our history. The first proposal of it in this negotiation was my own, and I trust it is now secured beyond the reach of revocation. . . . I record the first assertion of this claim for the United States as my own, because it is known to be mine perhaps only to the members of the present Administration, and may perhaps never be known to the public—and, if ever known, will be soon and easily forgotten.[2]

Jackson, who was some years later to berate Adams for the concessions made, had given the settlement his approval when the treaty was signed. He repeated his statement in a letter to Monroe a year later:

. . . I am clearly of your opinion, that for the present, we ought to be content with the Floridas—fortify them, concentrate our population, confine our frontier to proper limits, until our country, to those limits, is filled with a dense population; it is the denseness of our population that gives strength

---

[1] For notes to chap. vii, see pp. 197–201.

and security to our frontier. With the Floridas in our possession, our fortifications completed, Orleans, the great emporium of the west, is secure. The Floridas in the possession of a foreign power, you can be invaded, your fortifications turned, the Mississippi reached, and the lower country reduced.[3]

Jackson's belief that the public would be mollified for the loss of Texas by other acquisitions proved correct. Even the western Senators voted for the treaty. *Niles' Weekly Register* gave Jackson credit for the influence which his Florida campaign had had on the Spaniards:

Something, at last, has resulted from our long negociations with Spain—in which, by the bye, we apprehend that gen. *Jackson* has acted as a powerful mediator;—THE FLORIDAS ARE CEDED. We shall hear great grumblings about this on the other side of the Atlantic, and hope that matters are so fixed that we may get *possession* before the intrigues of jealous foreigners can interfere to prevent the ratification of a bargain which they have not any right to meddle with. The fact has long been evident, that sovereignty over these countries was needful to our peace and quietness, and that we would possess them by fair or foul means—by treaty or by force. We have preferred the former, and Spain has happily agreed to do that which her own interest prompted— for the Floridas, though so valuable to us, have always been a real incumbrance on her.[4]

The *National Register,* a journal which had supported William J. Crawford[5] for the presidency against Monroe in 1816, rejoiced in even broader terms, calling the yielding of Texas

... fully justified by the cession of the Floridas by Spain, ... for the first time, our government begins to see its way to the Northern Pacific Ocean with any thing like a clear and definite view of sovereignty. . . . It is thus we stride, from object to object; and shall eventually light upon the banks of the river Columbia and the shores of the Pacific! What magnificent prospects open upon us![6]

Clay's opposition, previously mentioned as a source of anxiety for Adams, seems to have been dictated largely by his antagonism toward Jackson and toward the administration, with which the hero of New Orleans was then on good terms. Congress had just declined (in votes taken on February 8, 1819) to censure Jackson for his Florida escapade, after a series of debates which developed into spectacular social events and drew to the House the largest crowds it had ever entertained. Clay's diatribe against Jackson had been the feature of this discussion, but even he agreed that the Spanish officials in Florida deserved punishment.[7]

Europe's Reception of the Treaty

Of even more immediate importance was the foreign reception of the treaty. In Madrid, after an early favorable reaction, serious resistance developed; whereas in this country the only serious deprecation came as a result of a political machination of twenty-five years later.

Onís was relieved at the conclusion of the "arduous and confused [*escabroso*] negotiation," and prepared to leave for home.[8] The purport of his whole series of despatches is that he felt he had made a good bargain in exchanging the Floridas for Texas (as he interpreted it), and that the concession in the Northwest was necessary to obtain a peaceful agreement.

Hyde de Neuville not only congratulated Onís on obtaining all that could be expected "in disputing the terrain foot by foot,"[9] but sent to Paris a 25-page memoir on the whole affair, wherein he described it by saying:

> In this long struggle of noble, but too easily irritable passions, I have seen at times force which offends, weakness which misleads, I have seen exaggerated pretensions, imprudent ideas, ill-studied calculations; but also more often honor, the interest of the Country, true patriotism in the struggle. . . . Reason, wisdom, generous sentiments have prevailed.[10]

Copies of the treaty were sent to Spain by Don Joaquín Zamorano, Spanish consul at Alexandria, Virginia, and by John Forsyth, the new United States minister, who sailed for Madrid on the U.S. sloop-of-war "Hornet" in March. Before an attempt is made to consider Forsyth and tell of his adventures in a field which proved foreign to his abilities and experience, it is important to note the arrival in Madrid on April 24 of Onís' messenger, and the reception accorded his news.

Throughout the study of diplomacy at Madrid in these years, one receives the impression that the most competent and cool-headed foreign observer there was the British ambassador, Henry Wellesley. His despatches to Castlereagh give one of the clearest accounts available of the complex procedure there. And although for part of the time the Russian Tatistcheff displaced him in the King's intimacy, no doubt Wellesley, because of his years of residence there, could perceive what was going on more readily than Erving or the inexperienced Forsyth.

Wellesley wrote on April 26 that Irujo had received word of the treaty, and "expressed himself to be on the whole satisfied with it." Wellesley saw, however, what was to prove to be the most significant objection to the document on the part of the Spanish government.

> I asked him [wrote the British ambassador] whether it contained any stipulations binding the Government of the United States not to acknowledge the Independence of Buenos Ayres. He said that it contained no such stipulation, but that he was satisfied that such a measure was not in the contemplation of the American Government.[11]

One must note that the United States had just informed England that it expected soon to recognize the consul-general appointee of Buenos Aires and would be pleased if Britain would concur. Castlereagh not only told Wellesley of this, but gave a less explicit statement of it to the Spanish ambassador at London, authorizing him to transmit it to Irujo if he wished.[12]

Possibly Irujo had sufficient judgment to perceive that, with the ratification of the treaty hanging in the balance, the United States would hardly give the deliberate affront of recognizing an insurgent Spanish colony. It is to be doubted that he knew that the British had declined to act in coöperation with the United States in the matter, or that he foresaw internal dissensions in the United Provinces of the La Plata which were temporarily to weaken their claim to recognition. But in his letter of November 28, 1818, Onís had written that the reports of Special Commissioners John Graham and Caesar Rodney on the condition of the insurgent provinces, and the delay in the return of their colleague, Theodorick Bland, would probably prevent the recognition of Buenos Aires in the coming session of Congress.[13] Irujo received this despatch shortly before his conversation with Wellesley, and perhaps it explains his statement to the latter.

The British ambassador also on that occasion told of asking Irujo

> whether there was any stipulation restraining the traffic in warlike stores with the Spanish Insurgents. He said that there was nothing in the treaty to that effect, but that effectual measures would be taken by the Government of the United States for preventing any such traffic in future.[14]

Onís indeed had turned to conversations on that problem with

Adams as soon as the treaty was signed; but the "effectual measures" of the United States were not forthcoming.

Erving was still in Madrid on May 1, 1819, and wrote then as follows:

> I understand that they are highly delighted with the treaty, and I have no doubt of it, Mr Irujo takes all the merit to himself, & I am told that it has given to him considerable security in his place; it has enabled him also to procure the restoration of Mr Heredia (one of those dismissed from the council of War) who has always been the principal person consulted on American affairs & who boasts that he drew up the last instructions to Mr Onís.[15]

Further evidence that at first the treaty was well received in Spain is seen in the fact that its negotiators were promptly rewarded in true eighteenth-century diplomatic style. To Onís, besides the Grand Cross of the Order of Isabella the Catholic, which he had received in 1817, came appointments as counselor of state and ambassador to Russia (the latter not long after was superseded by a similar appointment to Naples).[16] Orders were also given on April 30 to bestow upon Hyde de Neuville the Grand Cross of the Order of Isabella the Catholic, and lesser honors and appointments upon the various secretaries, messengers, and consuls associated with Onís.[17]

The approvals and rewards cited, though, were only the first-blush reactions of Irujo and the King. Wellesley reported that on the receipt of the treaty King Ferdinand VII approved it and ordered that it be ratified at once, but that Irujo, whose "chief endeavor ... was to avoid all responsibility ... desired that it might be submitted to the Council of State, alleging that the Council having seen and approved the instructions .·. . ought likewise to examine the act itself previous to its ratification."[18]

If one concedes that the Englishman knew whereof he spoke in that instance, this caution on the part of Irujo brought on his downfall. On the very day, May 1, 1819, that Erving wrote telling of the approval accorded the treaty, resistance to it appeared when it was submitted to the *Consejo de Estado.*

Irujo appeared before the King and his advisers, and read to them the minutes of the meeting of the previous October in which they had authorized giving wide discretionary powers to Onís. He assured them that the minister had accordingly executed the treaty within the terms of his instructions and declared that, although the treaty was not all that could be desired, it was the best which could have been obtained.[19] No effective charges, in fact, were ever made that Onís exceeded his instructions, and such an allegation was never used in the dispute over the ratification.

The majority of the members present favored ratification, but sufficient opposition arose to cause postponement of final action. It is essential to note that at this time no official resistance in the *Consejo* developed on account of the land grants. One Guillermo Hualde, a priest who was secretary of the *Consejo,* bemoaned the great concessions made, and carried his objection to the point of saying that the treaty should not be ratified. He maintained that the acquisition of the Floridas would only enable the United States, in whose good pretensions he had no faith, to expand into Cuba and the Caribbean, and that England would declare war on Spain rather than allow such a gain by its American rival. The Duke of Infantado (a prominent noble who had been in high positions since before the Napoleonic invasion) agreed, and insisted that the United States should be made to promise not to invade Spanish possessions nor to give its aid or protection to the Spanish American insurgents.

That the Florida cession was not to produce such resistance from England is foreseen in a pertinent comment by Sir Henry Wellesley, who wrote that

it is extraordinary that the cession of the Floridas should now be made a point of difficulty when it is notorious that that cession was always considered as inevitable, and that the only obstacle which impeded the negociation with the Government of the United States was the settlement of the Boundaries upon the North Western frontier. I have very little doubt however of the Treaty's being ratified, and the language which will be held upon the occasion of its ratification will be that the King could not in honor refuse to abide by a Treaty which had been signed by his Plenipotentiary but that he so much disapproved its conditions that he had disgraced those of his Ministers . . . who had prepared and issued the instructions under which it was negociated.[20]

Both Wellesley and Erving sensed at this time some uneasiness outside the ranks of the *Consejo* over the status of the grants which had been made in Florida by Ferdinand to his favorites just previous to the cession, an uneasiness which was confirmed by subsequent developments in Washington. And the whole Spanish court was growing irritated at the manner in which the new minister, Forsyth, conducted himself.

In view of previous manifestations it is not surprising to find that the difficulty over the land grants was brought forward by the treaty's one violent opponent in this country, Henry Clay. According to Adams, Clay on March 8 called on President Monroe to say that the concessions had been made on January 23, 1818, the day before the date stipulated in the treaty.[21] Clay was wrong in detail, but not in substance.

The secretary of state turned to the correspondence of the department and found that letters written by Erving the previous year had indeed warned him of the danger. It has been shown previously that Erving's despatches gave the date of the Puñonrostro grant as of December 17, 1817. Adams had been thrown off his guard, however, by Erving's statement that Pizarro had said enough to convince him that there would be no trouble on that score.[22] The Vargas grant clearly was made after the date set in the treaty, and it never seriously entered the controversy. The substantially correct assumption was that the most important grant, that to Alagón, had the same date as that to Puñonrostro.

The difficulties which followed are so notorious that they need be only summarized here.[23] Adams, contrite because he had not noticed the date of December, 1817, in the Puñonrostro grant, consulted Hyde de Neuville at once, and then wrote Onís asking an explanation. The Spanish minister replied with a specific declaration that he understood and intended that the Alagón, Puñonrostro, and Vargas grants should be void. Hyde de Neuville obliged with a letter saying that that was also his understanding during the negotiation.[24] I have previously advanced the belief that Onís did not consciously deceive Adams; that his instructions do not appear to have given him the exact dates of the land grants; and that, pursuant to directions to relinquish the land grants if he could not save them without blocking the negotiation, he had meant to give them up. Later Adams assumed the position that, inasmuch as the grantees had not taken possession of their lands, the concessions would not have been binding upon the King of Spain, and therefore, according to the treaty wording, were void no matter what their dates.[25]

None of the grantees had, indeed, occupied the extensive regions involved. But an agent of Alagón, one Garrido, was formally put in possession by the Spanish governor at St. Augustine, and arrived in Washington late in March.[26] Onís remarked that that action was unfortunate, since on such basis the grant would be upheld by the courts of the United States, and it might be impossible for the King to yield on the point, a step Onís considered necessary in order to keep peace with the United States.[27]

That such a yielding must be made became at once evident when Adams sent to Spain by Forsyth a form of declaration to be signed coincident with the King's ratification, affirming that the three disputed grants were void. At President Monroe's behest Forsyth was authorized to exchange the ratifications even though the declaration should not be signed, but this was not revealed at the time.[28]

FORSYTH'S MISSION FAILS

The new minister himself must be considered as one of the irritating factors contributing to the disappointing delay in ratification. Forsyth had been chairman of the Foreign Relations Committee of the House of Representatives until November, 1818, when he was elected to the Senate from Georgia to fill a vacancy.[29] He served a short time in that body, although he was offered and accepted the Spanish appointment in December. It was confirmed on February 15, 1819, and he then resigned from the Senate. Onís at the time said he was pleased, considering the "gentleness and talent" of the Georgian.[30] Adams was not so approving. He declared later that his bitter opponent, Secretary of the Treasury Crawford, was responsible for the appointment, and that Forsyth "had neither the experience, nor the prudence, nor the sincerity, nor the delicacy of sentiment suited for such a station."[31] Nor did he know Spanish.

The unfortunate complication of the land grants jeopardized Forsyth's mission from the first, and he went under the cloud of mutual suspicion, bearing a demand for a post-treaty declaration which would inevitably antagonize the Spanish officials. An annoying incident over the handling of his baggage at Cádiz, on April 15, gave him a bad initial taste of Spanish procedure.

Forsyth on his arrival at Madrid three weeks later conferred with Erving, who soon departed in disgust. Erving had recently engaged in a disagreeable controversy with Irujo over claims of certain merchants, the most notable case being that of Richard W. Meade, whose complications over a financial matter had resulted in his imprisonment for two years. Irujo found one note so offensive that he declined to receive it.[32] Erving, some years later when his ire had perhaps grown through meditation, wrote that he "returned in a state of great irritation and mortification, not, as Mr. Adams has supposed, because the negotiation had been removed to Washington, but because in the course of it I had been treated with indignity."[33]

After Erving's departure, Forsyth's presentation of the demand that the declaration concerning the land grants be signed produced a storm of protest and a violent court intrigue stirred up by Alagón and his associates. Most active among the latter was the minister of grace and justice, Juan Esteban Lozano de Torres, a former chocolate seller of Cádiz. The appointment of this illiterate and unscrupulous man is one of the notorious incidents in the corrupt reign of Ferdinand VII. Among the tales told of him are that he seldom presented himself to the King without shedding tears of affection, and that he always carried the King's picture conspicuously hanging from his neck.[34] He and the Duke of Alagón, both described by one Spanish writer as belonging in a "gallery of sinister figures,"[35] at the time appeared the most influential associates of Ferdinand, with the possible exception of Tatistcheff. Alagón, commander of the King's personal guards, was also his constant companion in revelry.

It can hardly be supposed that all the officials were subject to the same influences, and such a sane observer as Wellesley saw that the more fundamental bases of resistance to the Adams-Onís Treaty were concerns over the extremely large territorial cessions and over the recovery and protection of the Spanish colonial empire. Forsyth specifically noted as major objections that the United States' boundary should not have been allowed to extend to the "Pacifick," and that Britain would be offended.[36]

The results of this intrigue were the overthrow and banishment from the court on June 12 of Irujo and Heredia, an attempt to obtain English backing, and a continued refusal to give satisfactory replies to Forsyth. Wellesley reported that members of the *Consejo de Estado* approached him privately to ask if his government had remonstrated against the cession of the Floridas, and that he had replied that Britain had not chosen to interfere even in view of the "inconvenience" which might result from the United States' possession of the Floridas.[37]

The procrastination irritated Forsyth, whose ineptitude in the situation was revealed by his often-quoted note of June 21 to González Salmón (the brother-in-law of Onís), who temporarily succeeded Irujo as secretary of state. After disclaiming intention of threat, although the tone of his letter was ominous, Forsyth went on:

> I know too well the abundant resources, the expanding power, the youthful vigor of my country, to degrade her character by using language unworthy of it; if not by my respect for Spain, I should be prevented by the fear of the deserved resentment of my own country; I should not be easily forgiven for condescending to say how she would punish an act of perfidy. It is by her acts, and not by the railings of her ministers, that she will be known to those who violate the faith pledged to her. But there is this, which a just Government will more cautiously avoid than even the well-founded resentment of a powerful nation—the degradation of conscious baseness. No wise King will dare to do an act which would deprive him of the respect of all nations, sully the reputation of his kingdom in the eyes of the civilized world, and deprive his people of the strongest incentive to virtuous exertions, under every dispensation of Heaven—the confidence in the integrity of their Government.[38]

Such an insulting manner of address to a nation which, however temporarily demoralized, was extremely sensitive in its respect for regal eminence virtually ended any hope of success for Forsyth.

No reply was received to that note for seven weeks. Meanwhile Ferdinand called a session of the *Consejo* on June 30, in which a majority of the members agreed that the treaty was undesirable, because too much territory was ceded, because there was no guaranty in it by the United States not to recognize Buenos Aires, and because there was no promise from that country to enforce its neutrality toward the Spanish American rebels.[39] Extreme irritation was manifest over the demand for signature of the post-treaty declaration and over the insulting nature of Forsyth's notes. One member, the Duke of Parque, described the declaration request as "unjust, irritating, scandalous, and lacking in all reason," and said Forsyth's latest note "is irritating, insolent, audacious, and directly offends the respect which we all owe to Your Majesty."

On the next night at a meeting attended by the King, the *infante* Don Carlos, and six ministers, the conclusions reached at the previous meeting were discussed and means were sought to delay ratification until more favorable circumstances might arise. It was decided that, "taking as a pretext" the request for signature of the land-grant declaration, ratification should be withheld, but the decision should not be announced; that efforts should be made to obtain English support; and that in place of further dealings with Forsyth, a new minister should be sent to Washington in an attempt to gain a more favorable settlement.[40] At the same time a report was made on the defenses of Cuba and orders were given to strengthen the fortifications. On such bases ratification was withheld. The period provided therefor in the treaty expired on August 22, 1819.

It must be emphasized, in fairness to Onís and Pizarro, that the members of the *Consejo* did not seriously take into account the difficulties of the negotiation, or the stress of circumstances which had forced their minister at Washington to make the concessions he had. Their preoccupation with European affairs, court intrigues, a dispute with Portugal, and the Spanish American revolutions partly explains their attitudes. Further, it may be doubted that many of them were acquainted with the voluminous correspondence involved, or with the facts. Said Sir Henry Wellesley:

I am assured that M. Lozano de Torres who is now the King's principal adviser is ignorant even of the geographical position of the countries which form the principal objects of the negociations with Portugal and with the United States, and it may be doubted whether the King himself is much better informed upon these subjects.[41]

Allegations ran rife among the foreign observers concerning the real responsibility for nonratification, showing among other things that the land-grant issue was not regarded as the primary obstacle. Particularly prone were they to blame England, less so to hold Russia and France guilty. The official correspondence shows no justification for such charges, however.

To be sure, some Englishmen were greatly disturbed by the cession of the Floridas, as the Spanish declared that they would be. The Marquis of Lansdowne, a veteran leader of the Whig opposition in the House of Lords, in May, 1819, decried the cession of the Floridas and the threat to Caribbean commerce. But his demand for active interference was discountenanced by the prime minister, Lord Liverpool, and Castlereagh, who more highly valued peaceable relations with the United States.[42] Rumors were widespread that to offset the Florida cession England had acquired Cuba from Spain, and this aroused certain groups in the United States, although *Niles' Weekly Register* published the reports with some skepticism concerning their truth.[43]

Naturally, the extension of the United States into the Floridas made this country a formidable Caribbean power, with hundreds of miles of added shore line and with new strategic positions, and brought it within striking distance of Cuba. Toward that island many expansionists in the United States were already casting longing glances. Well might Spain hope that the dislike of the greatest maritime Power for such a menace to its own Caribbean plantation interests would arouse active English opposition. On that supposition Spanish officials based renewed appeals to British diplomats and, apparently, one more concrete scheme. Wellesley wrote in July, 1819, that the archplotter and former rebel José Alvarez de Toledo was being sent to England as a special emissary. It was alleged that he would offer the Floridas to England for a loan of six million dollars, which would be sufficient to meet the pecuniary claims of the United States against Spain. The plan fell through, however, as Toledo for some reason did not present himself at the foreign office, and the Spanish ambassador there falsely declared to Castlereagh that he had never heard of such a person.[44]

One possibility appears wherein British diplomacy might have contributed to the delay in ratification by Spain, although the policy of England was clearly otherwise. In March, before receiving word of the treaty's signature, Castlereagh gave San Carlos, the Spanish ambassador, a vague idea of the intention of the United States to recognize Buenos Aires.[45] This was based on a definite overture to England presented by the United States minister, Richard Rush, for concurrent action in that matter, which Castlereagh refused. It may be that such information stirred Spanish fears and strengthened the demands of the treaty's opponents for a guaranty of nonrecognition. On the other hand, it appears that Irujo used the knowledge of such menacing intentions on the part of the United States to show the necessity of settling at once, and at all costs, with that Power. Other indications of British policy lead to the belief that it was for that purpose that Castlereagh relayed the information to San Carlos.

The documents show that on numerous occasions the British officials, particularly Castlereagh and Wellesley in their diplomatic pursuits, emphasized the desire not to intervene nor to antagonize the United States. They pointed out to Spain the probability of aggression by the United States if offended, urged Ferdinand and his ministers to ratify, and frankly explained that policy to the United States ministers at Madrid and London.[46]

France was somewhat less definite, but anxiously pressed both parties to avoid a breach. Irujo reported to the King and ministers that the French ambassador at Madrid, Montmorency, Duke of Laval, had urged that Spain make up her mind promptly in the matter, in order to avoid the unfortunate results which it seemed would necessarily follow any delay.[47] He also stated, as is confirmed by Forsyth's despatches, that Montmorency had appealed to Forsyth to agree to ratification without requiring the explanatory declaration on the land grants. Montmorency "absolutely hooted" at the possibility of Ferdinand's signing the supplementary paragraph, and asked to be allowed to convey some indication that the grants might be recognized.[48]

In that recommendation Montmorency followed closely the policy of his government as outlined by the new foreign minister, Marquis Dessolle, to Albert Gallatin. The latter wrote in July, 1819, that Dessolle's disposition was very friendly and that

this Government is sensible of the danger which that of Spain would run by not ratifying. The French Ambassador will give his advice accordingly, but with what degree of energy and what effect, I cannot say: and, as it is only a ratification for which they are anxious, he may also advise Mr Forsyth to exchange the ratifications without minding the land claims.[49]

Such a procedure appears consistent with the general policy of the Powers to maintain peace in Europe and to further a pacification of the Americas which might open the Spanish colonies to European trade. Whatever rivalries for that commerce might develop, surely a war between Spain and the United States would be disadvantageous to all.

Despite rumors then current, Russia seems to have been equally amenable to the new arrangement. First reports had linked the Czar's minister Tatistcheff with the maneuverings of Lozano de Torres and Alagón against the treaty. Earlier evidence of the Russian's antipathy to Wellesley and his interference in Spanish court intrigues certainly make the existence of such a connection seem plausible. Indeed, Count Polética, the new Russian minister at Washington, admitted to Adams that, despite official Russian declarations, his colleague in Madrid might be playing a double game.[50] At the same time, Adams was convinced of the friendly attitude of Polética, as well as of that of Count Pozzi di Borgo, the Czar's ambassador at Paris.

These ministers evidently had instructions from St. Petersburg to favor the treaty, as is indicated in Nesselrode's letter to Polética of November 27, 1819, and in a despatch of the preceding month sent by George W. Campbell, then minister of the United States in the Russian capital.[51] Both emphasized Nesselrode's belief that Spanish ratification was necessary in order to preserve peace.

Tatistcheff, apparently likewise instructed, officially gave his support to the Adams-Onís agreement. He assured Forsyth that he "personally believed the ratification necessary and proper for Spain, and certainly the policy of Europe required it to be done."[52] He addressed a note to the Spanish foreign office in which he cited the probability of occupation of the Floridas and Texas by the United States, their recognition of Buenos Aires and Chile, and their aid to other insurgents in the event Spain failed to accept the treaty.[53] Meanwhile, Tatistcheff's personal influence at Madrid was on the wane. He had been instructed to support British policy there and thus lost favor with Ferdinand. In October, 1819, he departed, never to return.[54]

Interesting speculation can be undertaken concerning the effect on Russian policy of the expansion of the United States to the Pacific. During the negotiation, news of Adams' desire to draw the boundary to the Coast could not have reached St. Petersburg in time to arouse protest before the signing of the treaty. Nesselrode's views have been shown to be friendly toward the United States after that time. But within seven months after the ultimate ratification of the treaty, in September, 1821, Alexander issued his famous ukase claiming exclusive jurisdiction on the North Coast above the Fifty-first Parallel. Such an avowal, which drew immediate protest from Adams, seems paradoxical in view of the previous cordial attitude. It appears, however, to have resulted not from studied Russian foreign policy, but from a temporary *coup* of the Russian American Fur Company, which naturally would have liked to extend and protect its commercial domain. That the Czar's government did not commit itself to upholding the ukase is made clear in the reports of the United States minister, Henry

Middleton, and manifested in the concession made by Russia in the convention with the United States signed in 1824.[55] She withdrew at that time to the line of 54° 40′.

SPAIN'S ATTEMPTED EVASION

Such a conciliatory attitude as that evinced by Russia was not contemplated by the Spanish officials in 1819, however, and in spite of the counsel of other Powers they determined not to ratify the Adams-Onís Treaty. Their decision was due more to court intrigue and to lack of appreciation of the exigencies of the situation than to justifiable objections.

When the time limit prescribed in the treaty expired in August, 1819, Forsyth's ire increased, and in succeeding months the imperious tone of his notes mounted. The Duke of San Fernando (appointed foreign minister in September), on the contrary, suavely carried on with the procrastination which had been agreed upon as Spanish policy.

Captain Read, of the sloop-of-war "Hornet," who had brought Forsyth to Spain and hoped to take back the ratification, had meanwhile returned home in disappointment. In September he again arrived in Spain, bearing new instructions written by Adams after the latter had heard of the Spanish delay, but before he knew of the proposal to send a special envoy to Washington. The letter advised Forsyth to accept ratification even though it should come after the time limit, provided it could be returned in time for the opening of Congress in December, 1819.[56] In reply to the stated desire of Ferdinand to consider the treaty "with deliberation," Adams went into a lengthy argument on the obligation of a sovereign to ratify a treaty signed by a minister who had full powers, as did Onís, and who had not exceeded his instructions.[57] This was a generally accepted principle of international law at the time, so far as absolute monarchies were concerned, though it has since fallen out of favor owing to the rise of representative government with its constitutional checks on executive authority.

Adams went on to explain how the fact that the grantees of Florida land had not actually fulfilled the conditions of occupation was an additional argument against the validity of the grants, and said that the minister should under no circumstances exchange ratifications without presenting the declaration for signature.

Should the Spanish ratification not arrive by the opening of Congress, the President would explain the whole matter to that body, holding Spain responsible for damages resulting from the delay and leaving Congress to authorize whatever action it saw fit.

Forsyth presented a note accordingly. Not receiving a satisfactory reply, he followed it up with one so offensive that San Fernando returned it describing it as "expressed in terms ... equally unprecedented and repugnant to the delicacy and attention which are peculiar to and are invariably observed in all diplomatic communications." Forsyth replied that, in view of the King's serious offense in withholding ratification, "no doubt it occurred to the enlightened understanding of your Excellency that from the nature of the subject but few sacrifices could be made to diplomatick courtesy."[58] Such bickering could accomplish nothing in a court where monarchical dignity was as highly revered as in Madrid. The net result of Forsyth's mission must be considered to have been only heightened antagonism. It should be stated that the very firm tone of Adams' instructions of August 18 gave Forsyth appreciable backing for his peremptory communications.

While these compliments were being passed back and forth, Ferdinand, after a succession of futile efforts, had finally found a man for the new mission to Washington, Major General Francisco Dionisio Vives. But in keeping with the agreed policy of awaiting some favorable turn in circumstances, General Vives was taking an inordinately long time to perform certain quarantines and reach Madrid in preparation for his journey.

Circumstances developed in such a way as to make more and more inevitable the ultimate ratification. Early in November Lozano de Torres, chief opponent of the agreement, was removed from the ministry of grace and justice. During that same summer and fall the expedition preparing at Cádiz for the pacification of the Americas (which would have strengthened Spain's position toward the United States) collapsed, and ominous dissensions appeared among the military forces. These disturbances were a phase of the intense conflict between liberals and conservatives which marked all of Ferdinand's reign.

Forsyth, then, was unable to obtain the ratification before Congress convened in December, 1819. When Captain Read of the "Hornet" returned empty-handed in November, President Monroe and his Cabinet busied themselves with preparing an appropriate message to Congress.

In some quarters there was agitation in favor of immediate aggressive action. The western constituencies which had produced the "War Hawks" of 1812 were not to be expected to sit placidly by while European court intrigue thwarted their expansionist dreams. During the summer the President made a tour of the western and southern states, and at Nashville heard the following toasts drunk:

The Seminole campaign—a check to Spanish perfidy, British intrigue, and Indian barbarity; most approved where best understood. The Floridas; Indispensable to our property; essential to our security.[59]

The belligerent tone of popular opinion in this country was evident to Mateo de la Serna, who had become chargé at Washington on the departure of Onís in May. He wrote of the "mockery, scorn and contempt" with which Spain was regarded in this country, and of the general sentiment that the government should at once execute the treaty as if ratified, even going to the point of capturing Texas.[60] The Spanish consul at St. Louis wrote alarmingly that the exploring expedition of Major Stephen H. Long into the upper Missouri country was part of the government's plan to seize the Provincias Internas; and, although the consul at Natchitoches realized that the abortive effort of Dr. James Long to liberate Texas was without official sanction, he saw that it represented a restless and ambitious frontier sentiment.[61] At such a critical juncture these menacing circumstances in the West might well have put the diplomatic controversy beyond the possibility of a peaceable settlement. The warnings reached Madrid while the monarchy was still awaiting a favorable turn of affairs. In view of the threatening situation, Onís, who had returned to Spain, was asked to prepare a detailed statement of the United States' naval forces which might be called out in the event of war, and he acted accordingly.[62]

THE INEVITABLE RATIFICATION

The dire threats which were popularly made relative to Spanish North America could not be unreservedly backed by the government at Washington, however. In a depression year, with the wolves of the election of 1824 already showing their teeth, with a heated controversy looming over Missouri's admission, with all Europe committed to peace and the United States to a policy of friendship with England, with the outcome of the Spanish colonial revolts uncertain, and a great expedition still heralded from Cádiz, well might the administration measure cautiously its diplomatic strides.

Adams was offended by the objections to his treaty. In November, 1819, he advised the President not to wait for the Spanish negotiator but explicitly to order the occupation of the Floridas by a large enough force to take it over peacefully, as an assertion of a right rather than a hostility. When the negotiator came, Adams thought that he should refuse to reopen the negotiation and should demand not only ratification but damages for the delay.[63] Monroe at first concurred.

Throughout the discussions of ensuing weeks Adams argued for his theory of the eventual identical extent of the United States and North America, maintaining that it was inevitable that this country should expand. But in consideration of the peaceful dispositions of England, France, and Russia, and upon the urgent behest of Hyde de Neuville, he retracted to the extent of recommending a conditional clause on the seizure of the Floridas. The President agreed after a long dispute, in which Crawford obstructed Adams' program, simply, as the latter believed, out of hostility.[64]

The message, as finally delivered, after recounting the justice of the treaty and the events since its signature (being accompanied by substantiating documents), recommended that Congress pass a law for the occupation of the Floridas, contingent upon the success or failure of the mission of General Vives in settling the matter.[65] Monroe emphasized the justice of immediate execution of the treaty, but asked deference to courtesy among nations, saying there would be little loss from a slight delay. His belief that the delay would be short was substantiated by the knowledge that England, France, and Russia had declined to back the Spanish policy and had urged agreement. Congress was willing to wait, and took no action.

Vives finally arrived in April, 1820. His efforts hardly need detailed narration. He simply expounded the policies previously declared in the councils of the Spanish government. This naturally was futile. In a note of April 14 he offered Spanish ratification on condition, first, that the United States strengthen its neutrality laws against the privateers who were aiding the colonial revolts; second, that a guaranty of the integrity of Spanish American possessions be given; and, third, that a promise be made not to recognize any of the insurgent provinces. Adams replied that no new neutrality laws were necessary, though the government would exert its best efforts in that direction; and naturally complete refusal met the demands for a territorial guaranty and for a promise of nonrecognition.[66]

Inasmuch as Vives' instructions gave him no further latitude, Adams' negative answer on the second and third points resulted in the reference of the matter once again to Madrid. Meanwhile events in Spain had inaugurated a series of steps leading directly to ratification. The liberal movement, intermittently in evidence ever since Ferdinand's restoration, gained sufficient momentum to precipitate a widespread military revolution. On March 7, 1820, the King agreed to accept the Constitution drawn up by the patriot government at Cádiz in 1812. This act transferred the sovereignty from the King to the nation and made it necessary for the Cortes to approve any cessions of territory.[67]

Among the men, many of them returning from exile, who now took the reins for a three-year period of quasi-liberal government, Evaristo Pérez de Castro was named minister of state, and until he could arrive in Madrid one Jabat filled the position. Forsyth described them as being favorably inclined toward settlement of the treaty dispute.[68] Jabat and Pérez, however, contributed little to the negotiation.

Reports which arrived in Madrid from La Serna in Washington, warning of the danger of seizure of the Floridas and Texas by the United States, stirred the *Consejo de Estado* to action. On April 23, 1820, they recommended putting off the issue, if possible without hostilities, until the Cortes should meet to approve the treaty.[69] Before the Cortes was finally organized in July, more news arrived from Washington. President Monroe had on March 27 asked Congress to delay action on the Floridas still further. A week later Clay had spoken in the House against the relinquishment of Texas, offering a resolution condemning the treaty. Subsequently Vives' futile meetings with Adams had taken place. Then the President had again asked postponement in view of the change in the Spanish government.[70] Accordingly, no occupation of the Floridas had as yet been authorized.

Fully aware of the possibility of a rupture and mindful of the assurance the treaty would give to the boundaries of Spanish North America, Narciso de Heredia, now again in favor, recommended ratification in a notable memoir drawn up late in July, 1820.[71] The *Consejo* approved, and the King asked the Cortes for the necessary authorization, his request being forthwith turned over to a committee.

The committee had another important document to guide them in their deliberations, the first volume of the *Memoria* of Onís.[72] This included a general treatise on the United States, followed by a brief summary of the negotiation of the treaty. It carried also reprints of the Franco-Spanish treaty of 1800, the Convention of 1802 with the United States, the Adams-Onís Treaty, and the "Verus" pamphlets of 1810, 1812, and 1817. Besides, there was published with the book a map by the French geographer Adrien H. Brué, showing the new demarcation line. Forsyth reported that the *Memoria* had appreciable influence in Spain, but he was so irritated by some of its statements regarding the United States that he circulated among principal members of the Cortes some remarks he had prepared upon it.[73]

The committee of the Cortes in a secret session on September 30, 1820, recommended ratification.[74] That action was accordingly authorized by the Cortes itself on October 5, and the disputed grants were declared null and void. The King signed the ratification on October 24. In the closing days an attempt was made to obtain from the United States some concession for the grantees of Florida lands, but this effort was headed off by the firm attitude of Forsyth.[75]

The Spanish approval was at once despatched to Washington, where Monroe felt obliged to submit it to the Senate for its advice and consent. That body passed a second resolution of advice and consent on February 19, 1821. Only four Senators, all from western states, opposed ratification.[76] On the second anniversary of the original signature, ratifications were exchanged by Adams and Vives.

Adams had urged the submission of the Spanish ratification to the Senate because he wanted a vote of confidence. It was also considered advisable because of the long delay. In explaining the approval he wrote that

against this there were only four votes—Brown, of Louisiana, who married a sister of Clay's wife; Richard M. Johnson, of Kentucky, against his own better judgment, from mere political subserviency to Clay; Williams, of Tennessee, from party impulses, connected with the hatred of General Jackson; and Trimble, of Ohio, for some maggot in the brain, the cause of which I do not yet perfectly know.[77]

The secretary had no way of appreciating the lack of coöperation between the Spanish executive and the foreign office. He continued to believe that Onís knew the date of the land grants and had consciously deceived him. Describing the happy prospect which had prevailed two years before, he said the treaty "promised well for my reputation in the public opinion. Under the petals of this garland of roses the Scapin, Onis, had hidden a viper."[78] It has been demonstrated, however, that Onís appears to have had no intent to deceive when he signed the treaty.

In Spain, Onís' reputation fared better. Indeed, during the year 1819 there was a widespread rumor to the effect that he would be made foreign minister to succeed Irujo. At the time, however, he was not sure how he and his handiwork would be received at Madrid, and he tarried some time in London and Paris. He was presented at the Court of St. James's and talked with leading figures in both capitals.[79] He was subsequently appointed ambassador to Russia, then to Naples, but did not serve in either post. He did go in 1821 to England, where he was ambassador for nearly two years.[80] He retired after that mission and died in Madrid in 1827. The tradition of diplomatic service in the family was carried on by his son Mauricio de Onís y Mercklein, who was foreign minister in the following decade. The older of Onís' two daughters had married José de Heredia, younger brother of Narciso, who had been attached to the legation in Washington and later occupied prominent positions in Spain.

With respect to the treaty, which was Onís' greatest task, it had been accepted largely through necessity, but it was generally acknowledged that the minister had done all that he could. He himself made an effort to assuage dissatisfaction over it by publishing a second volume of his *Memoria* after the ratification. This presented almost all the notes exchanged between himself and Adams and a brief evaluation of the treaty. This last section, which is of especial interest, has been generally overlooked in the United States because the second volume was never published in English.

Onís pointed out that the Floridas were really of little value to Spain.[81] To lose the opportunity to exchange them would have meant abandoning them without recompense. In an earnest effort to justify his actions, he cited nine advantages accruing to Spain from the treaty: the retention of Texas; the acquisition of territory beyond longitude 100° west and north of the Red River, which he now said had belonged to Louisiana; the provision of a wide desert between the boundary line and the settled portions of New Spain; the removal of the Russian menace to California by the extension of the domain of the United States to the Pacific; release from payment of claims which would surely amount to several times the five million dollars' worth assumed by the United States; lightening of the obligations imposed by the article of Pinckney's Treaty which provided that "the flag covers the goods" in neutral maritime commerce; the promise for return of deserters to ships by consuls; the admission of Spanish ships to Florida ports with special customs privileges; and the restoration of harmony, which would lessen the probability of recognition of the insurgent colonies by the United States.

LEGACIES OF THE TREATY

Onís' return to Spain ended his active rôle in the negotiations with the United States. The Spanish government was soon to be shorn of interest in the matter by the effective independence of Mexico, which came later in 1821. But on the American side the treaty became the basis of complications which carried over into the twentieth century.

The execution of the treaty involved a series of controversies which covered many more years than its negotiation. President Monroe proclaimed the agreement on Washington's Birthday, 1821, just two years after its original signature, and subsequently the necessary enabling acts were passed in Congress. Jackson was appointed to receive the ceded area and to become the territorial governor of what is now the state of Florida. Parts of West Florida, the definition of which was intentionally left vague in the treaty, had already been incorporated into the states of Louisiana,

Alabama, and Mississippi. The actual transfer of what remained of Spanish West Florida (the section east of the Perdido) was effected in a transaction between Spanish Commissioner José Callava and Jackson on July 17, 1821. Jackson's imperious nature showed itself when over a small argument concerning the delivery of certain papers he peremptorily ordered Callava imprisoned. Meanwhile, on July 10, the transfer of East Florida had been made at St. Augustine by Governor José Coppinger to Colonel Robert Butler.[82]

Thus ended years of frontier rivalry in the southeast, a region in which the Indian policies of the two countries had long been in contrast and conflict. Whereas the Spaniards had endeavored to maintain the Indian communities and to exploit their trade, the United States had begun its campaign of extermination. The Spaniards had tolerated and even befriended the Indians as neighbors, albeit they sometimes proved troublesome. But there was no room for Creek or Cherokee on land the United States expected to occupy. As a result of this policy the southern frontier was not pacified until the last sizable group of Indians had been removed or wiped out in the so-called "Second Seminole War," 1834–1842.[83]

Claims settlements also entailed years of controversy. The commission which was provided for in Article 11 reported on June 8, 1824, after having considered eighteen hundred claims for a wide variety of damages to United States citizens, chiefly those incurred in maritime shipping, and many resulting from the blockade of the South American coast by the Spanish royalists. Several of the claims were thrown out for lack of information, among them one for $491,153.33 (a Spanish commission had adjudicated it at $373,-879.83) from Richard W. Meade for supplies furnished the Spanish government and for illegal imprisonment growing out of the debt. Meade had been a merchant in Cádiz since 1803 and was a man of influence. The controversy over his claim was widely discussed in Spain, England, and the United States, and resulted in the publication of an argumentative tract as late as 1910.[84]

The commission finally adjudicated all the claims at a total of $5,454,545.13; but as the treaty limit of indemnity was five millions, each of the awards had to be reduced proportionately by 8⅓ per cent.[85]

The Superior Court judges in East and West Florida were authorized to study and adjudicate, as provided in Article 9 of the treaty, claims for damages done by military operations in the Floridas. The Treasury Department threw out most of the claims with the declaration that the "late operations" in the Floridas mentioned in the document did not include those of 1812 and 1813, and that those of 1814 were acts of war. A dispute over interest payments continued late into the century, but on the value of the claims which were finally allowed slightly over a million dollars was paid.[86]

Spain attempted in 1827 to collect from France the amount of the damages incurred by United States ships captured by French corsairs and condemned in Spanish ports from 1797 to 1801, to which the United States waived claim in the treaty.[87]

The boundary in the southwest was approved by Mexico, inheritor of Spanish sovereignty, in her treaty with the United States of January 12, 1828. The ratification of that treaty was delayed until 1831, partly by President Jackson's efforts to acquire Texas.[88] No successful survey was made for many years. The expedition of Captain R. B. Marcy in 1852 was the first effective exploration of the Red River.[89] As late as 1896 a Supreme Court decision settled a dispute between Oklahoma and Texas by defining the south instead of the north branch of the Red as the line of 1819. In a dispute over oil rights under the river's bed, the same tribunal made the treaty the basis for its decision in 1921 that the boundary was the south bank instead of the center of the river.[90] This decision regarding the black gold of the twentieth century was founded upon a provision of Article 3 of the document, agreed upon after a last-minute argument between Adams and Onís over navigation of the stream. Little did they imagine to what remote concerns their conclusion would extend!

It has been seen that the United States yielded Texas with regret, but, considering the limited knowledge that Adams had of the circumstances of the negotiation, it was not unreasonable that she did so. Had the treaty taken Texas from Spain, her ratification would certainly have been even more difficult to obtain. Hostilities might even have resulted. It is interesting to note the extreme statement of the late Professor Latané that "the relinquishment of Texas was an unfortunate mistake that later cost us the war with Mexico and made the Civil War inevitable."[91] One might ponder how well the young nation could have assimilated at that early date Texas and even more Mexican territory, which might have come to it in a war, and what effect such expansion would have had on the sectional strife of the country. Furthermore, it must be remembered that the decision to yield Texas was taken in full Cabinet council, and that Adams was not in favor of it.

However that may be, the United States received the almost abandoned Floridas and the valid Spanish claim to Oregon in exchange for her own debatable claim to Texas. On the south, the acquisition increased slave territory and gave us a more direct interest in Caribbean affairs. On the southwest, the limit almost immediately did prove too much of a restriction on our expansion, and the seeds of the Texas revolution were laid. In the upper Missouri country the legend of a "great American desert," which became current after the Long expedition, delayed settlement for some time, but the region was definitely secured for the migration which was inevitable.

Over the mountains, recognition was obtained for title to a region then far distant, to which few people journeyed for some years thereafter. An international boundary line was drawn, however, which remained as established for twenty-seven years, and the southern limits of the joint-occupation territory were defined.[92]

The English in relinquishing Astoria in 1818 had not, to be sure, admitted our title to that region, and they did not after the Adams-Onís Treaty was ratified. They claimed in 1826 the right to settlement and navigation as far south as the Thirty-eighth Parallel below the Spanish treaty line.[93] They proceeded, however, with slight resistance, to sign an agreement on August 6, 1827, which indefinitely prolonged the period of joint occupation beyond the original ten-year period, but which defined the limits no more specifically. Clay, during this negotiation, indicated his understanding that effectively the region was bounded on the south by the Adams-Onís line and on the north by the line of 54° 40' established in treaties with Russia.[94] For some time the Oregon country was dominated by the Hudson's Bay Company; but its influence did not extend below the Columbia, and no claim to territory below the Forty-second Parallel appeared in the negotiation of the treaty of 1846. Furthermore, that England accepted the line of

1819 is indicated by the fact that she made no effort to negotiate such a limit directly with Spain, as she did with Russia for the northern line of the jointly occupied area. Her interests were not, to be sure, so direct in the southern part of the Oregon territory, where fur was scarce, as they were in the Alaska line. But theoretically she would have been as much entitled to make such a treaty with Spain as the United States was to make that of 1824 with Russia concerning the northern limit of the jointly occupied area.

Thus the United States had a good title to Oregon, which for some time she did not execute. But when in the 1830's westward migration began, the missionaries and pioneers going southwest found themselves obliged to become foreigners on foreign soil and under a religion that many of them did not like to accept. Their eyes then naturally turned northwest. Miss Ellen Semple, in a book emphasizing the influence of geographic conditions, conceded the importance of this political factor when she wrote:

At the time when American trappers and traders found their way to the Pacific, California was a foreign possession. This fact, reinforced by the length and difficulty of the journey thither, sufficed to discourage the immigration of families, especially after the rebellion of Texas under American leadership had rendered citizens of the United States undesirable tenants of Mexican soil. . . . Oregon was as remote as California, and like it was barred by two thousand miles of plains, mountains, and desert; but it was claimed on solid grounds by the United States. Hence in this direction Americans turned when the uneasy spirit of migration began to stir along the Missouri and Mississippi frontier.[95]

The great trek moved westward along a path of empire secured by the Adams-Onís Treaty, and, partly by coincidence, the Oregon trail skirted closely the line of that agreement. Almost all the pioneers settled south of the Columbia in territory President Monroe would once have been willing to relinquish, but which Adams insisted on holding. The growth of their numbers forced the diplomats of the 1840's to recognize existing conditions of settlement.[96] That region, together with an area north of the Columbia, which was still disputed, was definitely confirmed to the United States in 1846. But the line of 1819 did not lose its importance even then, and it remains to separate the present states of California and Oregon.

In diplomacy the Adams-Onís Treaty revealed the growing influence of the United States. The country was still taking advantage of Europe's distress, as had been done in Jay's and Pinckney's treaties;[77] this time the distress was Spain's almost alone. But after the Napoleonic Wars the Powers of Europe were so anxious to keep the peace and to develop their maritime commercial lanes that they courted the favor of the United States assiduously and were willing to give her a free hand with Spain. All kept clear of a negotiation in which they might have had to defend a weak ally against an ambitious and growing republic, whose prominence in American commerce and politics made her a nation which no discreet Power would antagonize. All were poignantly aware of the greatly stimulated national consciousness after our "second war of independence," a consciousness which was to develop into the feeling of "Manifest Destiny." Accordingly, England, Russia, and France in some degree neglected their own possible territorial ambitions in the Americas and instructed their ministers at Washington to strive for cordial relations.

Thus Spain was forced to stand on her own and to negotiate as best she could, with a weak absolutist régime at home and a rebellious empire overseas. Even so, she retained Texas through the firmness of her negotiator, obtained a definite frontier in the hope of protecting her colonies, and secured release from embarrassing financial claims. The opponents of ratification blindly ignored the circumstances of the negotiation and Spain's desperate position in the Americas. Eventually common sense and necessity forced approval of the agreement reached by Onís and Adams.

NOTES TO CHAPTER VII

¹ United States Senate, *Journal of Executive Proceedings* (Washington, 1828), III:178.

² John Quincy Adams, *Memoirs* (Philadelphia, 1874–1877), IV:274–275.

³ Jackson to Monroe, June 20, 1820, in Andrew Jackson, *Correspondence* (Washington, 1926–1933), III:28; Adams, *Memoirs*, IV:238–239.

⁴ *Niles' Weekly Register* (Baltimore), XVI (February 27, 1819):3.

⁵ Wilhelmus B. Bryan, *History of the National Capital* (New York, 1916), II:168–169.

⁶ *National Register* (Washington), VII (February 27, 1819):129.

⁷ Mrs. Samuel H. Smith, *The First Forty Years of Washington Society* (New York, 1906), pp. 144–146; *Annals of Congress* (Washington, 1834–1856), XXXIII:631–655 and *passim*.

⁸ Onís to Irujo, April 24, 1819, in A.H.N., Est., 5645.

⁹ Hyde de Neuville to Onís, February 19, 1819, *ibid.*, 5661.

¹⁰ "Negotiation entre les Etats Unis et l'Espagne," Hyde de Neuville to Richelieu, February 23, 1819, in A.M.A.E., Corr. Pol., E.U., Suppl. 9.

¹¹ Wellesley to Castlereagh, April 26, 1819, in P.R.O., F.O., 72/224.

¹² Adams to Richard Rush (minister to Great Britain), January 1, 1819, in D.S., United States Ministers, Instructions, VIII; Castlereagh to Wellesley, March 12, 1810, in P.R.O., F.O., 72/222.

¹³ Onís to Pizarro (received by Irujo), November 28, 1818, in A.H.N., Est., 5644.

¹⁴ Wellesley to Castlereagh, April 26, 1819, in P.R.O., F.O., 72/224.

¹⁵ Erving to Adams, May 1, 1819, in D.S., Despatches, Spain, XVI.

¹⁶ MS biography of Onís (Madrid, 1827). The Order of Isabella the Catholic was established in 1815 to reward those who might aid in the defense of the Spanish American empire.

¹⁷ Irujo to Mateo de la Serna (Spanish chargé at Washington), April 30, 1819, in A.M.E., 225; José Pizarro, *Memorias* (Madrid, 1894–1897), II:92, and III:364–366. Pizarro's memoirs contain a bitter complaint of the discrimination against him in these awards. He, Narciso de Heredia, and Irujo were the only ones not honored, and the latter two ultimately were well recompensed. Pizarro, who with Onís and Heredia contributed the largest services in the negotiation, and who was exiled for his pains, had reason for complaint.

¹⁸ Wellesley to Castlereagh (private), June 24, 1819, in P.R.O., F.O., 72/224.

¹⁹ *Minuta* of the *Consejo de Estado*, May 1, 1819, in A.H.N., Est., 5661.

²⁰ Wellesley to Castlereagh (private), June 24, 1819, in P.R.O., F.O., 72/224.

²¹ Adams, *Memoirs*, IV:287.

²² See above, chap. vi, p. 135; also Erving to Adams (private), February 10, February 26, April 5, and September 20, 1818, in D.S., Despatches, Spain, XV–XVI. The Alagón grant was estimated at some seven million acres, and covered most of the peninsula; the Puñonrostro grant extended across the northern part from the St. John's to the Perdido; the Vargas concession included most of the area west of the Perdido, already claimed and actually occupied by the United States.

²³ The highly complex details of the land grants, with texts, dates, references, and map, are presented in D. Hunter Miller, *Treaties and Other International Acts of the United States of America* (Washington, 1931—), III: 20–31, 42–49.

²⁴ Hyde de Neuville to Richelieu, March 9, 1819, in A.M.A.E., Corr. Pol., E.U., Suppl. 9; Adams to Onís and Onís to Adams, March 10, 1819, and Hyde de Neuville to Adams, March 18, 1819, in *A.S.P., F.R.*, IV:651–653; Onís to Irujo, March 10, 1819, in A.H.N., Est., 5661.

²⁵ Adams to Hyde de Neuville, July 14, 1819, in *A.S.P., F.R.*, IV:653–654.

²⁶ Adams, *Memoirs*, IV:314–315. Alagón on May 29, 1819, deeded his lands to Richard S. Hackley, former United States consul at Cádiz. For the deed and the opinions of several lawyers supporting Hackley's claim, see Richard S. Hackley (compiler), *Legal Opinions on the Title of Richard S. Hackley to Lands in East Florida* (New York, 1831).

²⁷ Onís to Irujo, March 24, 1819, in A.H.N., Est., 5661.

²⁸ Adams, *Memoirs*, IV:290. The declaration was included with a supplement to general instructions for Forsyth, March 10, 1819; see D.S., United States Ministers, Instructions, VIII.

²⁹ A sketch of Forsyth's life introduces Professor E. I. McCormac's account of his successful term as secretary of state (1834–1841); see *American Secretaries of State* (New York, 1927–1929), IV:299–343. See also United States Congress, *Biographical Dictionary of the American Congress, 1774–1927* (Washington, D.C., 1928), p. 980.

³⁰ Onís to Irujo, February 17, 1819, in A.H.N., Est., 5661.

³¹ Adams, *Memoirs*, IV:521–522; see also *ibid.*, pp. 187, 190, 192–193, 241.

³² Irujo to Onís, February 18, 1819, in A.M.E., 225; Erving to Adams, March 4, 1819, in D.S., Despatches, Spain, XVI.

³³ Jabez L. M. Curry, "Diplomatic Services of George W. Erving," Massachusetts Historical Society, *Proceedings*, Ser. 2, V (1889):31.

³⁴ Diego San José, *Vida y "milagros" de Fernando VII* (Madrid, 1929), p. 205. The best special account of this period is by the late Marqués de Villa-Urrutia, *Fernando VII*, [Vol. I] *Rey constitucional* (Madrid, 1922). On the complex Spanish background, intrigues, and diplomacy here concerned, consult the thorough study of the ratification controversy in Charles C. Griffin, *The United States and the Disruption of the Spanish Empire, 1810–1822* (New York, 1937), pp. 191–243.

³⁵ Anonymous, *Los ministros en España desde 1800 á 1869* (Madrid, 1869), II:705–710.

³⁶ Forsyth to Adams, August 22, 1819, in D.S., Despatches, Spain, XVII.

³⁷ Wellesley to Castlereagh, June 8 to 14, 1819, in P.R.O., F.O., 72/224.

³⁸ Forsyth to González Salmón, June 21, 1819, in *A.S.P., F.R.*, IV:654–655; and in A.H.N., Est., 5661.

³⁹ *Minuta* of the *Consejo de Estado*, June 30, 1819, in A.H.N., Est., 5661; Forsyth to Adams, August 22, 1819, in D.S., Despatches, Spain, XVI.

⁴⁰ *Acta* of the *Junta de Ministros*, July 1, 1819, in A.H.N., Est., 5661.

⁴¹ Wellesley to Castlereagh (private), June 24, 1819, in P.R.O., F.O., 72/224.

⁴² James M. Callahan, in *Cuba and International Relations* (Baltimore, 1899), narrates the controversies on the matter in England. Illustrative matter is found in *Niles' Weekly Register*, XVI (May 1 and August 7, 1819):161–162, 385, and in J. Freeman Rattenbury, "Remarks on the Cession of the Floridas to the United States of America, and on the Necessity of Acquiring the Island of Cuba by Great Britain," *Pamphleteer* (London), XV (1819):261–280. See also J. Fred Rippy, *Rivalry of the United States and Great Britain over Latin America (1808–1830)* (Baltimore, 1929), pp. 69–70.

⁴³ *Morning Chronicle and Baltimore Daily Advertiser* (Baltimore), I (May 6, 1819):2–3; *Niles' Weekly Register*, XVI (May 22 and 29, August 28, 1819):210–211, 237, 438.

⁴⁴ Arthur P. Newton, "United States and Colonial Developments, 1815–1846," *Cambridge History of British Foreign Policy* (Cambridge, 1922–1923), II:226–228; Wellesley to Castlereagh (private), July 6, 1819, in P.R.O., F.O., 72/225; Castlereagh to Wellesley (private), July 21, 1819, *ibid.*, 72/222; Joseph B. Lockey, "The Florida Intrigues of José Alvarez de Toledo," Florida Historical Society, *Quarterly*, XII (1934):145–178. Gallatin did not believe Toledo ever got farther than Bordeaux; see Gallatin to Adams, July 29, 1819, in D.S., Despatches, France, XIX.

⁴⁵ Castlereagh to Wellesley, March 12, 1819, in P.R.O., F.O., 72/222.

⁴⁶ Castlereagh to Wellesley (private), January 10, 1817, *ibid.*, 185/66; Castlereagh to Wellesley (private), July 21, 1819, *ibid.*, 72/222; Wellesley to Castlereagh, August 6 and 24, 1819, *ibid.*, 72/225; Castlereagh to San Carlos, April 28, 1819, and San Carlos to González Salmón, July 17, 1819, in A.H.N., Est., 5661; Forsyth to Adams, August 22, 1819, in D.S., Despatches, Spain, XVII; Rush to Adams, July 16 and 21, 1819, in D.S., Despatches, Great Britain, XXIV.

⁴⁷ *Acta* of the *Junta de Ministros*, July 1, 1819, in A.H.N., Est., 5661.

⁴⁸ Forsyth to Adams (private), June 11, 1819, in D.S., Despatches, Spain, XVII.

⁴⁹ Gallatin to Adams, July 6, 1819, in D.S., Despatches, France, XIX. Dessolle was foreign minister from December, 1818, to November, 1819, when he was replaced by Decazes.

⁵⁰ Adams, *Memoirs*, IV:458–459.

⁵¹ Extract from Nesselrode to Polética, November 27/December 9, 1819, in *A.S.P., F.R.*, IV:676; Campbell to Adams, October 20/November 1, 1819, in D.S., Despatches, Russia, VII.

⁵² Forsyth to Adams (private), August 22, 1819, in *A.S.P., F.R.*, IV:661–662.

⁵³ Tatistcheff to González Salmón, August 15, 1820, quoted in Jerónimo Bécker, *Historia de las relaciones exteriores de España durante el siglo XIX* (Madrid, 1924–1927), I:477–479.

⁵⁴ Charles K. Webster, *Foreign Policy of Castlereagh, 1815–1822* (London, 1925), p. 226.

⁵⁵ This division of Russian interests is considered in Edward H. Tatum, Jr., *The United States and Europe, 1815–1823: A Study in the Background of the Monroe Doctrine* (Berkeley, 1936). See also Middleton to Adams, August 8/20, 1822, in D.S., Despatches, Russia, IX. The ukase is discussed, and the Convention of 1824 is printed with notes, in Miller, *Treaties*, III:151–162.

⁵⁶ Adams to Forsyth, August 18, 1819, in D.S., United States Ministers, Instructions, VIII.

⁵⁷ Adams quoted Emmerich de Vattel, *Le droit des gens* (Leyden, 1758; *The Law of Nations*, Philadelphia, 1817), Book II, chap. xii, par. 156; and Georg F. von Martens, *Précis du droit des gens* (Göttingen, 1789; *Summary of the Law of Nations*, Philadelphia, 1795), Book II, chap. i, par. 3. Cf. John B. Moore, *A Digest of International Law* (Washington, 1906), V:184–193.

⁵⁸ Forsyth to San Fernando, October 2 and 18, November 20, 1819, and San Fernando to Forsyth, November 12, 1819; enclosed with Forsyth to Adams, October 28 and November 27, 1819, all in D.S., Despatches, Spain, XVII.

[59] *National Intelligencer* (Washington), VII (June 29, 1819):3.

[60] La Serna to González Salmón, October 15, 1819, in A.H.N., Est., 5645.

[61] Juan Ortega to Felipe Fatio (consul at New Orleans), San Luis de los Illineses, June 6 and 16, 1819; Felix Trudeaux to Fatio, Natchitoches, June 9, 1819; and other correspondence enclosed with Viceroy Conde de Venadito to the *secretario de estado*, September 30, 1819, in A.G.I., Est., 33. The viceroy's despatch, one of a series of monthly reports, is printed, without the enclosures but with an illuminating historical introduction, in Alfred B. Thomas (ed.), "Documents Bearing on the Northern Frontier of New Mexico, 1818–1819," *New Mexico Historical Review*, IV (1929):146–164. See also Thomas, "The Yellowstone River, James Long and Spanish Reaction to American Intrusion into Spanish Dominions, 1818–1819," *ibid.*, pp. 164–177.

[62] Onís to San Fernando, Madrid, December 23, 1819, in A.H.N., Est., 5661.

[63] Adams, *Memoirs*, IV:432.

[64] The preparation of the message is described at length in Adams, *op. cit.*, pp. 432–466.

[65] James Monroe, Message to Congress, December 7, 1819, in *Compilation of the Messages and Papers of the Presidents, 1789–1897* (Washington, D.C., 1896–1899), II:54–58.

[66] Vives to Adams, April 14, 19, and 24, 1820, and Adams to Vives, April 18 and 21, and May 3, 1820, in *A.S.P., F.R.*, IV:680–684.

[67] Villa-Urrutia, *Fernando VII*, [Vol. I] *Rey constitucional* (Madrid, 1922), pp. 184–185; Rafael Altamira, "Spain, 1815–1845," *Cambridge Modern History* (Cambridge, 1902–1912), X:214–220.

[68] Forsyth to Adams, March 30, 1820, in D.S., Despatches, Spain, XVIII.

[69] *Minuta* of the *Consejo de Estado*, April 23, 1820, in A.H.N., Est., 5662.

[70] Monroe, Message to Congress, March 27, 1820, in *Messages and Papers*, II:69–70; Debates in Congress, April 3–4, 1820, in *Annals of Congress*, XXXVI:1719–1738, 1743–1781.

[71] *Memoria* of Heredia, July 22, 1820, in A.H.N., Est., 5565, Expediente 4. Heredia had been recalled from exile and restored to his position as councilor of state following the revolution of March, 1820. See Narciso de Heredia, *Escritos del Conde de Ofalia* (Bilbao, 1894), p. 47.

[72] Onís, *Memoria sobre las negociaciones entre España y los Estados-Unidos de América, que dieron motivo al tratado de 1819* (Madrid, 1820).

[73] Forsyth to Adams, October 11, 1820, in D.S., Despatches, Spain, XVIII.

[74] *Informe of Comisión de Política*, September 30, 1820, in A.H.N., Est., 5662.

[75] Correspondence of Forsyth and Pérez de Castro, October 6 to October 11, 1820, in *A.S.P., F.R.*, IV:696–701.

[76] Senate, *Journal of the Executive Proceedings* (Washington, D.C.), III:242–244.

[77] Adams, *Memoirs*, V:285–286.

[78] *Ibid.*, p. 290.

[79] Rush to Adams, June 18, 1819, in D.S., Despatches, Great Britain, XXIII; Gallatin to Adams, July 6, 1819, in D.S., Despatches, France, XIX.

[80] Forsyth to Adams, January 3, 1820, in D.S., Despatches, Spain, XVIII; MS biography of Onís (Madrid, 1827).

[81] Onís, *Memoria*, II:209–213.

[82] See *A.S.P., F.R.*, IV:740–808.

[83] The "Second Seminole War" is treated in Grant Foreman, *Indian Removal; the Emigration of the Five Civilized Tribes of Indians* (Norman, 1932).

[84] Frank W. Hackett, *The Meade Claim* (Washington, 1910); see *A.S.P., F.R.*, IV:144–155, 704–736. Edwin M. Borchard, in *Diplomatic Protection of Citizens Abroad* (New York, 1915), pp. 389–390, discusses the injustice of ruling out the Meade claim.

[85] John B. Moore, *History and Digest of International Arbitrations* (Washington, 1898), V:4487–4518.

[86] *Ibid.*, pp. 4519–4531.

[87] See A.H.N., Est., 5574, Expediente on French claims.

[88] Miller, *Treaties*, III:405–420.

[89] Charles O. Paullin, *Atlas of the Historical Geography of the United States* (Washington and New York, 1932), p. 20 and plate 39.

[90] 162 *U.S. Reports* (1896) 1–91; 256 *U.S. Reports* (1921) 70–93, 602–610; Isaiah Bowman, "An American Boundary Dispute," *Geographical Review*, XIII (1923):161–189.

[91] John H. Latané, *History of American Foreign Policy* (new ed., New York, 1934), p. 119.

[92] Philip C. Brooks, "The Pacific Coast's First International Boundary Delineation, 1816–1819," *Pacific Historical Review*, III (1934):62–79.

[93] Gallatin (minister to Great Britain) to Clay (secretary of state), December 2, 1826, in *A.S.P., F.R.*, VI:655–656.

[94] Clay to Gallatin, June 19, 1826, and February 24, 1827, *ibid.*, pp. 644–647.

[95] Ellen C. Semple, *American History and Its Geographic Conditions* (New York, 1903), p. 201.

[96] Frederick Merk, in "The Oregon Pioneers and the Boundary," *American Historical Review*, XXIX (1924):681–699, clearly shows that only the region between the Columbia and the Forty-ninth Parallel was really in contest in 1846, appreciably diminishing the diplomatic significance of the pioneer settlement south of that river. The English relinquishment of the region south of the Columbia, however, shows that England maintained no claim beyond the southern limit of Oregon set by the treaty of 1819. And the fact still remains that the pioneers, encouraged by the strengthening of the United States' title in that treaty, put the area between the Forty-second Parallel and the Columbia beyond diplomatic bargaining.

[97] Samuel F. Bemis, *Pinckney's Treaty: A Study of America's Advantage from Europe's Distress, 1783–1800* (Baltimore, 1926).

APPENDIX

THE ADAMS-ONÍS TREATY, 1819

TREATY OF AMITY, SETTLEMENT, AND LIMITS, signed at Washington February 22, 1819. Original in English and Spanish. Submitted to the Senate February 22, 1819. Resolution of advice and consent February 24, 1819. Ratified by the United States February 25, 1819. Ratified by Spain October 24, 1820. The Spanish instrument of ratification was submitted to the Senate February 14, 1821. (Message of February 13, 1821.) Resolution of advice and consent February 19, 1821. Ratified by the United States February 22, 1821. Ratifications exchanged at Washington February 22, 1821. Proclaimed February 22, 1821.[1]

[ORIGINAL]

Treaty of Amity, Settlement and Limits between The United States of America, and His Catholic Majesty.

The United-States of America and His Catholic Majesty desiring to consolidate on a permanent basis the friendship and good correspondence which happily prevails between the two Parties, have determined to settle and terminate all their differences and pretensions by a Treaty, which shall designate with precision the limits of their respective bordering territories in North-America.

With this intention the President of the United-States has furnished with their full Powers John Quincy Adams, Secretary of State of the said United-States; and His Catholic Majesty has appointed the Most Excellent Lord Don Luis de Onis, Gonsalez, Lopez y Vara, Lord of the Town of Rayaces, Perpetual Regidor of the Corporation of the City of Salamanca, Knight Grand-Cross of the Royal American Order of Isabella, the Catholic, decorated with the Lys of La Vendée, Knight-Pensioner of the Royal and distinguished Spanish Order of Charles the Third, Member of the Supreme Assembly of the said Royal Order; of the Counsel of His Catholic Majesty; his Secretary with Exercise of Decrees, and his

[1] Taken from Miller, *Treaties*, III:3-20. See also U.S., Dept. of State, *Treaty* series, no. 327; and 8 *Statutes at Large* 252-273, for other publications of the treaty. The text here reproduced is from the manuscript original used by Miller.

Envoy Extraordinary and Minister Plenipotentiary near the United-States of America.

And the said Plenipotentiaries, after having exchanged their Powers, have agreed upon and concluded the following Articles.

ARTICLE. 1.

There shall be a firm and inviolable peace and sincere friendship between the United-States and their Citizens, and His Catholic Majesty, his Successors and Subjects, without exception of persons or places.

ART. 2.

His Catholic Majesty cedes to the United-States, in full property and sovereignty, all the territories which belong to him, situated to the Eastward of the Mississippi, known by the name of East and West Florida. The adjacent Islands dependent on said Provinces, all public lots and Squares, vacant Lands, public Edifices, Fortifications, Barracks and other Buildings, which are not private property, Archives and Documents, which relate directly to the property and sovereignty of said Provinces, are included in this Article. The said Archives and Documents shall be left in possession of the Commissaries, or Officers of the United-States, duly authorized to receive them.

ART. 3.

The Boundary Line between the two Countries, West of the Mississippi, shall begin on the Gulph of Mexico, at the mouth of the River Sabine in the Sea, continuing North, along the Western Bank of that River, to the 32^d degree of Latitude; thence by a Line due North to the degree of Latitude, where it strikes the Rio Roxo of Nachitoches, or Red-River, then following the course of the Rio-Roxo Westward to the degree of Longitude, 100 West from London and 23 from Washington, then crossing the said Red-River, and running thence by a Line due North to the River Arkansas, thence, following the Course of the Southern bank of the Arkansas to its source in Latitude, 42. North, and thence by that parallel of Latitude to the South-Sea. The whole being as laid down in Melishe's Map of the United-States, published at Philadelphia, improved to the first of January 1818. But if the Source of the Arkansas River shall be found to fall North or South of Latitude 42, then the Line shall run from the said Source due South or North, as the case may be, till it meets the said Parallel of Latitude 42, and thence along the said Parallel to the South Sea: all the Islands in the Sabine and the said Red and Arkansas Rivers, throughout the Course thus described, to belong to the United-States; but the use of the Waters and the navigation of the Sabine to the Sea, and of the said Rivers, Roxo and Arkansas, throughout the extent of the said Boundary, on their respective Banks, shall be common to the respective inhabitants of both Nations. The Two High Contracting Parties agree to cede and renounce all their rights, claims and pretensions to the Territories described by the said Line: that is to say. — The United States hereby cede to His Catholic Majesty, and renounce forever, all their rights, claims, and pretensions to the Territories lying West and South of the above described Line; and, in like manner, His Catholic Majesty cedes to the said United-States, all his rights, claims, and pretensions to any Territories, and East and North of the said Line, and, for himself, his heirs and successors, renounces all claim to the said Territories forever.

ART. 4.

To fix this Line with more precision, and to place the Land marks which shall designate exactly the limits of both Nations, each of the Contracting Parties shall appoint a Commissioner, and a Surveyor, who shall meet before the termination of one year from the date of the Ratification of this Treaty, at Nachitoches, on the Red River, and proceed to run and mark the said Line from the mouth of the Sabine to the Red River, and from the Red River to the River Arkansas, and to ascertain the Latitude of the source of the said River Arkansas in conformity to what is above agreed upon and stipulated, and the Line of Latitude 42. to the South Sea: they shall make out plans and keep Journals of their proceedings, and the result agreed upon by them shall be considered as part of this Treaty, and shall have the same force as if it were inserted therein. The two Governments will amicably agree respecting the necessary Articles to be furnished to those persons, and also as to their respective escorts, should such be deemed necessary.

ART. 5.

The Inhabitants of the ceded Territories shall be secured in the free exercise of their Religion, without any restriction, and all those who may desire to remove to the Spanish Dominions shall be permitted to sell, or export their Effects at any time whatever, without being subject, in either case, to duties.

ART. 6.

The Inhabitants of the Territories which His Catholic Majesty cedes to the United-States by this Treaty, shall be incorporated in the Union of the United-States, as soon as may be consistent with the principles of the Federal Constitution, and admitted to the enjoyment of all the privileges, rights and immunities of the Citizens of the United-States.

ART. 7.

The Officers and Troops of His Catholic Majesty in the Territories hereby ceded by him to the United-States shall be withdrawn, and possession of the places occupied by them shall be given within six months after the exchange of the Ratifications of this Treaty, or sooner if possible, by the Officers of His Catholic Majesty, to the Commissioners or Officers of the United-States, duly appointed to receive them; and the United-States shall furnish the transports and escort necessary to convey the Spanish Officers and Troops and their baggage to the Havana.

ART. 8.

All the grants of land made before the 24th of January 1818. by His Catholic Majesty or by his lawful authorities in the said Territories ceded by His Majesty to the United-States, shall be ratified and confirmed to the persons in possession of the lands, to the same extent that the same grants would be valid if the Territories had remained under the Dominion of His Catholic Majesty. But the owners in possession of such lands, who by reason of the recent circumstances of the Spanish Nation and the Revolutions in Europe, have been prevented from fulfilling all the conditions of their grants, shall complete them within the terms limited in the same respectively, from the date of this Treaty; in default of which the said grants shall be null and void.—All grants made since the said 24ᵗʰ of January 1818. when the first proposal on the part of His Catholic Majesty, for the cession of the Floridas was made, are hereby declared and agreed to be null and void.

ART. 9.

The two High Contracting Parties animated with the most earnest desire of conciliation and with the object of putting an end to all the differences which have existed between them, and of confirming the good understanding which they wish to be forever maintained between them, reciprocally renounce all claims for damages or injuries which they, themselves, as well as their respective citizens and subjects may have suffered, until the time of signing this Treaty.

The renunciation of the United-States will extend to all the injuries mentioned in the Convention of the 11ᵗʰ of August 1802.

2. To all claims on account of Prizes made by French Privateers, and condemned by French Consuls, within the Territory and Jurisdiction of Spain.

3. To all claims of indemnities on account of the suspension of the right of Deposit at New-Orleans in 1802.

4. To all claims of Citizens of the United-States upon the Government of Spain, arising from the unlawful seizures at Sea, and in the ports and territories of Spain or the Spanish Colonies.

5. To all claims of Citizens of the United-States upon the Spanish Government, statements of which, soliciting the interposition of the Government of the United-States have been presented to the Department of State, or to the Minister of the United-States in Spain, since the date of the Convention of 1802, and until the signature of this Treaty.

The renunciation of His Catholic Majesty extends,

1. To all the injuries mentioned in the Convention of the 11ᵗʰ of August 1802.

2. To the sums which His Catholic Majesty advanced for the return of Captain Pike from the Provincias Internas.

3. To all injuries caused by the expedition of Miranda that was fitted out and equipped at New-York.

4. To all claims of Spanish subjects upon the Government of the United-States arizing from unlawful seizures at Sea or within the ports and territorial Jurisdiction of the United States.

Finally, to all the claims of subjects of His Catholic Majesty upon the Government of the United-States, in which the interposition of His Catholic Majesty's Government has been solicited before the date of this Treaty, and since the date of the Convention of 1802, or which may have been made to the Department of Foreign Affairs of His Majesty, or to His Minister in the United-States.

And the High Contracting Parties respectively renounce all claim to indemnities for any of the recent events or transactions of their respective Commanders and Officers in the Floridas.

The United-States will cause satisfaction to be made for the injuries, if any, which by process of Law, shall be established to have been suffered by the Spanish Officers, and individual Spanish inhabitants, by the late operations of the American Army in Florida.

ART. 10.

The Convention entered into between the two Governments on the 11. of August 1802, the Ratifications of which were exchanged the 21" December 1818, is annulled.

ART. 11.

The United-States, exonerating Spain from all demands in future, on account of the claims of their Citizens, to which the renunciations herein contained extend, and considering them entirely cancelled, undertake to make satisfaction for the same, to an amount not exceeding Five Millions of Dollars. To ascertain the full amount and validity of those claims, a Commission, to consist of three Commissioners, Citizens of the United-States, shall be appointed by the President, by and with the advice and consent of the Senate; which Commission shall meet at the City of Washington, and within the space of three years, from the time of their first meeting, shall receive, examine and decide upon the amount and validity of all the claims included within the descriptions above mentioned. The said Commissioners shall take an oath or affirmation, to be entered on the record of their proceedings, for the faithful and diligent discharge of their duties; and in case of the death, sickness, or necessary absence of any such Commissioner, his place may be supplied by the appointment, as aforesaid, or by the President of the United-States during the recess of the Senate, of another Commissioner in his stead. The said Commissioners shall be authorized to hear and examine on oath every question relative to the said claims, and to receive all suitable authentic testimony concerning the same. And the Spanish Government shall furnish all such documents and elucidations as may be in their possession, for the adjustment of the said claims, according to the principles of Justice, the Laws of Nations, and the stipulations of the Treaty between the two Parties of 27th October 1795; the said Documents to be specified, when demanded at the instance of the said Commissioners.

The payment of such claims as may be admitted and adjusted by the said Commissioners, or the major part of them, to an amount not exceeding Five Millions of Dollars, shall be made by the United-States, either immediately at their Treasury or by the creation of Stock bearing an interest of Six per Cent per annum, payable from the proceeds of sales of public lands within the Territories hereby ceded to the United-States, or in such other manner as the Congress of the United-States may prescribe by Law.

The records of the proceedings of the said Commissioners, together with the vouchers and documents produced before them, relative to the claims to be adjusted and decided upon by them, shall, after the close of their transactions, be deposited in the Department of State of the United-States; and copies of them or any part of them, shall be furnished to the Spanish Government, if required, at the demand of the Spanish Minister in the United-States.

ART. 12.

The Treaty of Limits and Navigation of 1795. remains confirmed in all and each one of its Articles, excepting the 2, 3, 4, 21 and the second clause of the 22^{d} Article, which, having been altered by this Treaty, or having received their entire execution, are no longer valid.

With respect to the 15th Article of the same Treaty of Friendship, Limits and Navigation of 1795, in which it is stipulated, that the Flag shall cover the property, the Two High Contracting Parties agree that this shall be so understood with respect to those Powers who recognize this principle; but if either of the two Contracting Parties shall be at War with a Third Party, and the other Neutral, the Flag of the Neutral shall cover the property of Enemies, whose Government acknowledge this principle, and not of others.

ART. 13.

Both Contracting Parties wishing to favour their mutual Commerce, by affording in their ports every necessary Assistance to their respective Merchant Vessels, have agreed, that the Sailors who shall desert from their Vessels in the ports of the other, shall be arrested and delivered up, at the instance of the Consul—who shall prove nevertheless, that the Deserters belonged to the Vessels that claimed them, exhibiting the document that is customary in their Nation: that is to say, the American Consul in a Spanish Port, shall exhibit the Document known by the name of *Articles,* and the Spanish Consul in American Ports, the Roll of the Vessel; and if the name of the Deserter or Deserters, who are claimed, shall appear in the one or the other, they shall be arrested, held in custody and delivered to the Vessel to which they shall belong.

ART. 14.

The United-States hereby certify, that they have not received any compensation from France for the injuries they suffered from her Privateers, Consuls, and Tribunals, on the Coasts and in the Ports of Spain, for the satisfaction of which provision is made by this Treaty; and they will present an authentic statement of the prizes made, and of their true value, that Spain may avail herself of the same in such manner as she may deem just and proper.

ART. 15.

The United-States to give to His Catholic Majesty, a proof of their desire to cement the relations of Amity subsisting between the two Nations, and to favour the Commerce of the Subjects of His Catholic Majesty, agree that Spanish Vessels coming laden only with productions of Spanish growth, or manufactures directly from the Ports of Spain or of her Colonies, shall be admitted for the term of twelve years to the Ports of Pensacola and S⁺ Augustine in the Floridas, without paying other or higher duties on their cargoes or of tonnage than will be paid by the vessels of the United-States.—During the said term no other Nation shall enjoy the same privileges within the ceded Territories. The twelve years shall commence three months after the exchange of the Ratifications of this Treaty.

ART. 16.

The present Treaty shall be ratified in due form by the Contracting Parties, and the Ratifications shall be exchanged in Six Months from this time or sooner if possible.

In Witness whereof, We the Underwritten Plenipotentiaries of the United-States of America and of His Catholic Majesty, have signed, by virtue of Our Powers, the present Treaty of Amity, Settlement and Limits, and have thereunto affixed our Seals respectively.

Done at Washington, this Twenty-Second day of February, One Thousand Eight Hundred and Nineteen.

[Seal]   JOHN QUINCY ADAMS
[Seal]   LUIS DE ONIS

[THE SPANISH INSTRUMENT OF RATIFICATION]
[TRANSLATION]

Ferdinand the Seventh, by the Grace of God and by the Constitution of the Spanish Monarchy, King of the Spains.

Whereas on the twenty-second day of February of the year one thousand eight hundred and nineteen last past, a treaty was concluded and signed in the city of Washington between Don Luis de Onis, My Envoy Extraordinary and Minister Plenipotentiary, and John Quincy Adams, esq., Secretary of State of the United States of America, competently authorized by both parties, consisting of sixteen articles, which had for their object the arrangement of differences and of limits between both Governments and their respective territories; which are of the following form and literal tenor:

[Here follow both texts of the treaty]

Therefore, having seen and examined the sixteen articles aforesaid, and having first obtained the consent and authority of the

General Cortes of the Nation with respect to the cession mentioned and stipulated in the second and third articles, I approve and ratify all and every one of the articles referred to, and the clauses which are contained in them; and, in virtue of these presents, I approve and ratify them, promising, on the faith and word of a King, to execute and observe them and to cause them to be executed and observed entirely as if I Myself had signed them; and that the circumstance of having exceeded the term of six months fixed for the exchange of the ratifications in the sixteenth article may afford no obstacle in any manner, it is My deliberate will that the present ratification be as valid and firm, and produce the same effects, as if it had been done within the determined period. Desirous at the same time of avoiding any doubt or ambiguity concerning the meaning of the eighth article of the said treaty in respect to the date which is pointed out in it as the period for the confirmation of the grants of lands in the Floridas, made by Me or by the competent authorities in My royal name, which point of date was fixed in the positive understanding of the three grants of land made in favor of the Duke of Alagon, the Count of Puñonrostro, and Don Pedro de Vargas, being annulled by its tenor; I think proper to declare that the said three grants have remained and do remain entirely annulled and invalid, and that neither the three individuals mentioned, nor those who may have title or interest through them, can avail themselves of the said grants at any time or in any manner; under which explicit declaration the said eighth article is to be understood as ratified. In the faith of all which I have commanded to despatch these presents, signed by My hand, sealed with My secret seal, and countersigned by the underwritten, My Secretary of Despatch of State. Given at Madrid the twenty-fourth of October, one thousand eight hundred and twenty.

FERNANDO.

EVARISTO PEREZ DE CASTRO.

THE MELISH MAP, 1818

ADAMS AND ONÍS labored over, and cited in the treaty, the "Map of the United States with the contiguous British & Spanish Possessions, Compiled from the latest & best Authorities by John Melish; Engraved by J. Vallance & H. S. Tanner. . . . Improved to the 1st of January 1818." This was apparently the seventh, eighth, ninth, or tenth edition of a map well known at the time, the first having been published in 1816. Slight alterations appeared in the portrayal of the southern states through the various editions, but none up to 1819 related to the boundary delineation. Necessary revisions were made whenever a new hundred copies was issued. Colonel Lawrence Martin, chief of the Division of Maps and incumbent of the Chair of Geography at the Library of Congress, has thus far identified twenty different issues, or editions, six of them dated 1816, four 1818, two 1819, five 1820, two 1822, and one 1823.[1]

The map was printed on a scale of sixty miles to the inch, being originally approximately fifty-six and a half by thirty-five inches in size. The last seven editions were enlarged to include all of Mexico. It was issued whole or cut into sections and mounted for carrying. A book entitled *A Geographical Description of the United States* (first and second editions, Philadelphia, 1816; third edition, revised, 1818) was published to accompany it.

A survey of libraries in the United States, Canada, England, and France has revealed nine copies of the 1818 editions now available. This is believed to be the first time any edition of the map has been reproduced entire for publication. The copy here reproduced is now with the treaty in the Division of State Department Archives in the National Archives. No copy of the map was officially signed or made a part of the treaty by the negotiators. The map now with the treaty was acquired by the Department of State in 1840. The fact that it bears no superimposed lines or

---

[1] Preliminary statements regarding Colonel Martin's research appear in his annual reports of the Division of Maps for 1936–1938 (Library of Congress, *Report of the Librarian for the Fiscal Year* [Washington, 1936–1938]: 1936, pp. 125–127; 1937, p. 121; 1938, p. 141).

annotations indicates that it is not the copy used in the negotiation, as Adams in his *Memoirs* speaks as if a line had been drawn on a Melish map to illustrate his maximum boundary proposal.[2]

A copy of an 1816 edition was sent by Onís to his government in April, 1817, and one of an 1818 edition in March, 1819.[3] In transmitting the latter, Onís said that it was "that which was in hand in the negotiation of the Treaty." But such identification might apply either to the particular copy of the map sent, or just to the Melish map in general. These maps are not now in the Archivo Histórico Nacional, where the originals of Onís' despatches are filed.

Other copies of one or another of the 1818 editions, without as much data as would be desired regarding previous ownership or use, are preserved by the New York Public Library, the Harvard College Library, the Boston Public Library, the Provincial Library and Archives of British Columbia, the Dauphin County Historical Society (Harrisburg, Pennsylvania), and Dr. W. E. Wrather, of Dallas, Texas. There is one, bearing a superimposed red line along most of the Adams-Onís delineation, but without identification concerning previous ownership or use, in the Library of Congress, which also has half of another without annotations of interest here.

John Melish (1771–1822) was a traveler, merchant, and commercial geographer.[4] He was born in Scotland and studied at the University of Glasgow. He journeyed to the West Indies in 1798, and to Savannah in 1806. In the latter place he set up an importing and exporting house, and while operating it traveled extensively. After going back to Scotland in 1807, he returned to the United States two years later, this time to remain. He soon made his permanent home in Philadelphia.

Melish began publishing with an account of *Travels in the United States of America* (2 vols., Philadelphia, 1812), and his first notable maps were issued in *A Military and Topographic Atlas of the United States* (Philadelphia, 1813), to illustrate the campaigns of the war. Following these enterprises he published

---

[2] Adams, *Memoirs*, IV:110, 239.

[3] Onís to Pizarro, July 18, 1818, in A.H.N., Est., 5643; Onís to Irujo, March 5, 1819, *ibid.*, 5661.

[4] *Dictionary of American Biography*, XII:513.

tions and in those of 1818) located it in about latitude 41° north, instead of its true position of 39° 20'. The Forty-second Parallel, along which it was agreed the limit should run after leaving the head of the Arkansas, is some 183 miles north of that point.[10] Later editions of the map incorporated the results of both the Convention of October 20, 1818, between the United States and Great Britain, and the Adams-Onís Treaty of February 22, 1819.

---

[10] On the first of the 1816 editions of the map the headwaters of the Arkansas were placed in approximately 42°, and it is conceivable that the ultimate treaty delineation derived from that fact. Since Adams' first proposal was for the Forty-first Parallel and was made after several later editions were published, however, it seems more probable that bargaining between the extreme demands of the negotiators brought the final result.

REFERENCES

CONCERNING THE VOLUMINOUS MATERIAL bearing on the Adams-Onís Treaty the salient facts are that there is a surprising amount of source material which has either been insufficiently studied or not exploited at all, that there has been no satisfactory comprehensive monograph with the treaty as its central theme, and that the innumerable writings incidentally touching on it have been liable to gross misstatements on account of the lack of such a monograph.

The very extent of the material has no doubt been one factor prohibiting an adequate investigation of the subject. Most of the records used herein have been known or presumed to exist. Many have been used for other purposes, particularly the manuscripts from the United States Department of State, the British Public Record Office, and the French Foreign Office. The material used, and some additional records listed here, have been selected as either contributing directly to an understanding of the negotiation of the treaty or explaining how conditions of frontier settlement guided the diplomacy. This has meant the elimination of those records dealing with minor related topics, and a great many concerned with routine administrative, diplomatic, and military details.

Although monographs, articles, and general histories have been studied and are listed, particularly for the previous views and interpretations of the subject, the greater part of this work has been based upon manuscripts and printed documents representing the actual instruments of the negotiation.

The following list of references does not purport to be a complete list of all materials relating to the subject. It is rather an indication of those I have used, those significant in the historiography of the treaty, and some others which are suggested for readers wishing to pursue the matter farther. Special mention should be made of Samuel Flagg Bemis and Grace Gardner Griffin's *Guide to the Diplomatic History of the United States, 1775–1921* (Washington, 1935), which contains notes on all kinds of material.

The comments are designed to give explanations of the hitherto obscure items, and for those that have been well known simply to indicate their value in this study. The references have been listed according to the following arbitrary classification with respect to type:

A. Manuscripts
B. Printed materials
    1. Documents
    2. Periodical matter
      a) Contemporary
      b) Later and recent
    3. Memoirs and biographies
    4. General works and special treatises
C. Maps

A. MANUSCRIPTS

With four countries directly concerned, and numerous individuals figuring prominently, the files of papers run into many thousands of pages. Most of them are well preserved, and with one exception the archives and libraries cited were open and the materials easily accessible at the time of my study. I am informed that the Archivo Histórico Nacional at Madrid was not damaged during the recent siege there. In the Spanish archives the manuscripts are kept in bundles of several hundred pages each, known as *legajos*. These are frequently divided into *expedientes,* small files of records from various sources assembled at the time of their use as treating certain subjects at hand. Nearly all the other collections listed which are in libraries or archives are in the form of bound volumes of manuscripts.

A number of selections of this material have been published for one purpose or another. For the official correspondence of the various governments, however, thoroughness has required direct reference to the originals, and they are accordingly cited in the notes. The one notable exception to this practice is the reference to the *American State Papers* for such of the Adams-Onís and Pizarro-Erving correspondence as is printed there with reasonable completeness.

Various guides and indexes accessible to competent investigators in the archives and libraries have not been listed. Special attention should be directed to the series of guides to materials for the history of the United States in various foreign archives published by the Carnegie Institution of Washington, and to the indexes to records in the National Archives, the Division of Manuscripts of the Library of Congress, the British Public Record Office, and the French Foreign Office, all available at the archives named.

The Library of Congress now has photographic copies of nearly all the regular series of correspondence of the foreign governments mentioned with their representatives at Washington for the period of this study. This material, acquired through the Library's "Project A" under a grant from the Rockefeller Foundation, makes available to students in this country identical copies of a vast collection of records. The Library of Congress and other institutions in this country have transcripts of varying quality of certain other manuscripts at Sevilla. For this study almost all the foreign manuscripts cited have been studied in the archives abroad.

The private collections in Spain have not been exploited, but some information has been obtained concerning them. Those of prominent men in this country are well known. The greatest obstacle to a complete study of this subject is the fact that the papers of the Adams family are not available.

Official manuscripts are classified according to archival distribution, and for convenience the abbreviations used are repeated after each archives title.

Archivo General de Indias, Sevilla (A.G.I.).

Sección de Estado, Legajos 31–33 (Mexico).

Correspondence of the viceroys of Mexico, 1812–1819, including reports on frontier conditions, heading up correspondence with various other officials in North America.

Sección de Estado, Legajos 86–90 (América en general).

Papers dealing with the "pacification" of the insurgent colonies, 1816–1824. Correspondence, records of meetings, and special reports. These deal largely with the possibility of an English mediation in the dispute with the colonies; but in connection with northern frontier defense and international policy they intimately concern the United States.

Indiferente General, Legajo 1603.

Correspondence with diplomatic representatives in the United States, ·1792–1835. This bundle includes a number of Onís' letters regarding the Floridas, Louisiana, and the Provincias Internas.

Papeles procedentes de Cuba.

This large collection of papers transferred from Havana late in the nineteenth century contains much correspondence with the diplomatic representatives in the United States, and a great deal of material on frontier affairs in the Floridas. Most of this is summarized in the reports of the various officials to their home governments. It is chiefly concerned with routine details of military, administrative, and commercial character. Its value can readily be ascertained from Roscoe R. Hill's *Descriptive Cata-*

logue of the Documents Relating to the History of the United States in the "Papeles procedentes de Cuba" (Washington, 1916).

For Onís' correspondence in this collection, see especially Legajos 104, 1708, 1837, 1898, 1944, and 1945.

For information of Jackson's activities in the Floridas, see especially Legajos 158, 1877, 2356.

On the cession and transfer of the Floridas, see Legajo 1963.

Archivo General de la Nación, Mexico.

There are in this depository many papers representing Onís' relations with the viceroy and other colonial officials. This phase has not been covered in this study further than to indicate its general nature, and to point out the frequent interweaving of diplomatic negotiations and colonial policy. Many of these papers are duplicated or their contents summarized in the reports of Onís and of the viceroys to their home government.

The nature of the materials in Mexico is described in Herbert E. Bolton's *Guide to Materials for the History of the United States in the Principal Archives of Mexico* (Washington, 1913). Most important of the items in the Mexican collection is the treatise of Padre José Pichardo on the limits of Louisiana and Texas. Transcripts of this document are to be found in the Bancroft Library at the University of California, the Library of Congress, the Newberry Library, the Texas State Library, and the library of the University of Texas. It is from the last-named copy that Charles W. Hackett is publishing a translation of the treatise.

Archivo General de Simancas, Simancas (A.G.S.).

Sección de Estado, Inglaterra, Legajos 2675–2676 moderno.

The "Inglaterra" papers at Simancas are the records of the Spanish embassy at London. These *legajos* include copies of despatches from and originals of instructions to Count Fernán Núñez, the Duke of San Carlos, and Onís, Spanish ambassadors, from 1814 to 1822. There is also considerable correspondence with diplomatic agents in other courts, including Onís at Washington.

Faulty transcripts of this material are in the Library of Congress, the Newberry Library, and other institutions of this country. The supplementary versions of most of the letters, however (originals instead of office copies of despatches, and vice versa for instructions), are to be found in the more accessible archives of the offices to or from which the correspondence was sent.

Archivo Histórico Nacional, Madrid (A.H.N.).

Sección de Estado.

These papers consist largely of files removed from the archives of the foreign office late in the nineteenth century. They include records of that office, of the *Consejo de Estado*, and of various special commissions, reports of administrative officials in many places, special files (*expedientes*) on specific subjects, drafts of letters to ministers abroad and to foreign representatives in Spain, and originals of despatches of ministers abroad and notes from foreign representatives in Spain.

Legajos 5635–5646.

The regular series of records covering relations with the United States, containing originals of despatches and drafts of many instructions.

Despatches of chargés Valentín de Foronda (1809), José Viar (1809), minister Luis de Onís (1809–1819), chargé Mateo de la Serna (1819–1820), and special minister Francisco Vives (1820). Legajo 5643 also includes correspondence with agents in other courts for the years 1817–1818.

The files are incomplete because of the removal of many letters for the *expedientes*. In numerous instances, however, as the letters were sent in two or three copies they now appear in both places.

Legajos 5660, 5661, 5662.

Various papers concerning the negotiation with the United States, 1817–1820. Sometimes referred to at the time as the "great *expediente*" on the subject. Includes despatches from and drafts of instructions to diplomatic agents in Washington, London, St. Petersburg, Berlin, and Vienna; special reports prepared in the foreign office; minutes of sessions of the *Consejo de Estado* and of other meetings; and correspondence between various officials in Spain. Most of the basic instructions to Onís appear in draft here, and several not elsewhere.

Legajo 5574.

Correspondence, 1801–1827, on the spoliations on American commerce by French cruisers in Spanish waters previous to 1801, compensation for which Spain set out in 1827 to collect from France.

Legajo 6797.

Papers of the Spanish embassy in Paris, 1804–1818. The most important of these papers for this study are duplicated in Legajos 5660, 5661, 5662, and 5643.

Expedientes.

These are special files made up of papers from various sources relating to particular topics. Those listed here are contained in a series of *legajos* made up entirely of such material. The numbers used are those originally applied and now employed in the archives. As the *expediente* numbers arbitrarily assigned to the Library of Congress photographs often do not correspond, the latter numbers are given in parentheses.

Legajo 5552, expediente 6. (L.C. no. 6.) 1810.

Decision of the *Consejo* of the Regency to instruct Onís to stay in the United States though unrecognized.

Legajo 5554, expediente 30. (L.C. no. 12.) 1811–1823.

Activities of José Alvarez de Toledo.

Legajo 5555, expediente 60. (L.C. no. 12.) 1811–1821.

Services of Miguel Cabral de Noroña.

Legajo 5556, expediente 1. (L.C. no. 1.) 1812.

Spanish policy in the war between the United States and Great Britain.

Legajo 5557, expediente 1. (L.C. no. 1.) 1813.

On the state of relations with the United States.

Legajo 5557, expediente 2. (L.C. no. 2.) 1813–1815.

On the recognition of Onís and Erving.

Legajo 5559, expediente 5. (L.C. no. 5.) 1816.

Report of Narciso de Heredia on relations with the United States.

Legajo 5560, expediente 14. (L.C. no. 11.) 1817.

Onís' project of a treaty to be drawn up with the United States.

Legajo 5562, expediente 4. (L.C. no. 4.) 1814.

British activities in Florida. Documents from Pensacola.

Legajo 5562, expediente 8. (L.C. no. 8.) 1818.

Jackson's seizure of Pensacola.

Legajo 5562, expediente 11. (L.C. no. 11.) 1818.

Plan for fortification of the mouth of the Columbia.

Legajo 5563, expediente 37. (L.C. no. 17.) 1818.

French colonists in Alabama and Texas.

Legajo 5565, expediente 4. (L.C. no. 4.) 1820.

Memoria of Narciso de Heredia on the ratification problem.

Legajo 5566, expediente 2. (L.C. no. 1.) 1821.

Negotiations of Jackson, Callava, Butler, and Coppinger on disposition of Spanish supplies in the Floridas.

Legajo 5566, expediente 6. (L.C. no. 5.) 1821–1822.

Relative to the expulsion of Spanish officers from the Floridas.

Legajo 5567, expediente 10. (L.C. no. 2.) 1821.

Memoria of José de Heredia on the negotiation and ratification.

Legajo 94, expediente 16. (L.C. no. 16.) 1820.

Records of session of the *Consejo de Estado* in which Irujo's support of the treaty in May and June, 1819, was approved, and his banishment rescinded.

Archives du Ministère des Affaires Etrangères, Paris (A.M.A.E.).

Correspondance politique, Etats Unis, volumes 72–77.

Home office copies of the correspondence with the minister to the United States, Baron Guillaume Hyde de Neuville, and supplementary documents, covering the years 1815–1820. The despatches of Hyde de Neuville contain references to the negotiation of Adams and Onís, and the copies of instructions sent to him indicate clearly the policy of the French government.

Correspondance politique, Etats Unis, Supplément, volumes 8–9.

These files, numbered three and four in a subseries dealing with "Louisiane et Florides," contain some diplomatic correspondence of Hyde de Neuville and other agents, and special reports relating to various problems concerning those regions. These volumes cover the years 1803–1835.

Correspondance politique, Etats Unis, Supplément, volume 10.

Various papers on relations with the United States, 1803–1830, including some despatches of Hyde de Neuville concerning the Adams-Onís negotiation.

Correspondance politique, Espagne, volumes 695–707.

Correspondence to and from the French ambassador at Madrid, Montmorency, Duke of Laval, 1815–1820. Originals of the representations of Pizarro to the French ambassador, copies of which are in the Spanish archives. Despatches of the ambassador concerning the negotiation and the delay in ratification, and instructions informing him of the procedure of the French court in the matter.

Archivo del Ministerio de Estado, Madrid (A.M.E.).

Estados Unidos, Legajos 216–225, 227–228, 237.

Instructions to diplomatic agents in the United States, 1809–1821. Many of the important letters on the negotiation with the United States do not appear in these *legajos*. For them, the drafts are to be found in the bundles in the Archivo Histórico Nacional, chiefly in Legajos 5660, 5661, and 5662. Two of the long series of important instructions have not been found, those of July, 1809, and August 27, 1817. Their contents have been learned definitely from other sources, particularly the records of the *Consejo de Estado*. The original instructions given to Onís at Sevilla in 1809 were missing in 1817, according to a letter of Pizarro to him, July 30, 1817, in A.H.N., Est., 5660. Their lack would be more serious if it were not for the fact that, by the time Onís was recognized as minister and could negotiate, circumstances had altered Spanish policy.

These *legajos* consist of papers returned to Spain late in the century from the legation at Washington, and contain the originals of the instructions. Historical scholars have not been given access to the foreign office archives in recent years. This fact enhances the value of typewritten transcripts of the instructions to the ministers in the United States made under the direction of Dr. Samuel F. Bemis and now available in the Division of Manuscripts of the Library of Congress. The *legajos* here listed have been studied by means of these transcripts.

Biblioteca Nacional, Madrid, Sección de Manuscritos (B.N.M.).

MS no. 18636:28.

Letter of Manuel de Salcedo (governor of Texas) to Miguel de Lardizábal (deputy from New Spain to the Spanish *Junta Central*), San Fernando de Bexar (Texas), November 15, 1809. Long exposition of conditions and needs of the province, disparaging the boundary claims of the United States as unjust, and discountenancing the "neutral ground agreement" of 1806.

Department of State, Washington (D.S.). *See* The National Archives.

Erving Papers.

Besides the Erving correspondence in the Department of State files, a number of his private letters, mostly to James Madison, September 25, 1798, to February 17, 1830, were given to the Massachusetts Historical Society by Robert C. Winthrop, Jr., in

1896. The manuscript volume bears Winthrop's comment that "it may be added that the greater part of the letters addressed to Mr. Erving by Madison and other public men of that period perished in the great New York fire of 1835."

Fernán Núñez Papers.

For the purposes of this study the work of Carlos José Gutiérrez de los Ríos, seventh Count and first Duke of Fernán Núñez, ambassador to England and later to France, is sufficiently explained in the official correspondence and the work of the Marqués de Villa-Urrutia. There were in 1936, however, private papers belonging to him and other prominent members of the family in the possession of the present Duke of Fernán Núñez, at Santa Isabel, 42, Madrid.

Irujo Papers.

There is little biographical information available concerning Carlos Martínez de Irujo y Tacón, Marqués de Casa Irujo, Spanish *secretario de estado* and earlier minister to the United States. Much information about his work occurs in the official correspondence cited, however. For further personal data, one might refer to certain of the private papers for 1818–1819 which were in 1936 in the possession of the Duke of Sotomayor, in Madrid.

Library of Congress, Division of Manuscripts.

Outside of the photographic material previously mentioned, there are in the wealth of papers in this division several collections bearing more or less directly on the Adams-Onís negotiation. They have been cited accordingly if quoted or referred to in the text. Those which should be mentioned particularly are the Monroe, Madison, and Jackson papers. The most important of these documents have been published, and the official correspondence of these men is to be found in the archives of the executive departments.

In addition to the Monroe correspondence in the regular collection so labeled in the Division of Manuscripts, there is a volume of private papers of the secretary of state labeled "Spanish Affairs," covering the years 1810–1816. It includes memoranda of a conversation in 1811 between Monroe and Juan Bernabeu, who served as intermediary for Onís, and a copy and translation of the notorious letter of Onís to the captain-general of Caracas, February 2, 1810, which was inaccurately published in *A.S.P., F.R.*, III:404. These papers were transferred from the State Department in 1906, but their import had been hidden owing to the manner of binding. My attention was directed to them by Mr. Donald H. Mugridge, of the Division of Manuscripts.

Private papers of Monroe also appear in other collections, notably that of the New York Public Library.

The National Archives, Washington.

Division of Legislative Archives.

The originals of the Presidential messages to Congress concerning the treaty negotiation, with accompanying documents, referred to herein as duplicated in the Department of State files or published in the *American State Papers*, are among the Senate archives transferred to the National Archives in 1937.

Division of Navy Department Archives.

The logbook of the sloop-of-war "Hornet," bearing brief notes concerning the mission on which it carried John Forsyth and the exchange copy of the Adams-Onís Treaty to Spain in 1819, is now filed in the National Archives.

Division of State Department Archives (D.S.).

The diplomatic records formerly in the Archives Section of the Department of State were transferred to the National Archives in 1938. The identity and integrity of the series are of course scrupulously maintained, and citations prepared previously are still valid.

These well-known collections have been used by many investigators, but heretofore no satisfactory exposition of our relations with Spain during or after the War of 1812 has resulted. This study is primarily concerned with the later of those two periods, but the records of the earlier have been surveyed for the backgrounds of the Adams-Onís negotiation.

The papers dealing with Spain are home office copies of letters sent out, originals of despatches and other correspondence received. The legation files are still in Madrid.

—Instructions to United States Ministers, volumes VII–IX.

For the period of these instructions, 1808–1823, the copies of letters sent to all ministers abroad were entered into the same volume. This includes, therefore, material relating to United States policy toward other countries than Spain but indirectly affecting the Adams-Onís negotiation. In these volumes are instructions sent to Anthony Morris, Thomas Brent, and ministers George W. Erving and John Forsyth.

These records not only show what the agents of the United States were directed to do in Madrid, but also provide the best available exposition of the policy of this government, much more frank, of course, than the statements made to Onís.

—Despatches, Spain, volumes XI–XIX.

Letters, 1808–1821 inclusive, of Erving, Morris, Brent, and Forsyth. Various accompanying documents are included. Even though the major portion of the negotiation was conducted at Washington, these despatches are of vital importance in giving an account, albeit often a biased one, of events at Madrid. Further, in view of infrequent communication and the lack of press services in Madrid, the Department of State here depended on these despatches and on the statements of Onís for its knowledge of the Spanish viewpoint and activities. On that knowledge, naturally, the policy of the United States was formulated.

—Despatches, France, volume XIX.

Despatches of Albert Gallatin, minister, 1819–1820, several of which relate to the problems of the negotiation and the delayed ratification.

—Despatches, Great Britain, volumes XXIII–XXIV.

Correspondence from Richard Rush, minister, 1817–1820, including information on the rôle of England in the controversies over the Adams-Onís negotiation, the proposed British mediation, and the unfounded suspicion that England was contributing to the delay of ratification of the treaty.

—Despatches, Russia, volumes VII–IX.

Letters from ministers George W. Campbell and Henry Middleton, 1818–1822, a few of which relate to our relations with Spain.

—Notes to Foreign Legations, volume II.

Office copies of the notes delivered to representatives of all countries at Washington were bound together for the period of this volume, 1810–1821.

The most important of these are printed in the *American State Papers, Foreign Relations* series. It should be pointed out that they do not reveal true policy as frankly as the correspondence between the officials of one country, or the accounts in despatches or diary entries of personal conversations in which diplomatic formalities played a less prominent rôle. Of the more than seventy-five notes to Onís included in this volume, most have to do with commercial affairs or matters of protocol.

—Notes from the Spanish Legation, volumes II–VI.

The quantity of this material is one indication of the industry of Onís and his aides. These volumes altogether include the originals of notes received from 1805 to 1821, signed by minister Casa Irujo, chargés Valentín de Foronda and José Viar, consuls Juan Bernabeu and Pablo Chacón, minister Onís, and chargé Mateo de la Serna; but two entire volumes, IV and V, are taken up by the period of the negotiations between Adams and Onís, 1817–1819. The most significant of these notes also appear in *A.S.P., F.R.*, IV.

—Special Agents, volume VI.

Reports and other correspondence relative to the mission of John B. Prevost and James Biddle to South America and the Northwest Coast, 1817–1818, on the sloop-of-war "Ontario."

—Miscellaneous Letters, August–September, 1816.

Letters to the department from various persons, including John Jacob Astor.

—Treaties.

The file includes three signed manuscript originals of the Adams-Onís Treaty. There is also an original of the Spanish instrument of ratification, and one of the first United States ratification, of February 25, 1819. There is no copy of the second United

States instrument of ratification, February 22, 1821, but it is quoted in the proclamation of the treaty of the same date, an original of which appears. There are also three originals, two in Spanish and one in English, of the certificate of exchange of ratifications, February 22, 1821. Attested copies of the Senate resolutions of advice and consent, February 24, 1819, and February 19, 1821, are also included. There is a copy of the full power given to Adams by Monroe. In addition, there is a copy of the Melish map, which is reproduced herein, and regarding which some comments are made in Appendix II.

Onís Papers.

The family archives, including records not only of Onís but of his uncle and son, who were also diplomats, have been preserved in the ancestral home near Cantalapiedra, province of Salamanca, Spain. Their present proprietor is Professor Federico de Onís, of the Department of Romance Languages of Columbia University, a descendant in direct line through eldest sons.

I am indebted to Professor Onís for the use of a manuscript biography of Don Luis, written at Madrid in 1827, now in his possession. This paper was prepared shortly after the diplomat's death, apparently by someone in the foreign office.

Professor Onís is also the owner of two portraits of Don Luis, one of which was done not far from the time of the signing of the treaty, and shows the Grand Cross of the Order of Isabella the Catholic which was awarded for his services in the United States in 1817. That portrait is reproduced as frontispiece in this book.

Public Archives of Canada, Ottawa.

Bagot Papers, American Correspondence.

Correspondence of Charles Bagot, British minister to the United States, 1816–1819. There are two groups, of which one was obtained from his grandson about 1891. In that collection, Volume M. 157 includes copies of letters to Sir John C. Sherbrooke, governor-in-chief of British North America, referring to the Northwest Coast. The second group were copied from the family archives at Levens Hall, in England. Among them, Volume II contains letters of interest regarding the Adams-Onís negotiation.

Public Record Office, London (P.R.O.).

The manuscript volumes used in this institution are the regular series of diplomatic correspondence between the foreign office and its representatives at Washington and Madrid. They have been examined by many persons, but not in such a way as to produce what I consider a satisfactory account of the scheme for a British mediation in the negotiation between the United States and Spain. That could only be done by using these papers in direct connection with those in the Spanish archives. As in other manuscript collections referred to, more series and volumes than those cited have been examined, but the ones listed have been used or quoted.

Foreign Office Papers (F.O.), series 5. America, United States. Volumes 130–131.

Despatches of Sir Charles Bagot, 1818–1819. Originals.

F.O., series 115. Embassy and Consular Archives, United States. Volumes 29, 34.

Originals of instructions to Bagot, 1817, and to Bagot and G. Crawford Antrobus, chargé, 1819.

F.O., series 72. Spain. Volumes 197–200, 210–213, 224–226.

Despatches of Sir Henry Wellesley, British ambassador to Spain, 1817–1819. Originals.

F.O., series 72. Spain. Volumes 196, 209, 222.

Instructions to Wellesley, 1817–1819. Office copies.

F.O., series 72. Spain. Volumes 204, 216.

Correspondence with the Duke of San Carlos, Spanish ambassador to England, 1817–1818. Originals of notes received, copies of those sent.

F.O., series 185. Embassy and Consular Archives, Spain. Volumes 66, 71, 75.

Originals of instructions to Wellesley, 1817–1819.

SCHELLENBERG, THEODORE R. "The European Background of the Monroe Doctrine, 1818–1822." Ph.D. dissertation in the University of Pennsylvania Library, now in process of revision.

The first part of this work analyzes the interests and policies of Europe toward America; the second, through a detailed study of the press and other sources, portrays popular and official opinion in this country toward Europe.

STEWART, CHARLES L. "Martínez and López de Haro on the Northwest Coast, 1788–1789." Ph.D. dissertation in the University of California Library.

This study is informative concerning the rivalries of Spain, England, and Russia in the North Pacific.

B. PRINTED MATERIALS

1. DOCUMENTS

ADAMS, JOHN QUINCY. "Address before the Boston Young Men's Whig Club" (October 7, 1844), *Boston Advertiser and Patriot,* October 10 and 11, 1844.

A commentary on the Texas annexation question, refuting statements of Erving and of Jackson concerning the negotiation of the Adams-Onís Treaty.

————. "Reply to the Appeal of the Massachusetts Federalists," *Documents Relating to New England Federalism, 1800–1815,* HENRY ADAMS, ed., pp. 107–329. Boston, 1877.

An argumentative analysis of his own activities during Jefferson's administration, including his views on the Louisiana Purchase.

————. *Writings of John Quincy Adams.* 7 vols. WORTHINGTON C. FORD, ed. New York, 1913–1917.

These seven volumes of selected correspondence cover the period up to 1823. For this study, material relating to the negotiation has been used in the original in the State Department files.

BAGOT, CHARLES. "Charles Bagot's Notes on Housekeeping and Entertaining at Washington, 1819," S. E. MORISON, ed., Colonial Society of Massachusetts, *Proceedings,* XXVI (1927):438–446.

A letter written to Stratford Canning, Bagot's successor, counseling him on the vicissitudes of life in Washington and on the projected use of "the Onís house" for the legation. Canning annotated it and passed it on to his successor, Charles Vaughan.

BOLTON, HERBERT E., ed. *Athanase de Mézières and the Louisiana Texas Frontier, 1768–1780; Documents Published for the First Time, from the Original Spanish and French Manuscripts, Chiefly in the Archives of Mexico and Spain.* 2 vols. Cleveland, 1914.

A collection of correspondence of a Spanish official, with a historical introduction which is valuable for an understanding of the boundary questions.

CALHOUN, JOHN C. *Correspondence between Gen. Andrew Jackson and John C. Calhoun, President and Vice-President of the United States, on the Subject of the Latter, in the Deliberations of the Cabinet of Mr. Monroe, on the Occurrences in the Seminole War.* Washington, 1831.

Illustrative documents on the controversy over Jackson's activities in the Floridas between him and Calhoun, then secretary of war.

CALLAVA, JOSÉ. *Manifesto sobre las tropelías y bejaciones que cometió el gobernador americano de Panzacola contra Don José Callava, nombrado para la entrega de la Florida Occidental a los Estados Unidos.* Havana, 1821.

> Complaints concerning the dealings between Jackson and the Spanish official in the transfer of the Floridas.

CANTILLO, ALEJANDRO DEL, ed. *Tratados, convenios y declaraciones de paz y de comercio que han hecho con las potencias estranjeras los monarcas españoles de la casa de Borbon desde el año de 1700 hasta el día.* Madrid, 1843.

> Treaty collection, with notes. In connection with this and certain later publications one should use the *Indices generales de los tratados, convenios y otros documentos de caracter internacional ... 1801 á 1897*, published at Madrid in 1900.

GREAT BRITAIN. FOREIGN OFFICE. *British and Foreign State Papers.* London, 1841—.

> Volume I includes most of the British diplomatic agreements referred to in this study.

HEREDIA, NARCISO DE, CONDE DE OFALIA. *Escritos del Conde de Ofalia, Publicados por su Nieto el Marqués de Heredia.* Bilbao, 1894.

> Selected state papers and correspondence of Heredia, who was Pizarro's chief aide in the conduct of the Adams-Onís negotiation, and who later became *secretario de estado* and ambassador at London and at Paris. His account of the negotiation helps to show that Pizarro did not know of the land grants to Alagón and Puñonrostro at the time they were made, and the documents concerning his banishment throw some light on the ratification controversy at Madrid. The introductory biographical sketch was lifted from Díaz and Cardenas' *Galería de españoles célebres contemporáneos* (Madrid, 1841–1847).

JACKSON, ANDREW. *Correspondence of Andrew Jackson.* 6 vols. JOHN SPENCER BASSETT, ed. Washington, 1926–1933.

> Volume II: correspondence, 1814–1819; Volume III: correspondence, 1820–1828.

JEFFERSON, THOMAS. *Writings of Thomas Jefferson.* 20 vols. ANDREW LIPSCOMB, ed. Washington, 1903–1904.

> The "Memorial Edition." Volumes X–XV: correspondence, 1798–1823.

———. "The Limits and Bounds of Louisiana," American Philosophical Society, *Documents Relating to the Purchase and Exploration of Louisiana,* pp. 5–45. New York, 1904.

> A paper prepared in the fall of 1803, copies of which were sent to the United States ministers at Paris and Madrid.

LONDONDERRY, ROBERT STEWART, [VISCOUNT CASTLEREAGH,] SECOND MARQUIS OF. *Memoirs and Correspondence of Viscount Castlereagh.* CHARLES W. V. STEWART, ed. London, 1850–1853.

> Memoir of Viscount Castlereagh, by the editor, I:1–68. Volumes XI–XII (Third series, Military and Diplomatic, III–IV): correspondence, 1815–1822.

MADISON, JAMES. *Writings of James Madison, Comprising His Papers and Private Correspondence.* 9 vols. GAILLARD HUNT, ed. New York, 1900–1910.

> Volumes VIII–IX: correspondence, 1808–1836.

MANNING, WILLIAM RAY, ed. *Diplomatic Correspondence of the United States concerning the Independence of the Latin-American Nations.* 3 vols. New York, 1925.

> Volumes I and II contain selections, largely excerpts, from correspondence on the

treaty. It is more accurately prepared than in the *American State Papers*, but the latter set is more complete for this topic. The greater part of this material has been consulted in the original manuscripts.

MARTENS, GEORG FRIEDRICH VON. *Recueil des principaux traités d'alliance, de paix, de trêve ... &c. conclus par les puissances de l'Europe.* 7 vols. Göttingen, 1791–1801.

Continued in a *Supplément* (10 vols., 1802–1828), and various later series. Useful for the European treaties involving American colonial possessions.

MILLER, D. HUNTER. *Secret Statutes of the United States.* Washington, 1918.

An official memorandum prepared in the State Department explaining the secrecy of the discussions and resolutions of the Eleventh and Twelfth Congresses in regard to the Floridas, 1811–1813.

———. *Treaties and Other International Acts of the United States of America.* 5 vols. to 1939. Washington, 1931—.

The most accurate publication of our treaties available, with excellent historical and legal notes. Volume I: descriptive matter, tables, and lists. Volumes II–V: documents, 1776–1852.

MONROE, JAMES. *Writings of James Monroe.* 7 vols. STANISLAUS M. HAMILTON, ed. New York, 1898–1903.

Volumes IV–VI: writings, 1803–1823. These documents contain little of value for this study except material which has been examined in the original, and cited accordingly in the notes.

Official Correspondence between Luis de Onis, Minister from Spain to the United States, and John Quincy Adams, Secretary of State, in Relation to the Floridas and the Boundaries of Louisiana. London, 1818.

The documents here are duplicates of those in the *American State Papers*, but their publication in England at the time is of some interest. They may have been published at the behest of the Duke of San Carlos, Spanish ambassador there, as it was Spain's constant policy to publish information on the affair in Europe, hoping that the merits of her case would be self-evident.

PICHARDO, JOSÉ ANTONIO. *Pichardo's Treatise on the Limits of Louisiana and Texas.* 2 vols. to 1939. CHARLES W. HACKETT, ed. Austin, 1931—.

Translation by C. W. Hackett, Charmion C. Shelby, and Mary R. Splawn. This document, prepared in pursuance of a royal order of 1805, and completed in 1812, was intended to support the Spanish claims in the boundary controversy with the United States. Research in connection with the present study of the Adams-Onís Treaty has produced evidence showing how it actually reached the hands of the men directing the negotiation.

PIKE, ZEBULON M. *Zebulon Pike's Arkansaw Journal: In Search of the Southern Louisiana Purchase Boundary Line (Interpreted by His Newly Recovered Maps).* STEPHEN H. HART and ARCHER B. HULBERT, eds. Colorado Springs and Denver, 1932.

A new edition of the record of Pike's expedition of 1806, which provided information used by the United States in the negotiation, and which figured in the pecuniary claims controversy; with a bibliographical résumé and historical notes based on recent detailed research.

ROBERTSON, JAMES A., ed. *Louisiana under the Rule of Spain, France, and the United States, 1785–1807.* 2 vols. Cleveland, 1911.

This important collection includes papers of Claiborne, Casa Calvo, and others valuable for an understanding of Louisiana's rôle in the diplomacy of the Borderlands.

SMITH, MRS. SAMUEL HARRISON. *The First Forty Years of Washington Society Portrayed by the Family Letters of* . . . . GAILLARD HUNT, ed. New York, 1906.

Illuminating accounts of persons and events in Washington by the wife of the founder of the *National Intelligencer,* a prominent Washington banker and for part of 1814 *ad interim* secretary of the treasury.

TATE, VERNON D., ed. "Spanish Documents Relating to the Voyage of the 'Racoon' to Astoria and San Francisco," *Hispanic American Historical Review,* XVIII (1938) :183–191.

Correspondence of Spanish officials showing favor to England in the War of 1812, and aid given the ship whose officers effected the official seizure of Astoria in 1813.

THOMAS, ALFRED B., ed. "An Anonymous Description of New Mexico, 1818," *Southwestern Historical Quarterly,* XXXIII (1929) :50–74.

————. "Documents Bearing Upon the Northern Frontier of New Mexico, 1818–1819," *New Mexico Historical Review,* IV (1929) :146–164.

————. "The Yellowstone River, James Long and Spanish Reaction to American Intrusion into Spanish Dominions, 1818–1819," *ibid.,* pp. 164–177.

Translations of documents from the archives at Sevilla and Mexico showing the anxiety of Spanish officials over conflicts with traders and adventurers of the United States along the frontier from the Sabine to the Yellowstone. These warnings and accounts of disturbances indicate clearly why Onís considered the delineation of the boundary in the upper Red and Arkansas river region important, and why he was anxious to keep that line as far as possible from Santa Fé itself as a defensive measure.

UNITED STATES. CONGRESS. *American State Papers.* 38 vols. J. W. GALES, JR., and W. W. SEATON, compilers. Washington, 1832–1861.

These volumes contain transcripts of documents on subjects relating to which Congress received information from the executive departments. The compilers took them from the earlier published House and Senate documents issued separately from time to time. Minor errors in transcription appear, and the selection of documents is not what the historian would desire. They are nevertheless the most valuable printed source for such a study as the present one.

Class I, *Foreign Relations.* Volumes III–VI,.1803–1828. It has been estimated that the *State Papers* include only a fourth of the diplomatic correspondence of the period. Naturally, instructions to and despatches from ministers abroad were kept confidential at the time, and are not included. It was the custom of the government, however, to publish the notes exchanged with the representatives of foreign governments, much to the irritation of Onís and others. Such material, with accompanying documents, comprises the bulk of the *Foreign Relations* series. One must go to the originals in the archives for an absolutely complete view of the negotiations. Certain of the instructions and despatches were published, to be sure, but not in complete form.

Volume IV, pages 422–626 and 650–703, and Volume V, pages 263–282, contain the matter submitted to Congress relating to the Adams-Onís Treaty. Many related documents of importance appear elsewhere in the set.

Class II, *Indian Affairs.* Volume II, 1815–1827. Documents relative to the Indians of the Floridas at the time of the first "Seminole War," and after the cession to the United States.

Class V, *Military Affairs.* Volume I, 1789–1819. Documents on military activities in the Floridas, those on Andrew Jackson's invasion being of especial interest here.

Class VIII, *Public Lands.* Volume III, 1815–1824. Includes translations of Spanish documents and records of commissioners dealing with land titles in the Floridas.

Class X, *Miscellaneous.* Volume II, 1809–1823. Material relative to Jackson's activities as transfer agent and territorial governor of the Floridas; also to the history of Astoria and proposals for the occupation of the Columbia River region.

————. *Debates and Proceedings in the Congress of the United States . . . Comprising the Period 1789 to 1824.* 42 vols. J. W. GALES, JR., and W. W. SEATON, compilers. Washington, 1834–1856.

The well-known *Annals of Congress.* Volumes XX–XXXVII: Eleventh to Sixteenth Congresses, 1809–1821.

————. SENATE. *Journal of the Executive Proceedings of the Senate, from the Commencement of the First, to the Termination of the Nineteenth Congress.* 1789–1829. 3 vols. Washington, 1828.

Records the brief consideration given the treaty before its unanimous approval in 1819 and almost unanimous reapproval in 1821.

UNITED STATES. DEPARTMENT OF STATE. *Report to the President on Claims under Article IX of the Treaty of 1819, with the Opinion of the Legal Adviser, Henry O'Connor, Favoring Payment.* Washington, 1878.

————. *Statement Showing the Payments of Awards of the Commissioners Appointed under the Conventions between the United States and France, Concluded April 30, 1803, and July 4, 1831, and between the United States and Spain, Concluded February 22, 1819.* Washington, 1886.

These two publications are illustrative of one of the legacies of the Adams-Onís Treaty—years of dispute over the payment of claims.

UNITED STATES. PRESIDENT. *Compilation of the Messages and Papers of the Presidents, 1789–1897.* 10 vols. JAMES D. RICHARDSON, ed. Washington, 1896–1899.

UNITED STATES. SUPREME COURT. *Opinion of the Supreme Court in the Case of the United States v. Texas, regarding the Possession of Land between the North Fork and the Prairie Dog Fork of the Red River, on the Basis of the Treaty of 1819 and Subsequent Agreements,* 162 *U. S. Reports* (October term, 1895) 1, 20–91.

Decision of March 16, 1896, that the Melish map of 1818 was in error and that the true 100th meridian should be followed; and that the south or Prairie Dog Fork was the boundary according to the Adams-Onís Treaty.

————. *State of Oklahoma v. State of Texas, United States Intervener,* 256 *U. S. Reports* (October term, 1920) 70–93, 602–615.

Decision of April 11, 1921, in a case involving oil rights under the bed of the Red River, concluding that the south bank of the river was the boundary according to the Adams-Onís Treaty.

WHITAKER, ARTHUR P., ed. *Documents Relating to the Commercial Policy of Spain in the Floridas with Incidental Reference to Louisiana.* Deland, Florida, 1931.

Translations of material relative to the regulations of commerce during the second Spanish occupation of the Floridas, 1783–1821, with an excellent historical introduction by the editor.

2. PERIODICAL MATTER

a) Contemporary

Annual Register, or a View of the History, Politics, and Literature, for the Year [1758—]. Printed for J. Dodsley. London, 1761—.

Includes texts of official documents and treaties, and accounts and statistics of annual events.

BRACKENRIDGE, HENRY M. "The Florida Question Stated," *American Register* (Philadelphia), I (1817) :128–148.

A quasi-official popular statement of the United States' claim to West Florida, refuting the arguments of Onís in the "Verus" pamphlet of that year. Brackenridge, a young lawyer and author, was close to the administration, and later, in 1817, went to South America as secretary to one of the special commissioners.

Morning Chronicle and Baltimore Advertiser. 1 vol. Baltimore, 1819.

One of the journals voicing the fear of trouble with England, and of the latter's seizure of Cuba, in 1819.

The National Intelligencer. 112 vols. Daily. Washington, 1800–1870.

The administration organ, published by J. W. Gales, Jr., and W. W. Seaton.

The National Register. 9 vols. in 7. Weekly. Washington, 1816–1820.

A political journal which supported William J. Crawford against Monroe.

Niles' Weekly Register. 75 vols. Baltimore, 1811–1849.

As reliable as any publication of the time for a fair representation of public opinion. Published by Hezekiah Niles.

RATTENBURY, J. FREEMAN. "Remarks on the Cession of the Floridas to the United States of America, and on the Necessity of Acquiring the Island of Cuba by Great Britain," *Pamphleteer* (London), XV (1819) :261–280.

A widely circulated political tract, expressing fear of United States expansion.

b) Later and Recent Periodical Matter

BARRY, J. NEILSON. "Oregon Boundaries," *Oregon Historical Quarterly*, XXX (1932) :259–267.

Survey, with diagrams and statistics, of various boundary settlements.

BÉCKER Y GONZÁLEZ, JERÓNIMO. "La cessión de las Floridas," *España moderna* (Madrid), 240 (1908) :41–70.

This study of the Adams-Onís Treaty is almost entirely reproduced in his *Relaciones exteriores de España*.

BOWMAN, ISAIAH. "An American Boundary Dispute; Decision of the Supreme Court of the United States with Respect to the Texas-Oklahoma Boundary," *Geographical Review*, XIII (1923) :161–189.

A geographical study of the case decided in 1921 (referred to in chapter vii).

BROOKS, PHILIP C. "The Pacific Coast's First International Boundary Delineation, 1816–1819," *Pacific Historical Review*, III (1934) :62–79.

An account of the drawing of the California-Oregon line in the Adams-Onís Treaty.

———. "Pichardo's Treatise and the Adams-Onís Treaty," *Hispanic American Historical Review*, XV (1935) :94–99.

A documentary note tracing a copy of Pichardo's study to Narciso de Heredia, who used it in the preparation of his *Exposición* of June 4, 1817. A part of the documents accompanying the treatise were sent to Onís in 1818.

BURNS, FRANCIS P. "West Florida and the Louisiana Purchase—An Examination into the Question of Whether or Not It Was Included in the Territory Ceded by the Treaty of 1803," *Louisiana Historical Quarterly*, XV (1932) : 391–416.

This sketch of the controversy discusses two cases in which the Supreme Court declined to answer the question, saying it was a political, rather than a legal question, and accepting the opinions of the legislative and executive branches that it was so included.

CAULEY, TROY J. "The Southwestern Boundary of the Louisiana Purchase," *Texas Monthly*, V (1930):541–553.

A brief sketch of the negotiations from 1803 to 1819, based largely on the work of Thomas M. Marshall.

COX, ISAAC J. "The Southwest Boundary of Texas," Texas State Historical Association, *Quarterly*, VI (1902):81–102.

———. "The Louisiana-Texas Frontier," *ibid.*, X (1906):1–75, and *Southwestern Historical Quarterly*, XVII (1913):1–42, 140–187.

———. "The Significance of the Louisiana-Texas Frontier," Mississippi Valley Historical Association, *Proceedings*, III (1909):198–213.

———. "Monroe and the Early Mexican Revolutionary Agents," American Historical Association, *Annual Report*, 1911:197–215.

———. "The American Intervention in West Florida," *American Historical Review*, XVII (1912):290–311.

———. "The Pan American Policy of Jefferson and Wilkinson," *Mississippi Valley Historical Review*, I (1914):211–239.

———. "General Wilkinson and His Later Intrigues with the Spaniards," *American Historical Review*, XIX (1914):794–812.

———. "The Louisiana-Texas Frontier during the Burr Conspiracy," *Mississippi Valley Historical Review*, X (1924):274–284.

———. "Hispanic-American Phases of the 'Burr Conspiracy'," *Hispanic American Historical Review*, XII (1932):145–175.

Professor Cox's careful studies present a great amount of detailed information and clarifying interpretation concerning the complex frontier problems centering about the Sabine River and New Orleans, and other developments considered in chapters i and ii. They are based on extensive research in this country and in Europe.

CURRY, JABEZ L. M. "The Acquisition of Florida," *Magazine of American History*, XIX (1888):286–301.

———. "Diplomatic Services of George W. Erving," Massachusetts Historical Society, *Proceedings*, V (1889):17–33.

Two sketches by a United States minister to Spain, based in part on the legation archives there. The biography is more personal than political.

DAVIS, T. FREDERICK. "McGregor's Invasion of Florida," Florida Historical Society, *Quarterly*, VII (1928):3–71.

———. "United States Troops in Spanish East Florida," *ibid.*, IX (1930–1931):3–23, 96–116, 135–155, 259–278; X (1931):24–34.

Two useful detailed accounts of border developments which complicated the problems of Onís.

ELLIOTT, T. C. "An Event of One Hundred Years Ago," and "The Surrender at Astoria in 1818," *Oregon Historical Quarterly*, XIX (1918):181–187, 271–282.

Narratives, with documentary quotations, of the visits to the Columbia River of Captain James Biddle with the sloop-of-war "Ontario," August 19 and 20, 1818, and Special Commissioner John B. Prevost aboard the British sloop-of-war "Blossom," October 1 to 6, 1818.

FICKLEN, JOHN R. "The Northwestern Boundary of Louisiana," Louisiana Historical Society, *Publications,* II, pt. 2 (1899) :26–39.

———. "Was Texas Included in the Louisiana Purchase?" Southern Historical Association, *Publications,* V (1901) :351–387.

These are among the earliest scholarly studies of the Louisiana boundary problems. The first refutes a number of statements, particularly that of the United States Land Office map of 1896, indicating that Oregon was included in the purchase. The second questions the validity of Henry Adams' decision that the United States had a good claim to Texas.

FISHER, LILLIAN E. "American Influence on the Movement for Mexican Independence," *Mississippi Valley Historical Review,* XVIII (1932) :463–478.

A sketch of various coöperative schemes to liberate Mexico operating across the border or by sea.

FOREMAN, GRANT. "The Red River and the Spanish Boundary in the United States Supreme Court," *Chronicles of Oklahoma,* II (1924) :298–310.

Brief history of litigations, based on the treaty of 1819, settled in 1896 and 1921.

GALPIN, W. FREEMAN. "American Grain Trade to the Spanish Peninsula, 1810–1814," *American Historical Review,* XXVIII (1922) :24–44.

This statistical view of the trade in relation to war and diplomacy treats an interesting neglected phase of the War of 1812, and is important for an understanding of Onís' activities.

GUINNESS, RALPH B. "The Purpose of the Lewis and Clark Expedition," *Mississippi Valley Historical Review,* XX (1933) :90–100.

Argues that Jefferson's main objective was the development of the fur trade, not any contemplated acquisition of the territory. Scientific aims were incidental, according to this work, which is based on well-known published materials.

HINSDALE, BURKE A. "Establishment of the First Southern Boundary of the United States," American Historical Association, *Annual Report,* 1893:331–366.

The first historical study of the relations of the United States to the Mississippi and the Gulf, 1779 to 1819.

LOCKEY, JOSEPH B. "The Florida Intrigues of José Alvarez de Toledo," Florida Historical Society, *Quarterly,* XII (1934) :145–178.

An able survey of the activities of Toledo in connection with the negotiations concerning the cession of the Floridas, 1813–1820, based on investigation of parts of the Spanish diplomatic correspondence.

MANNING, MABEL M. "East Florida Papers in the Library of Congress," *Hispanic American Historical Review,* X (1930) :392–397.

Historical and bibliographical description of some 65,000 manuscripts, largely local records of Spanish East Florida, handed over in accordance with the terms of the Adams-Onís Treaty.

MANNING, WILLIAM R. "The Nootka Sound Controversy," American Historical Association, *Annual Report,* 1904:279–478.

A thorough review of the Anglo-Spanish negotiations, 1790 to 1794, useful for the background of territorial claims on the North Coast.

MARTIN, THOMAS P. "Some International Aspects of the Anti-Slavery Movement, 1818–1823," *Journal of Economic and Business History,* I (1928) :137–148.

This study of the rivalry between the East Indian and the growing American cotton industries shows something of the British manufacturers' attitude toward slavery and the southward expansion of the United States.

MEANY, EDMOND S. "Three Diplomats Prominent in the Oregon Question," *Washington Historical Quarterly*, V (1914) :207–214.
Traces the interests of Adams, Gallatin, and Clay in Oregon from 1814 on, neglecting the significance of the Adams-Onís Treaty.

MERK, FREDERICK. "The Oregon Pioneers and the Boundary," *American Historical Review*, XXIX (1924) :681–699.
Diminishes the diplomatic significance of United States settlers of the early 'forties by showing that the Willamette Valley where they settled was not in the region disputed between 1826 and 1846.

PERKINS, DEXTER. "Russia and the Spanish Colonies, 1817–1818," *American Historical Review*, XXVIII (1923) :656–673.
Emphasizes the conciliatory policy and sincerity of Alexander I, in contrast to whatever Tatistcheff may have done. Suggests that the latter's desire for a complete reconquest of Spanish America brought about the fall of Pizarro late in 1818. Discusses the Russian desire to have the United States join the mediation between Spain and her colonies.

PHINNEY, A. H. "The First Spanish-American War," Florida Historical Society, *Quarterly*, IV (1926) :114–129.

———. "The Second Spanish-American War," *ibid.*, V (1926) :103–111.
Sketches of military activities on the border, 1811–1815 and 1818, respectively.

RICHIE, ELEANOR L. "The Background of the International Boundary Line of 1819 Along the Arkansas River in Colorado," *Colorado Magazine*, X (1933) : 145–156.

———. "The Disputed International Boundary in Colorado, 1803–1819," *ibid.*, XIII (1936) :171–180.
Two important articles which are helpful in studying the interweaving of geographic and diplomatic factors.

SÁNCHEZ ALONZO, BENITO. Review of W. R. de Villa-Urrutia, *Fernán Núñez, el embajador* (Madrid, 1931), in *Revista de Filología Española*, XVIII (1931) :75–76.
An interesting discussion of Ferdinand's representatives in European diplomacy, and their comparative obscurity.

SCHAFER, JOSEPH. "British Attitude toward the Oregon Question, 1815–1846," *American Historical Review*, XVI (1911) :273–299.
An analysis of the bases of the rival claims to Oregon, suggesting, less clearly than Professor Merk in his later article, that the British did not seriously contest the possession south of the Columbia.

STENBERG, RICHARD. "The Boundaries of the Louisiana Purchase," *Hispanic American Historical Review*, XIV (1934) :32–64.
An inconclusive effort to prove that the boundaries of Louisiana were defined secretly between Spain and France in 1762, based wholly on well-known printed materials. The statements that Onís knew of such an agreement and that Adams knew Onís was specifically instructed to yield Texas as a last resort are particularly at variance with my beliefs.

WYLLYS, RUFUS K. "The East Florida Revolutions of 1812–1814," *Hispanic American Historical Review*, IX (1929) :415–445.

———. "The Filibusters of Amelia Island," Georgia Historical Society, *Quarterly*, XII (1928) :297–325.
The most useful of the various portrayals of the escapades of the St. Mary's frontier. The second article covers the affairs of 1817–1818.

3. MEMOIRS AND BIOGRAPHIES

ADAMS, JAMES TRUSLOW. *The Adams Family.* Boston, 1930.
>A fine characterization of John Quincy Adams is included; valuable for any study of his diplomacy, especially in the lack of a satisfactory biography.

ADAMS, JOHN QUINCY. *Memoirs of John Quincy Adams, Comprising Portions of His Diary from 1795 to 1848.* 12 vols. CHARLES FRANCIS ADAMS, ed. Philadelphia, 1874–1877.
>Volumes IV and V of this monument to the Puritan conscience contain accounts and comments concerning Adams' service as secretary of state. They are a guide to Adams' policy, and, for the times at which he made full entries, a narrative of events.

Appleton's Cyclopedia of American Biography. 6 vols. JAMES G. WILSON and JOHN FISKE, eds. New York, 1887–1889.
>Volume IV contains the only biographical sketch found in English of Luis de Onís. It is generally correct, but has certain errors, including the dates of both his birth and his death (giving 1769 for 1762, and 1830 for 1827).

BAGOT, JOSCELINE, ed. *George Canning and His Friends, Containing Hitherto Unpublished Letters, jeux d'esprit, etc.* 2 vols. London, 1909.
>A portrayal of characters and personal life, consisting largely of quotations from letters to Charles Bagot, and dealing mostly with European matters. The few letters written by Bagot in Washington are of interest.

BASSETT, JOHN S. *Life of Andrew Jackson.* 2 vols. New York, 1916; rev. ed., New York, 1929.
>A standard work, containing a concise summary of Jackson's invasions of Florida and their relation to diplomacy.

BEMIS, SAMUEL F., ed. *The American Secretaries of State and Their Diplomacy.* 10 vols. New York, 1927–1929.
>Volume III: "James Madison," by Charles E. Hill; "Robert Smith," by Charles C. Tansill; and "James Monroe," by Julius W. Pratt.
>Volume IV: "John Quincy Adams," by Dexter Perkins; and "John Forsyth," by Eugene I. McCormac.
>Professor Hill's carefully wrought narrative is a useful guide through the complex problems of Madison's secretaryship. Although Robert Smith was generally ignored until this sketch appeared, Professor Tansill shows that the irritating episodes of his dealings with Foster and Jackson make him worthy of attention in connection with the War of 1812. With the same vivid exposition that marked his *Expansionists of 1812,* Professor Pratt has written here an analysis of Monroe's services that is of basic importance for the present study. Professor Perkins' account, marked by clarity and candid expression, is the most useful single study of Adams' secretaryship. Certain points in the subject matter will be open to varying interpretations at least until a satisfactory biography of Adams is written. That in turn must await the opening of the Adams family papers to historians. It is only natural that the author of a monograph on one phase of Adams' services would disagree occasionally with such a necessarily general summary, and would feel that the portrayal of the Onís negotiations is incomplete, lacking a study of the Spanish manuscripts.

CLARK, BENNETT CHAMP. *John Quincy Adams, "Old Man Eloquent."* Boston, 1932.
>A readable, rapid characterization, based largely on standard published authorities.

DÍAZ, NICOMEDES PASTOR, and CARDENAS, FRANCISCO DE. *Galería de españoles célebres contemporáneos.* 9 vols. Madrid, 1841–1847.
>Volume III contains a sketch of Narciso de Heredia, Conde de Ofalia, which was reprinted verbatim without acknowledgment in the Introduction to the *Escritos del Conde de Ofalia* (Bilbao, 1894), edited by the Marqués de Heredia (*q.v.*).

Dictionary of American Biography. ALLEN JOHNSON and DUMAS MALONE, eds. 20 vols. New York, 1928–1936.

The sketches in the series most used in this study have been: In Volume I: "John Quincy Adams," by Worthington C. Ford; "John Armstrong," by Julius W. Pratt; "John J. Astor," by W. J. Ghent. In Volume III: "John C. Calhoun," by Ulrich B. Phillips. In Volume IV: "Henry Clay," by E. Merton Coulter; "William H. Crawford," by Ulrich B. Phillips. In Volume VI: "George W. Erving," by Charles E. Hill; "John Forsyth," by Robert P. Brooks (the statement therein that Forsyth "succeeded . . . in securing the ratification of the treaty" is in error). In Volume VII: "Albert Gallatin," by David S. Muzzey; "John Graham," by Armistead C. Gordon, Jr. In Volume IX: "Andrew Jackson," by Thomas P. Abernethy. In Volume XII: "James Madison," by Julius W. Pratt; "Richard W. Meade," by John H. Frederick; "John Melish," by Joseph Jackson. In Volume XIII: "James Monroe," by Dexter Perkins.

Dictionary of National Biography . . . from the Earliest Times to 1900. LESLIE STEPHEN and SIDNEY LEE, eds. 66 vols. London, 1885–1901. Reprinted in 22 vols., including Supplement, London, 1921.

All references are to the 1921 printing. The notices most used have been: In Volume III: "George Canning," by Thomas E. Kebbel. In Volume VII: "Augustus J. Foster," by Henry Morse Stephens. In Volume X: "Francis J. Jackson," by Henry M. Chichester; "Robert Jenkinson, Second Earl of Liverpool," by Lord Sumner. In Volume XIII: "John P. Morier," by Stanley Lane-Poole. In Volume XVIII: "Robert Stewart, Viscount Castlereagh," by Lord Sumner. In Volume XX: "Arthur Wellesley, First Duke of Wellington," by Ernest M. Lloyd; "Henry Wellesley, First Baron Cowley," by George LeG. Norgate; "Richard Wellesley, Marquis Wellesley," by Alexander J. Arbuthnot. In Volume XXII: "Charles Bagot," by T. B. Browning.

GILMAN, DANIEL C. *James Monroe.* Boston, 1883.

This account in the *American Statesman* series is unfortunately still the best biography of Monroe available.

HYDE DE NEUVILLE, JEAN GUILLAUME, BARON. *Mémoires et souvenirs du Baron Hyde de Neuville.* 3 vols. Paris, 1890–1892.

Volume II (1814–1822) covers the Frenchman's services as minister to the United States, but with only slight references to the Spanish affairs. The abridged edition of the memoirs, translated into English by Frances Jackson (2 vols., London, 1913), contains but one insignificant passage relating to the treaty of 1819.

JAMES, MARQUIS. *The Border Captain.* Indianapolis, 1933.

A readable, highly informative biography and colorful characterization of Andrew Jackson up to the end of his services as territorial governor of Florida, 1821.

Los ministros en España desde 1800 á 1869, historia contemporánea por uno que siendo español no cobra del presupuesto. 2 vols. Madrid, 1869.

Hardly more than a series of anecdotes, published anonymously, but useful to a limited extent for biographical data, and entertaining for its comments on individual characters. Narciso de Heredia, Juan Lozano de Torres, and the Duke of Alagón are among those considered.

MORSE, JOHN TORREY. *John Quincy Adams.* Boston, 1882.

This well-known volume in the *American Statesmen* series clearly reveals the prevailing lack of knowledge concerning Spanish affairs and the lack of appreciation of the significance of the treaty of 1819 in Adams' career and in the territorial and diplomatic development of the nation.

ONÍS, LUIS DE. *Memoria sobre las negociaciones entre España y los Estados Unidos de América, que dieron motivo al tratado de 1819. Con una noticia sobre la estadística de aquel pais. Acompaña un apéndice, que contiene documentos importantes para mayor ilustración del asunto. Por D. Luis de Onís, ministro plenipotenciario que fué cerca de aquella república, y actual embajador de S.M. en la Corte de Nápoles.* 2 vols. Madrid, 1820.

Onís, Luis de. *Memoir upon the Negotiations between Spain and the United States of America, Which Led to the Treaty of 1819. . . . Translated from the Spanish, with Notes, by Tobias Watkins.* Washington, E. De Krafft, printer, 1821; Baltimore, published by Fielding Lucas, Jr., 1821.

Volume I of Onís' memoir, published before the decision of the Spanish Cortes in favor of ratification, contains a general account of the foreign relations of the United States, a brief narrative of the negotiation, and in the Appendix the Franco-Spanish treaty of 1800, the Convention of 1802 between Spain and the United States, the Adams-Onís Treaty, and the three "Verus" pamphlets written by or for Onís in 1810, 1812, and 1817.

Volume II has not received due historical notice because it was not published in the English version. It appeared in the winter of 1820, after ratification had been approved, and contained, in addition to transcripts of most of the notes exchanged by Onís and Adams, a highly significant note upon the value of the treaty as Onís saw it, which is discussed in chapter vii, *supra.*

The general account of the United States in all probability was drawn up pursuant to an order of May, 1818, to the effect that each Spanish diplomatic representative abroad should submit at the end of his term of service a historical-political memoir concerning the country to which he was assigned (Pizarro to Onís, May 22, 1818, in A.M.E., 224). At least the material assembled for that task was conveniently at hand when he essayed to defend his treaty by a published statement.

The translator in his Preface wisely observed that, for Onís to prove that he had not accepted a disgraceful treaty, and that he had not been influenced by fear or partiality for the United States, "it was important, that he should show the political and physical strength of the United States, in its utmost magnitude: that he should demonstrate the impossibility of defending the Spanish provinces in America from the ambitious grasp of this colossal power: and that he should draw such a picture of the people, as might lead to the inference that contempt, rather than admiration or dread, supplied him with the colouring." This provides a reasonable explanation for the often paradoxical characterization of the potentialities of the land and its people, and of the vainglorious iniquity of both individual and national attitudes.

Tobias Watkins, the translator, was a physician who became active in public affairs. He was assistant surgeon-general of the United States in 1818 and 1819, and from 1824 to 1829 was fourth auditor of the United States Treasury. He had edited a periodical, *The Portico,* with a partner in Philadelphia from 1816 to 1820, and had translated certain medical matter from French when he undertook the Onís memoir.

The memoir was reprinted in Spanish at Mexico City in 1826.

John Forsyth's *Observations,* which he wrote in reply to Onís' book and circulated among certain members of the Spanish Cortes in 1820, were published in Madrid in 1822. The translation into Spanish was done by the Reverend Thomas Gough, who had once been an unofficial representative of the United States there. The title was *Observaciones sobre la memoria del Señor Onís, relativas á la negociación con los Estados Unidos.*

Parton, James. *Andrew Jackson.* 3 vols. New York, 1860.

A standard pioneer work, in large measure replaced by Bassett's biography.

Pizarro, José García de León y. *Memorias de la vida del Excmo. Señor ... escritos por el mismo.* 3 vols. Madrid, 1894–1897.

An apologia comprising a vivid account of the long public service of one of the most able Spanish officials of the period. It covers the entire Napoleonic era and eighteen years thereafter, although Pizarro's public service ended, much to his dismay, in 1818. That dismay colors the memoirs, which were written, certainly with some reference to records, in and after 1833. The third volume contains transcripts of important documents.

Porter, Kenneth W. *John Jacob Astor, Business Man.* 2 vols. Cambridge, 1931.

A highly detailed account, with the emphasis on business activities. It leaves unanswered certain questions concerning Astor's relationship with the State Department.

RUSH, RICHARD, *Memoranda of a Residence at the Court of London, Comprising Incidents Official and Personal from 1819 to 1825*. Second series. Philadelphia, 1845.

> These well-known memoirs of the United States minister at London include occasional items concerning San Carlos, Onís, and Spanish affairs, with considerable information on British policy.

Russkiĭ biograficheskiĭ slovar'. 25 vols. St. Petersburg, 1896–1913.

> A biographical dictionary. Volume XX contains a sketch of Dmitri Pavlovitch Tatistcheff, Russian ambassador to Spain, 1815–1819, with bibliographical references. For the translation, I am indebted to Mr. Vladimir Gsovksi, of the Library of Congress.

SAN JOSÉ, DIEGO. *Vida y "milagros" de Fernando VII*. Madrid, 1929.

> A popular biography, employing various of the entertaining anecdotes which have developed about the period of Ferdinand's rule.

SHREVE, ROYAL O. *The Finished Scoundrel, General James Wilkinson*. Indianapolis, 1933.

> A readable and illuminating book, useful here for the study of his activities on the Louisiana-Texas frontier.

SMITH, ARTHUR D. H. *John Jacob Astor, Landlord of New York*. New York, 1929.

> A popular account of some value. Uses the account of Astor's opinion of the Treaty of Ghent, taken from C. A. Bristed's *Letter to the Hon. Horace Mann* (*q.v.*).

UNITED STATES. CONGRESS. *Biographical Dictionary of the American Congress, 1774–1927*. Washington, 1928.

> Contains useful sketches of the official services of Forsyth, Adams, and others who figure in this work.

VAN DEUSEN, GLYNDON G. *The Life of Henry Clay*. Boston, 1937.

> This new biography is of value here as a portrayal of Adams' prime opponent in foreign affairs.

VILLA-URRUTIA, WENCESLAO R. DE. *Fernando VII*. 2 vols. Madrid, 1922–1931.

> Although Volume I of this work is primarily concerned with the period 1820–1823, and Volume II with the succeeding decade, the introductory chapters comprise one of the most scholarly treatments of Ferdinand's rule before 1820.

———. *Fernán Núñez, el embajador*. Madrid, 1931.

> The late Marqués de Villa-Urrutia was one of the few thorough scholars of the whole era of Ferdinand VII, from 1808 to 1833, a period which has been generally neglected by historians and passed over lightly in comprehensive histories of Spain. This biography of the second Fernán Núñez to be an ambassador is valuable for the background of the Adams-Onís affair, and for some direct information on its ramifications in London and Paris. (See Benito Sánchez Alonzo, under "Later and Recent Periodical Matter" in this Bibliography.)
>
> Carlos José Gutiérrez de los Ríos, sixth Count of Fernán Núñez, was Spanish ambassador to France from 1787 to 1791. His son, Carlos José Francisco, who became first Duke of Fernán Núñez, in 1817, was ambassador to England, 1812 to 1817, and to France, 1817 to 1820. The latter is the subject of Villa-Urrutia's study.

WELLESLEY, HENRY, BARON COWLEY. *Diary and Correspondence of Henry Wellesley, First Lord Cowley, 1790–1846*. COL. THE HON. F. A. WELLESLEY, ed. London, 1930.

> A disappointing work both in content and in execution, edited by the diplomatist's grandson. No diary was available for the period of Wellesley's mission to Spain (1810–1822), and the account of that period, made up from correspondence with notes is wholly inadequate.

Reference Works: In addition to material primarily biographical, data of this kind have been obtained from numerous authorities, of which three encyclopedias should be mentioned. They are: JOSÉ ALEMANY Y BOLÚFER, *Diccionario enciclopédico ilustrado de la lengua española* (Barcelona, 1927); ESPASA-CALPE, S.A., *Enciclopedia universal ilustrada Europeo-Americana* (70 vols., Barcelona, 1907–1930; *Apéndice*, 10 vols., Madrid, 1930–1933); and *La Grande encyclopédie, inventaire raisonné des sciences, des lettres et des artes* (31 vols., Paris, 1886–1902), all of which contain biographical sketches.

4. GENERAL WORKS AND SPECIAL TREATISES

ADAMS, HENRY. *History of the United States*. 9 vols. New York, 1889–1891.

The classic and the most complete history of the country in the period 1801 to 1817, and one which marked a notable advance in the study of foreign sources. Adams supports the United States' claim to Texas, but deprecates that to West Florida.

AGUADO BLEYE, PEDRO. *Manual de historia de España*. 2 vols. Bilbao, 1914; 5th ed., rev., 1927–1931.

A concise account by an outstanding Spanish historian, with excellent bibliographies throughout. It is one of the few general works dealing in any thoroughness with the reign of Ferdinand VII.

ALTAMIRA, RAFAEL. *Histoire d'Espagne*. Paris, 1931.

———. "Spain, 1815–1845," *Cambridge Modern History* (1902–1912), X: 205–243. London, 1907.

Like most other comprehensive Spanish histories of Spain, Professor Altamira's great *Historia de España y de la civilazación espanola* (Barcelona, 1900–1911) does not cover the nineteenth century, but in these two works he considers the reign of Ferdinand VII. The first, though short, is marked by pungent characterizations. The second is the best account of the period available in English.

BALLESTEROS Y BERETTA, ANTONIO. *Historia de España y de su influencia en la historia universal*. 8 vols. to 1939. Barcelona, 1918—.

The seventh volume of this exemplary series covers the period from 1808 to 1841, and continues the thorough treatment of internal affairs and the unusually extensive bibliographical data. For diplomatic history the work is not so satisfactory. The one paragraph on the Adams-Onís Treaty includes the erroneous statement that it was effected by Erving.

BANCROFT, HUBERT H. *History of Arizona and New Mexico*. San Francisco, 1889.

———. *The Northwest Coast*. 2 vols. San Francisco, 1884.

Bancroft's pioneer comprehensive works have formed an essential foundation for any study of the West, though they have been improved upon in many details.

BÉCKER, JERÓNIMO. *Historia de las relaciones exteriores de España durante el siglo XIX*. 3 vols. Madrid, 1924–1927.

The only general history of nineteenth-century Spanish diplomacy, prepared by the late archivist of the Archivo del Ministerio de Estado. It is of value, but is as one-sided in its account of the Spanish interests in the treaty negotiations as most works written in this country have been in the other direction.

BEMIS, SAMUEL F. *A Diplomatic History of the United States*. New York, 1936.

———. *Pinckney's Treaty: A Study of America's Advantage from Europe's Distress, 1783–1800.* Baltimore, 1926.

The first of these scholarly accounts contains in one chapter the best existing brief narrative of the negotiation, signature, and ratification of the Adams-Onís Treaty, under the title "The Transcontinental Treaty." The book on Pinckney's Treaty gives an essential explanation of the background of relations between Spain and the United States in the early nineteenth century. Its title expresses a thesis which can be accurately applied to the result of the Adams-Onís affair.

BOLTON, HERBERT E. *The Spanish Borderlands; A Chronicle of Old Florida and the Southwest.* New Haven, 1921.

———. *Texas in the Middle Eighteenth Century; Studies in Spanish Colonial History and Administration.* Berkeley, 1915.

Two works invaluable for an understanding of the political, economic, and geographical background of the frontier controversies concerned in the Adams-Onís negotiations. I am indebted to Dr. Bolton for permission to use the term the "Borderlands" in my title, since my narrative continues the history of those regions for a period from the date his *Chronicle* left off.

BOND, FRANK. *Historical Sketch of "Louisiana" and the Louisiana Purchase.* Washington, 1912.

Discussion of five maps exhibited by the General Land Office at the Louisiana Purchase Exposition at St. Louis in 1904. Concludes that the United States acquired West Florida but not Texas in the purchase.

BORCHARD, EDWIN M. *Diplomatic Protection of Citizens Abroad, or the Law of International Claims.* New York, 1915.

A standard treatise, in which the ruling out of the Meade claim is termed an injustice, inasmuch as it was one of those for which the United States assumed responsibility in the treaty of 1819.

BRACKENRIDGE, HENRY M. *Views of Louisiana.* Pittsburgh, 1814.

A descriptive and historical tract of contemporary fame, asserting that West Florida and Texas were included in the Louisiana Purchase, on the basis of French maps and writings.

BREVARD, CAROLINE M. *History of Florida from the Treaty of 1763 to Our Own Times.* 2 vols. JAMES A. ROBERTSON, ed. Deland, Florida, 1924.

In addition to a clear survey of the period here concerned, this work contains useful appendixes with statistics and data on officials.

BRISTED, CHARLES A. *A Letter to the Hon. Horace Mann.* New York, 1850.

A tract written in reply to Mann's criticisms of John J. Astor and Stephen Girard. Contains the account of Astor's conversation with Gallatin about the Treaty of Ghent (see pp. 151–152).

BROOKS, PHILIP C. "Spanish Royalists in the United States, 1809–1821," in *Colonial Hispanic America.* A. CURTIS WILGUS, ed. Washington, 1936.

A narrative of the troubles of Onís and the men who aided him with agents of the insurgent Spanish American colonies.

BRYAN, WILHELMUS B. *History of the National Capital.* 2 vols. New York, 1916.

Includes useful accounts of the scene, press, and personalities of the period.

CALLAHAN, JAMES B. *Cuba and International Relations.* Baltimore, 1899.

A general treatise containing information on the attitudes of England and the United States toward Cuba in 1819–1820, with illustrative quotations.

CHADWICK, FRENCH E. *The United States and Spain: Diplomacy.* New York, 1909.

The first of two volumes written with particular attention to the war of 1898, presenting therefore a cursory but reasonably accurate summary of the century preceding

CHAMBERS, HENRY E. *West Florida and Its Relations to the Historical Cartography of the United States* (Johns Hopkins Studies in History and Political Science, Ser. XVI, no. 5). Baltimore, 1898.

One of the earliest modern historical studies of the controversy over the inclusion of West Florida in the Louisiana Purchase. A standard account so far as the materials then available would allow. Chambers believed, as does the present writer, that the claim of Livingston and Madison to West Florida was unsound.

COX, ISAAC J. *The West Florida Controversy, 1798–1813: A Study in American Diplomacy.* Baltimore, 1918.

A highly detailed analysis of the problems of colonization and diplomacy involved, based upon research in the Spanish colonial archives as well as in those of this country.

CRANDALL, SAMUEL B. *Treaties, Their Making and Enforcement.* New York, 1904.

An international law text with several references to legal points involved in the ratification and execution of the Adams-Onís Treaty.

CROCKETT, GEORGE L. *Two Centuries in East Texas.* Dallas, 1932.

A local hisory of the region about Nacogdoches, of which chapter vi is a detailed account from 1790 to 1821.

DARBY, WILLIAM. *A Geographical Description of the State of Louisiana.* Philadelphia, 1816; 2d ed., enlarged, New York, 1817.

———. *Memoir upon the Geography, and Natural Civil History of Florida.* Philadelphia, 1821.

Darby, a prominent geographer, published both of these books with accompanying maps. The first includes as an Appendix an argument that the United States should push its claims to the maximum view of the Louisiana Purchase limits: the Perdido, the Río Grande, and a midpoint between the Columbia River and San Francisco on the West Coast.

DOUGLAS, EDWARD M. *Boundaries, Areas, Geographic Centers and Altitudes of the United States and Several States with a Brief Record of Important Changes in Their Territory.* 2d ed., Washington, 1930.

A useful historical and statistical summary giving concise data on all parts and possessions of the United States. Published by the United States Geological Survey. First edition, 1923. This supplanted the earlier (1885, 1900, 1904, 1906) *Boundaries of the United States*, by Henry Gannett.

FAIRBANKS, GEORGE R. *History of Florida from ... 1512, to ... 1842.* Philadelphia, 1871.

Long accepted as one of the standard works. This sketch gives no detailed account of the treaty of 1819.

FORBES, JAMES G. *Sketches, Historical and Topographical, of the Floridas; More Particularly of East Florida.* New York, 1821.

A descriptive work dealing largely with East Florida, and preceded by a history of the region since 1492.

FOREMAN, GRANT. *Pioneer Days in the Early Southwest.* Cleveland, 1926.

———. *Indian Removal: The Emigration of the Five Civilized Tribes of Indians.* Norman, 1932.

———. *Advancing the Frontier, 1830–1860.* Norman, 1933.

These books, by a scholar who has studied intensively the whole story of the Indians who eventually settled in Oklahoma, are important for the early history of the upper Red River and Río Grande regions, and for an account of the liquidation of the Florida Indian problem.

FORTIER, ALCÉE. *History of Louisiana.* 4 vols. New York, 1904.

A comprehensive work, especially valuable for the later nineteenth century. For the earlier periods, it does not improve greatly on Gayarré.

FUGIER, ANDRÉ. *Napoléon et l'Espagne, 1799–1808.* 2 vols. Paris, 1930.

A thorough and illuminating study of Franco-Spanish relations and their place in European politics, based upon research in the archives of Spain, France, and other countries.

FULLER, HUBERT B. *The Purchase of Florida.* Cleveland, 1906.

This book, long accepted as the standard account of the Adams-Onís Treaty, was based largely on the *American State Papers*, Adams' *Memoirs*, and a cursory reference to the archives of the State Department. Its narrative of Florida border plots and conflicts is its strongest point.

The author failed to see the transcontinental aspect of the treaty, and consequently established in popular usage the erroneous interpretation expressed in the title. Had the negotiation involved only a "purchase" of the Floridas, Adams would have had no reason to consider it his greatest diplomatic achievement.

Fuller's work is, further, a notable example of the limitations of one-sided diplomatic study. Not a single Spanish item is cited, Onís is neglected, and the Spanish negotiation appears only as seen in the notes published in the *American State Papers* and in Adams' caustic comments. Upon such an inadequate foundation Fuller built a lamentation over our sins of aggrandizement.

GALLATIN, ALBERT. *The Oregon Question.* New York, 1846.

Most of the controversial literature of the 'forties referred slightly, if at all, to the treaty of 1819. Since, as Professor Merk has shown, the area in dispute then was between the Columbia and the Forty-ninth Parallel, the California-Oregon line was not in the limelight. Gallatin, however, in urging mutual concessions and an amicable settlement with England, deprecated the validity of the Spanish title acquired in the Adams-Onís Treaty. His arguments do not preclude the conclusion of the present writer that this country obtained an equity of appreciable legal value from Spain.

GARRISON, GEORGE P. *Texas, A Contest of Civilizations.* New York, 1903.

A useful survey, although supplanted in many details by later research.

GAYARRÉ, CHARLES. *History of Louisiana.* 4 vols. in 3. New Orleans, 1854–1866.

The classic history of Louisiana, this work remains an invaluable authority. See especially volumes III and IV, covering the Spanish and American periods.

GEOFFROY DE GRANDMAISON, CHARLES A. *L'Espagne et Napoléon.* 3 vols. Paris, 1908–1931.

A detailed account, 1804 to 1814, but one in which affairs of the United States appear infrequently.

GHENT, W. J. *The Early Far West.* New York, 1931.

A semipopular sketch including information on explorers and fur traders on the Spanish frontier.

GOLDER, FRANK ALFRED. *Russian Expansion on the Pacific, 1641–1850.* Cleveland, 1914.

This book deals largely with the seventeenth-century Russian explorations which became the basis of territorial claims.

GOODWIN, CARDINAL L. *The Trans-Mississippi West, 1803–1853.* New York, 1922.

A valuable outline and narrative for any study of Western expansion.

GREENHOW, ROBERT. *History of Oregon and California, and the Other Terri-tories on the Northwest Coast of America.* Boston, 1844.

A widely known pioneer work by a physician who had become translator for the State Department. Originally published in smaller form in 1840, this painstaking study was the broadest expression of the attitude of the United States in the contro-versy with England. A perfunctory account of the Adams-Onís Treaty appears in an early chapter.

GRIFFIN, CHARLES C. *The United States and the Disruption of the Spanish Empire, 1810–1822.* New York, 1937.

A careful analysis, based on study of archival materials in Europe and the United States, which shows the relationship of the Adams-Onís treaty negotiations to other international problems. It grew out of a study of the delay in ratification of the treaty of 1819, and emphasizes the close connection between that diplomatic complication and the recognition of the Spanish American republics. It is notable for its evaluation of the motives affecting the nations and persons concerned.

HACKETT, FRANK W. *The Meade Claim.* Washington, 1910.

An argumentative tract reviewing the circumstances of the waiver of claims by the United States in the Adams-Onís Treaty, its ratification, and the subsequent disallow-ance of the long-standing claim of Richard W. Meade, merchant and naval agent of the United States in Spain, against the Spanish government. One of numerous writ-ings decrying that action by the United States Claims Commission, and significant for its recent date.

HACKLEY, RICHARD S., compiler. *Legal Opinions on the Title of Richard S. Hackley to Lands in East Florida.* New York, 1831.

Collection of documents relative to the futile effort of the former United States consul at Cádiz to have this government acknowledge him as owner of the Alagón grant in East Florida. Includes an alleged deed from the Duke of Alagón giving Hackley title to all the lands granted the former, dated May 29, 1819. The claim de-pended of course upon the argument that the King could not legally invalidate the Alagón grant, as he did in ratifying the treaty.

HAMILTON, PETER J. *Colonial Mobile.* New York, 1897; rev. ed., New York, 1910.

A complete and readable history of Mobile, and of the Southwest in which it was an important center, to 1821.

HERMANN, BINGER. *The Louisiana Purchase, and Our Title West of the Rocky Mountains, with a Review of Annexation by the United States.* Washington, 1898.

A brochure, by the commissioner of the General Land Office, to correct a map issued by that office in 1896. Asserts that Oregon was included in the Louisiana Pur-chase. Hermann's statement that Adams accepted a line on the Forty-second Parallel because it was the northern limit of Spanish occupation is groundless, and his con-clusion regarding Oregon has not been upheld. It was promptly attacked in a paper by John R. Ficklen in the *Publications* of the Louisiana Historical Society (*q.v.*).

HILDT, JOHN C. *Early Diplomatic Negotiations of the United States with Russia* (Johns Hopkins Studies in History and Political Science, Ser. XXIV, nos. 5 and 6). Baltimore, 1906.

A useful though now outdated general sketch, containing no mention of Russia's view toward the Adams-Onís negotiations.

HILL, CHARLES E. *Leading American Treaties.* New York, 1922.

A clear, concise account, notably accurate considering the lack of any previous thorough account of the matter, in which both Spanish and English sources were used.

HISTORICAL RECORDS SURVEY. *Inventory of the County Archives of Louisiana, No. 35, Natchitoches Parish.* Baton Rouge, 1938.
The historical introduction contains valuable information, largely drawn from the records themselves, relative to the vicinity of Natchitoches and Los Adaes (now Robeline, Louisiana).

HOUCK, LOUIS. *The Boundaries of the Louisiana Purchase.* St. Louis, 1901.
One of a number of controversial pieces called forth by the approaching Centenary Exposition (1904). The author refutes various arguments and maintains the extreme interpretation of the purchase boundaries, including West Florida, Texas, and Oregon. Houck's later collection of documents, *The Spanish Regime in Missouri* (Chicago, 1909), contains nothing of interest for this study.

HUNT, GAILLARD. *The Department of State.* Washington, 1914.
A convenient summary of the growth of the department in organization, personnel, and activities.

LATANÉ, JOHN H. *History of American Foreign Policy.* New York, 1927; rev. ed., enlarged, New York, 1934.
The revised edition contains no change in the original comments on the Adams-Onís Treaty, which seem to berate Adams unduly for the relinquishment of Texas.

LOCKEY, JOSEPH B. *Pan-Americanism; Its Beginnings.* New York, 1920.
An interpretive study of relations between the American republics through the first three decades of the nineteenth century. The author emphasizes the influence of England in the diplomacy of Spain and the United States, without an explanation of the steps in which it was apparent. He does not give as much credit as do either Mr. Charles C. Griffin or I to fear of United States recognition of the new republics as a motive for the Spanish delay in ratifying the Adams-Onís Treaty. Most valuable in this book are numerous quotations from Hispanic American writings of the time showing the close relationship of the Adams-Onís discussions to Hispanic American problems.

E. WILSON LYON. *Louisiana in French Diplomacy, 1759–1804.* Norman, 1934.
An incisive analysis of the European background, unusually informative for an appreciation of the complex arguments concerning the title to Louisiana.

MCCALEB, WALTER F. *The Aaron Burr Conspiracy.* New York, 1903; expanded ed., New York, 1936.
In the analysis of Burr's actions, McCaleb included considerable information on Wilkinson and the Louisiana-Texas frontier, especially on the "neutral ground" agreement of 1806, useful in this study.

MARSHALL, T. M. *History of the Western Boundary of the Louisiana Purchase, 1819–1841.* Berkeley, 1914.
The introductory chapters of this book present a concise summary of the diplomacy concerned, from 1803 through 1819. Marshall was a pioneer in seeing the broader view of the Adams-Onís Treaty and considering the Floridas, Texas, and Oregon as interdependent elements in the general settlement. The work was seriously limited, however, in that only printed authorities were used, chiefly the *American State Papers* and Adams' *Memoirs*.

MARTENS, GEORG FRIEDRICH VON. *Précis du droit des gens.* 2 vols. Göttingen, 1789. (*Summary of the Law of Nations.* Philadelphia, 1795.)
One of the standard treatises on international law cited by Adams in his arguments over the obligation of Spain to ratify the treaty.

MICHAEL, WILLIAM H. *History of the Department of State of the United States.* Washington, 1901.
Includes brief biographical sketches of numerous officials.

MOORE, JOHN BASSETT. *History and Digest of the International Arbitrations to Which the United States Has Been a Party.* 6 vols. Washington, 1898.

————. *A Digest of International Law.* 8 vols. Washington, 1906.
> Volume V of the first of these notable compilations includes statements and discussions of the claims settlements made under the treaty of 1819.

MOWAT, ROBERT B. *Diplomatic Relations of Great Britain and the United States.* New York, 1925.
> A quite general survey, which suffers from being grounded too exclusively on British materials, and portrays as too placid the diplomacy following the War of 1812. It gives a convenient summary, nevertheless, of the work of Charles Bagot.

NEWTON, ARTHUR P. "United States and Colonial Developments, 1815–1846," *Cambridge History of British Foreign Policy* (1922–1923), II:220–283. Cambridge, 1923.
> British attitudes as revealed in various negotiations, those concerning the slave trade and British, Spanish, and Russian territorial interests in North America being of particular interest here. Some consideration of the effects of the Adams-Onís Treaty on British policy.

PAXSON, FREDERIC L. *History of the American Frontier, 1763–1893.* Boston, 1924.
> A factual account of value for an understanding of the actual conditions of settlement which affected diplomacy, and containing a good summary of the Adams-Onís negotiations.

PERKINS, DEXTER. *The Monroe Doctrine, 1823–1826.* Cambridge, Massachusetts, 1927.
> The outstanding monograph on a manifestation of foreign policy the roots of which lay in certain of the same problems confronted by Adams and Onís.

PHILIPS, EDITH. *Les réfugiés Bonapartistes en Amérique (1815–1830).* Paris, 1923.
> A thorough investigation of the French exiles who attempted to colonize Alabama and Texas. The author considers their relations with officials in this country, especially Monroe, and the efforts of Onís and Hyde de Neuville to head them off.

PHILLIPS, W. ALISON. "Great Britain and the Continental Alliance, 1816–1822," *Cambridge History of British Foreign Policy* (1922–1923), II:3–50. Cambridge, 1923.
> This analysis of British relations with the Continental Powers brings in to good effect the problems of Spain, Britain's ally, and her colonies. Russian intrigues in Spain and the conciliatory attitude of Castlereagh toward the United States in the settlements growing out of the Treaty of Ghent are also explained.

PI Y MARGALL, FRANCISCO, and PI Y ARSUAGA, FRANCISCO. *Historia de España en el siglo XIX.* 6 vols. Barcelona, 1903.
> Verbose and anecdotal, without satisfactory documentation, more useful for internal condition of Spain than for foreign policy.

PRATT, JULIUS. *Expansionists of 1812.* New York, 1925.
> This notable work, which revamped and expanded our conception of the frontier problems and the genesis of the war with England, is essential for an understanding of Onís' early years in this country, and for the background of the larger problems which he faced later.

REEVES, JESSE S. *Napoleonic Exiles in America—A Study in American Diplomatic History, 1815–1819* (Johns Hopkins Studies in History and Political Science, Ser. XXIII, nos. 9 and 10). Baltimore, 1905.
> An early study of the attempted French colonization projects and some consideration of the relations between their organizers and the United States government.

RICHMAN, IRVING BERDINE. *California under Spain and Mexico, 1535–1847.* Boston, 1911.
> Narrative of exploration, settlement, and administration, heavily documented, of value here for the conflicting territorial claims on the Pacific Coast.

RIPPY, J. FRED. *Rivalry of the United States and Great Britain over Latin America (1808–1830).* Baltimore, 1929.
> An able study based on extensive archival research, necessarily including an interpretation of the policies of the two countries toward Spain and the problems of the Adams-Onís negotiations.

ROSENGARTEN, JOSEPH G. *French Colonists and Exiles in the United States.* Philadelphia, 1907.
> Little more than a compilation of information regarding numerous French settlements and prominent individuals in all periods, but chiefly since the Revolution. Hyde de Neuville is treated at some length.

SEMPLE, ELLEN C. *American History and Its Geographic Conditions.* New York, 1903; rev. ed., Boston, 1933.
> An essential basis for any understanding of westward expansion, this book is of particular interest here in connection with the political and geographical conditions affecting the direction of the Oregon migration.

SWANTON, JOHN R. *Early History of the Creek Indians and Their Neighbors.* Washington, 1922.

———. *Indian Tribes of the Lower Mississippi Valley and Adjacent Coast of the Gulf of Mexico.* Washington, 1911.
> Two important historical and statistical treatises, with maps, necessary for the study of rivalries of the white nations for control of the Floridas.

TATUM, EDWARD HOWLAND, JR. *The United States and Europe, 1815–1823; A Study in the Background of the Monroe Doctrine.* Berkeley, 1936.
> An able analysis of the popular attitude in the United States, based largely on studies of the public press and of published speeches. The views of relations with England and with Russia are pertinent here, as is the stimulating chapter on John Quincy Adams. For comments on Dr. Tatum's description of relations with England, see above, p. 128, note 2.

THOMAS, ALFRED B. *Forgotten Frontiers, A Study of the Spanish Indian Policy of Don Juan Bautista de Anza, Governor of New Mexico, 1777–1787.* Norman, 1932.
> One of the few scholarly monographs dealing with the advance of the Spanish frontier northward into the Red and Arkansas River country, which was concerned in Adams' and Onís' negotiations over the boundary.

THOMAS, BENJAMIN P. *Russo-American Relations, 1815–1867* (Johns Hopkins Studies in History and Political Science, Ser. XLVIII, no. 2). Baltimore, 1930.
> A survey of the activities of the respective envoys of the two countries. Of slight value here because Minister Daschkoff was not on speaking terms with the government at Washington during the Adams-Onís discussions, and Russia's connection with the affair was entirely manifest in the actions of her ambassador at Madrid, Tatistcheff.

UPDYKE, FRANK A. *The Diplomacy of the War of 1812.* Baltimore, 1915.
  This narrative of the negotiations between the United States and Great Britain leading to and growing out of the war, with a consideration of Russian activities, reveals how limited has been the standard interpretation of the subject. Hardly a word appears concerning Spain, which was allied with Great Britain in the European struggle, used the British envoys as mouthpieces at Washington, shared the British opposition to our territorial ambitions, and tried twice to have its interests considered at the peace negotiations.

URRUTIA, FRANCISCO JOSÉ. *Los Estados Unidos de América y las repúblicas Hispano-Americanas de 1810 á 1830, páginas de historia diplomática.* Madrid, 1918.
  Heavily documented accounts of the work of various agents, chiefly those from the embryonic republics to the United States, including information on the commissions from South American governments held by such adventurers as Gregor McGregor and Louis Aury.

VATTEL, EMMERICH DE. *Le droit des gens.* Leyden, 1758. (*The Law of Nations.* Philadelphia, 1817.)
  A treatise used by Adams in his argument that the King of Spain was obliged to ratify the treaty.

VIGNOLES, CHARLES B. *Observations on the Floridas.* New York, 1823.
  A history and description of the then newly acquired territory, with numerous quotations from diplomatic documents. Published a year later as *The History of the Floridas.*

VILLA-URRUTIA, WENCESLAO R. DE. *Relaciones entre España é Inglaterra durante la guerra de independencia, 1808 á 1814.* 3 vols. Madrid, 1911–1914.
——. *España en el congreso de Viena.* 2d ed., rev., Madrid, 1928.
  Two scholarly, well-documented studies, somewhat prone to narration of personal intrigues, but easily the most thorough Spanish diplomatic works dealing with the period.

WAGNER, HENRY R. *Spanish Explorations in the Strait of Juan de Fuca.* Santa Ana, California, 1933.
  A historical and cartographic study, of use for the background of Spanish and Russian claims on the Northwest Coast.

WALIZEWSKI, KAZIMIERZ. *Le regne d'Alexandre Ier.* 3 vols. Paris, 1925.
  Volume III (1818–1825) contains some references to the activities of Tatistcheff.

WEBSTER, CHARLES K. *Foreign Policy of Castlereagh, 1815–1822.* London, 1925.
  A scholarly analysis of the problems and purposes of Castlereagh's diplomatic services, including his attitude toward Spanish and United States affairs, and some consideration of the British reaction to the Adams-Onís Treaty.

WHITAKER, ARTHUR P., ed. *Documents Relating to the Commercial Policy of Spain in the Floridas.* Deland, Florida, 1931.
  The documents here published are largely not pertinent to this study, but the historical introduction is a valuable portrayal of the second Spanish occupation of the Floridas, especially in the early nineteenth century.

WHITE, ELIZABETH BRETT. *American Opinion of France, from Lafayette to Poincaré.* New York, 1927.
  This study of popular opinion, especially as expressed in the press, includes accounts of the actual developments concerned, such as the activities of the French exiles in this country, and of Hyde de Neuville.

C. MAPS

Only those maps are included here which have been referred to in the text, as the listing of a number of well-known maps which figured in the backgrounds of the Louisiana-Texas boundary controversy has been deemed outside the scope of this study. Earlier maps which influenced the work of Melish have been indicated in Appendix II.

BRUÉ, ADRIEN HUBERT. *Carte de l'Amérique septentrionale*. Paris, 1820.

This edition of the work of a prominent French geographer was published with Onís' *Memoria sobre las negociaciones* (Madrid, 1820), and was colored to show the boundary as drawn in the Adams-Onís Treaty.

HUMBOLDT, ALEXANDRE DE. *Carte générale du royaume de la Nouvelle Espagne*. Paris, 1809.

One of the maps appearing in the noted traveler and scholar's *Atlas geographique et physique de la Nouvelle Espagne* (Paris, 1811). Figured in the controversy over the names of the Texas rivers.

LÁNGARA Y HUARTE, JUAN DE. *Carta esférica que comprehende las costas del Seno Mexicano*. Madrid, 1799.

The work of a prominent Spanish maritime officer, used by Jefferson in the preparation of his tract on the limits of Louisiana. It indicated the Sabine as the boundary between the Spanish provinces of Louisiana and Texas.

MELISH, JOHN. *Map of the United States with the Contiguous British and Spanish Possessions*. Philadelphia, 1816. Improved to the first of January, 1818. Philadelphia, 1818.

See Appendix II.

PAULLIN, CHARLES O. *Atlas of the Historical Geography of the United States*. JOHN K. WRIGHT, ed. Washington and New York, 1932.

This extensive work includes discussions and reproductions of numerous maps indicating the growth of colonial boundary problems and is indispensable for any study of early United States diplomacy. See review of the *Atlas* by Frederick Merk, and correspondence concerning it, in *New England Quarterly*, VI (1933):620–625, 847–852.

PICHARDO, JOSÉ ANTONIO. "El nuevo México y tierras adyacentes." [Mexico, 1811].

Manuscript map in Archivo General de la Nación, Mexico. Published in *Pichardo's Treatise on the Limits of Louisiana and Texas*, Charles W. Hackett, ed. (Austin, 1931—), Vol. II, pocket. Drawn to accompany the report prepared by the Mexican priest for use in the boundary negotiations, supporting the Spanish claim to Texas.

PIKE, ZEBULON M. *Map of the Internal Provinces of New Spain*. Philadelphia, 1810.

Published with Pike's narrative of his western trip, his arrest by the Spaniards, and his trip to Mexico, this work was an important authority on the near-by Spanish territory in the time of the Adams-Onís negotiation, and contributed greatly to the prevailing ideas of the Red and Arkansas River courses.

INDEX

INDEX

Adams, John Quincy, 1–2, 71, 74, 78, 84, 87, 88–89, 110–111, 151, 159, 162, 182, 183, 187; dealings of, with Onís, 89, 93–94, 94–97, 122, 126–127, 132, 139–140, 142, 145, 147, 160, 163, 176, 190; and British mediation, 113 ff.; and Spanish land grants, 135, 176, 177; Jackson upheld by, 143, 144, 148–150; ultimatum of, 145–146, 155–157 *passim*; on yielding the claim to Texas, 156, 194; Adams-Onís Treaty signed by, 164

Aguayo, Marquis of, 41

Alabama River, 37, 87, 91

Alagón, Duke of, land grants to, 135, 145, 176, 197 (n. 22)

Albuquerque, trade at, 44

Alexander of Russia, 24, 108, 183

Allende, Pedro, 46

Ambrister, Robert Christie, 94, 117, 140, 141, 149, 150

Amelia Island, 31, 86, 87, 90, 91, 92, 94, 100, 116, 123

"Anglo-Americans," 31, 35, 43, 44, 45, 86, 117, 120

Anian, Strait of, 50

Anza, Juan Bautista de, 45

Apalache, 31, 34

Apalachicola River, 30, 31, 34, 35, 94, 100, 116

Aranjuez, 11, 13

Arbuthnot, Alexander, 116–117, 140, 141, 149, 150

Arizona, 30, 46

Arkansas River, 46, 84, 134, 158, 159, 161, 162

Armstrong, General John, 6–8

Arroyo Honda, 39, 41, 42, 142, 144

Astor, John Jacob, 48, 51, 151–152

Astoria (Fort George), 48, 51–52, 72, 150–152, 167 (n. 49), 194

Aury, Louis, 86

Bagot, Charles, 112–114, 117–118, 121, 125, 150

Bahama, 31, 94

Bahía del Espíritu Santo, 40, 41

Baker, Anthony St. John, 52

Baltimore, trade with East Florida, 31

Banda Oriental, 107–108

Barataria Lake, 42

Bardaxi y Azara, Eusebio, 16–17, 19

Baton Rouge, revolt at, 36

Bayou La Fourche, 84

Bayou Pierre, 39

"Beaver" (ship), 51, 151

Bering, Vitus, 49

Bernabeu, Juan Bautista de, 18

Big Horn River, 47

Bland, Theodorick, 87, 173

Bodega Bay, 50

Bodega y Cuadra, Juan Francisco de la, 49–50

Bolívar, 86

Bonaparte, Joseph, 10–11, 15, 19, 61, 87, 120–122 *passim*

Borgo, Count Pozzi di, 183

Bosquejo, 75–76, 110

Bowdoin, James, 7, 8

Bowlegs, Chief, 100, 140

Brazil, program of, 107–108

Brazos de Dios, 160

Brent, Thomas, 12, 60

British: rivalry between, and Russians at Madrid, 106, 109; commercial ambitions, 108; aloofness, 116; mediation scheme, 132, 134; Northwest fur trade dominated by, 151; established north of the Columbia, 158; appeals to, diplomats, 181

British Columbia, 51, 66; *see also* Pacific Northwest

Brué, Adrien H., 189

Buenos Aires, 76, 86, 88, 99, 173, 179, 181

Burr, Aaron, 39, 42

Bustamente, 44

Butler, Colonel Robert, 192

Cadiz, 11–12, 21, 62, 98, 177, 178, 185, 187, 188

Calcasieu River, 84, 134, 144

Calhoun, John C., 96, 143, 149